武士道
BUSHIDO

新渡戸稲造［著］
須知徳平［訳］

D0773136

Bilingual Books

新渡戸稲造夫妻。ご子息の結婚披露宴の折、東京・小日向の自宅パーラーにて。
Inazo Nitobe and his wife Mary at the reception held at his home in Kobinata,
Tokyo following his son's wedding.

ニューヨークにて。(この写真は、記念切手にも用いられた)
This photo, taken in New York, was used for a commemorative stamp.

国際聯盟事務次長として。ジュネーブの執務室で1925年頃。
At his office in Geneva about 1925, when he was serving as Under-Secretary General of the League of Nations.

目　次

CONTENTS

はしがき

　世界は急速にボーダレス化している。日本に
いるとそれほど感じなくても、欧州を旅行
したり、アセアン諸国を訪れるつど、このことに
驚かされる。それでは、世界の物の考え方、価値
観までがボーダレス化し、同質化されていくのだ
ろうか。これは、真の国際人・新渡戸稲造の名著
『武士道』を読み返すたびに、私が考えされられ
る疑問である。

　おそらく、好むと好まざるとにかかわらず、同
質化の方向に進むだろう、と私は考えている。し
かし、経済のボーダレス化とはかなりの時間的ず
れがあるだろうとは思う。もうひとつの疑問は、
その同質化はアジア的考え方が欧米化の方向に進
むことをも意味するだろうか、ということである。
だが、この結論を出すのは早急すぎるかもしれな
い。日本をはじめとしてアジア諸国には抵抗感が
あまりにも強く、また欧米もアジアに学ぶものが
多々あると思うからである。

Foreword

THE world is rapidly becoming "borderless." Even if we don't feel this so much when we are in Japan, every time we travel to Europe or visit the ASEAN countries we are surprised by this fact. But will there be a similar trend toward homogeneity, a similar "borderless" transformation, in the world's way of thinking, in its values? This is something I am made to ponder every time I reread the famous book *Bushido* by that true internationalist Nitobe Inazo.

I think that, whether we like it or not, the trend toward homogeneity will probably continue. However, I think there will probably be a considerable "time lag" in comparison with the borderless transformation in the economic field. Another question I have is whether this trend toward homogeneity will mean that "Asian" ways of thinking will move in the direction of "Europeanization" or "Americanization." It may still be too early, however, to give a conclusion. This is because there is too strong a feeling of resistance on the part of Japan and other Asian countries, and also because I think there is a great deal for Europe and America to learn from Asia.

　国連には人権委員会があって、日本は毎回アジア地域を代表して、この委員会に選出される。そしてアジアの国々は、アジアに位置してアジア的価値観を共有する日本こそ、欧米に向ってアジアの人権に関する考え方を説明し、説得してくれることを期待する。他方、欧米諸国は、日本の憲法を読んで、欧米以上に欧米的人権尊重の価値観に貫かれていることを見る。そして日本こそ、アジアにあってアジア諸国に対し、西欧型民主主義の下における真の人権とはいかなるものか、そしてアジアの伝統的価値観がなぜ改革を要するか、中国をはじめとするアジア諸国に説得してくれることを期待する。

　しかし現実の日本は、欧米からも、アジアからも期待されつつ、双方から失望される存在になっているのではないだろうか。これは日本が自らの明確な価値観を喪失していることに基因するように思う。

　元外務大臣のある政治家の事務所の壁に、横2メートルほどの大きな額が掛かっている。それには墨痕鮮かに「ボーイズ・ビー・アンビシャス」（青年よ、大志を抱け）と英語で記されていて、イナゾー・ニトベと英語でサインがある。しかし私には、日本の社会は個人が大志を抱き、それを実現しやすい社会ではなくなってしまっているように思われる。その大志とは、国のため、社会のため、あるいは自分個人の大成功を目指すものか

In the United Nations there is a Commission on Human Rights, and Japan is always selected to represent the Asian region on this Commission. The Asian countries look to Japan, a country located in Asia and sharing Asian values, to explain Asian thinking on human rights to Europe and America and to persuade them of its validity. On the other hand, the European and American countries read Japan's Constitution and see that it is characterized through and through, to an extent even greater than in Europe and America, with Euro-American values of "respect for human rights." And they look to Japan as the country in Asia that can best persuade China and other Asian countries of what true human rights under Western-type democracy should be and why changes are needed in Asia's traditional values. But I often think that in fact Japan, while having these great expectations placed on it by both Asia and by Europe and America, is probably a disappointment to both. I think this is probably because Japan is losing its own clear values.

On the wall of the office of a certain politician who has formerly served as Japan's Foreign Minister is a framed piece of large handwriting, about two meters in length. Boldly written in ink with a thick brush are the English words "Boys, be ambitious" and the signature, in Latin letters, "Inazo Nitobe." However, it seems to me that Japan's society is becoming one where it is no longer easy for an individual to have great ambitions and to bring these to fruition. "Great ambitions" can be for one's country, for society, or for one's personal success. In whichever case,

もしれない。しかしいずれにせよ、最近の日本の
社会は、大成功を祝福せず、逆にその足を引っ張
るようになっているのではないだろうか。

　クラーク博士が「大志を抱け」と言ったアメリ
カの社会は、多くの欠点を有してはいるが、成功
者を祝福するという長所をもつ社会である。アメ
リカン・ドリームを達成した成功者を称え、自ら
もその社会の一員として、同様な成功のチャンス
に恵まれていることを誇りとする。一方、日本は
成功者を嫉妬し、批判する社会になっているよう
だ。

　国際連盟事務次長として活躍した新渡戸先生の
著作を読むたびに、私は国際人としての先生の偉
大さに感動すると同時に、いま日本が国際化から
取り残されつつあるという危惧を感じる。国際人
になるためには、まず第一に世界に関心を持たな
ければならない。しかし日本人は多数の人が海外
に出掛けながらも、心理的には世界から孤立して
いると言える。

　その一例をあげよう。日本の大新聞の一面に、
近隣アジア諸国以外の世界の問題が報ぜられるこ
とは異例である。また40ページほどの紙面の中
で、国際面はほんの2ページ程度で、しかも6面と
か7面とかにあり、多くの人に読み飛ばされてし
まう程度の扱いである。これは世界の大国では異
常な現象である。

however, it seems to me that Japan's society in recent years has become one which does not celebrate "great success" but, on the contrary, puts obstacles in its way. The American society with which Dr. William Clark, who taught at the Sapporo Agricultural School (where Nitobe studied between 1877 and 1881) and originated the phrase "Boys, be ambitious," was familiar has many faults but has the strong point of congratulating persons who have achieved success. It still gives honor to those successful persons who have achieved the American dream, and each individual member of that society is proud that he or she has a chance for similar success. Japan, on the other hand, seems to be a society that envies and criticizes the successful.

Every time I look at the writings of Dr. Nitobe, who served as Under-Secretary General of the League of Nations, I am both moved by Nitobe's greatness as an internationalist and gripped by the apprehension that today's Japan is being left behind in matters of international concern. To be an internationalist, you must first of all have an interest in the world. Yet the Japanese people may be said to be isolated from the world psychologically, even though a great many have traveled abroad. Let me give an example. On the front pages of Japan's major newspapers it is an uncommon thing for there to appear any news about parts of the world other than nearby countries of Asia. Among the 40 pages or so of a typical major daily newspaper, only about 2 pages are devoted to international matters. Such write-ups begin usually on only the sixth or seventh page and so tend to be skipped by

　真の国際人であるためには、第二に自らの明確な主張を持ち、これを堂々と披瀝する覚悟がなければならない。これはきわめて重要なことであって、新渡戸先生の偉大なる所以もここにあると言える。しかし、われわれ日本人には、世界の重要問題で白と黒に別れて議論が重ねられていると、灰色で妥協を図るという発想がいまだに生まれがちである。

　私事であるが、40年以上前、外務省に入省後、アメリカの大学に留学した最初の年に、ある科目で多くの先生の本を読破し論文をまとめ、自信をもって提出したところ、意外と低い点数がついて戻ってきた。失望しながらページを繰ってみると、最後に、採点した高名な教授のコメントが、「あなたの意見は何ですか」と書かれてあったのを、いまも鮮明に覚えている。

　じつはこれは、日本の教育のあり方の基本にまで関わってくる重要な点である。勉強とは先生の教えを記憶することではなく、自ら考えることなのである。そして多くの日本人にとって必要なことは、たとえ少数意見であっても、自らの意見を明確に発言し、主張することなのである。

　現代において、国際人たるためには、第三に人

many readers. Among the world's major countries, this is a very strange phenomenon.

A second requirement for being a true internationalist is to have one's own clear points of view and to be prepared to express them in a way that will carry weight with others. This is something that is really very important and can be said to be one of the reasons for Dr. Nitobe's greatness. However, when we Japanese encounter discussions of major problems of the world where opinions are divided, so to speak, between "black" and "white," there is always the tendency for us to look for "gray" compromises.

This is a personal story, but I well remember how over 40 years ago, after I had entered the Ministry of Foreign Affairs and was studying, during my first year abroad, at an American university, I had for one of my classes confidently submitted a paper after reading through many books written by many different professors. But the paper came back to me with an unexpectedly low mark. Disappointed, I went through the pages of the paper and at the end came across a comment by the eminent professor who had graded it. I vividly recall his comment even today. It was: "What is your opinion?" This is in fact an important point that goes to the very fundamentals of Japan's system of education. Study should not be memorizing what our teachers teach us but learning how to think on our own. And what many Japanese need is to be able to clearly express and advocate our own opinions, even if these might be "minority opinions."

In our present-day world, a third requirement for

道的問題に敏感でなければならない。そしてこれこそ新渡戸先生の最大の教えかもしれない。日本は世界第一の援助大国でありながら、そのわりに世界からの評価が高くないのも、日本の援助が経済問題に偏していて、人道援助となるとお付き合い的発想が強いためであろう。

　日本の場合、国連における人道援助というと、まず諸外国がいくら援助するかを見た上で、横並び的発想から日本の分担額を考えることが多い。世界の人道援助プロジェクトにおいて、日本が音頭をとった事例は数少ない。

　国際人の条件の第四として、平和の問題にも触れざるを得ない。「戦争なき状態が平和にあらず」という新渡戸先生の言葉はきわめて重要であるが、その解釈は容易ではない。私なりに判断すれば、そして国連の主張に沿って解釈すれば、日本では平和は常に正義であるが、国連は正義ある平和と、正義なき平和を峻別する。そして正義なき平和は平和と呼ぶに値せず、これを打ち破ってでも正義ある平和を樹立すべし、ということである。この考え方が国連の平和維持軍、いわゆるPKO

being an internationalist is being sensitive to humanitarian concerns. And here may be the most important of all the things taught by Dr. Nitobe. Japan may be the world's number one provider of official development assistance (ODA) to developing countries, but the fact that this assistance is not evaluated by the world as highly as we might expect is probably because preponderant attention is given to "economic" matters while, when it comes to "humanitarian assistance," there is a strong Japanese tendency to want to take a secondary role, helping perhaps, but not exercising real leadership. When matters of humanitarian assistance come up at the United Nations, the tendency is for Japan to first wait and see how much assistance other countries are willing to provide and then, as a sort of "side-wave" reaction, to consider what Japan's contribution might be. In the world's projects for humanitarian assistance there are very few examples of Japan's leading a proposal for action.

Coming now to a fourth condition for being an internationalist, I must say something about the problems of peace. Dr. Nitobe's remark that "a situation without war is not peace" is very important but is not easy to understand. In my judgment, and making an interpretation in conformance with United Nations vocabulary, it seems that Japan always considers "peace" to be just, whereas the United Nations makes sharp distinctions between "just peace" and "unjust peace," considering that "unjust peace" should not really be called peace and in some cases advocating its being broken down and replaced with a "just

の基礎となっているのだ。これは日本の安全保障
理事会入りを論ずる際に避けて通れない問題点で
もある。

　このように私には、日本の常識は世界の常識と
相当かけ離れたものになっているように思えてな
らない。新渡戸先生が「早すぎた国際人」と言わ
れた所以も、ここにあるのかもしれない。日本は
国際化の必要性を長い間唱えてきながら、いまだ
に国際化からは程遠い。いま、日本が生んだ偉大
な国際人の大先達である新渡戸先生の代表作『武
士道』を通じて、その教えをもう一度振り返って
みるとき、学ぶところはすこぶる多い。

波多野 敬雄
（前国連大使）

peace." This is the sort of thinking which lies at the base of the United Nations' so-called "peace-keeping operations" (PKO). It is a point that cannot be avoided when we talk about Japan's having a permanent seat on the UN's Security Council.

Considering these various points, I can't help but feel that Japan's customary thinking is rather far apart from that of the world as a whole. Here, too, may be one reason why Dr. Nitobe has been called "an internationalist who was ahead of his time." Although Japan has for a long time been voicing the need for "becoming more international," it is still rather far from making this a reality. There is much we can learn by reading *Bushido* and other later works by Japan's great pioneer internationalist Nitobe Inazo, who had much to teach that we can still learn from today.

Yoshio Hatano
(Former Ambassador to the UN)

武士道

BUSHIDO

日本の魂
The Soul of Japan

——日本思想の解明——

An Exposition of Japanese Thought

新渡戸 稲造 著

Inazo Nitobe, A.M., Ph.D.

須知 徳平 訳

translated by
Tokuhei Suchi

第1版　序　文

　およそ10年前のことである。私はベルギーの法政学の大家、故ド・ラヴレー氏の家に招かれ、数日を過ごしたことがあった。ある日二人で散歩をしていたとき、私たちの話題が、宗教問題になって、私はこの尊敬すべき老教授から、「それでは、あなたの説によると、日本の学校においては、宗教教育はなされていない、ということなんですか」と、聞かれた。「ありません」私がそう答えると、氏は驚いたように突然歩みをとめて、「宗教がない！　それでどうして、道徳教育を授けることができるのですか」と、くり返したその声を、私は簡単には忘れられないだろう。そのとき私は、この質問にどう答えていいかわからなかった。というのは、私が少年時代に学んだ道徳の教えは、学校で教えられたものではなかったからである。私自身の中の善悪や、正不正の観念を形成しているのは一体何なのか。そのいろんな要素を分析してみて、はじめてこれらの観念を私自身の中にふき込んだものは、実に、武士道であったことを、ようやくに見出したのである。

　私がこの小著を著すことに至った直接のきっかけは、妻（のメリー）が、現代の日本であまねく行われている、思想や習慣について「それはどのような理由で行われているのか」と、しばしば私に質問したことによるのである。

　私は、ド・ラヴレー氏ならびに妻に対して、満足のゆくよ

Preface to the First Edition

ABOUT ten years ago, while spending a few days under the hospitable roof of the distinguished Belgian jurist, the lamented M. de Laveleye, our conversation turned during one of our rambles, to the subject of religion. "Do you mean to say," asked the venerable professor, "that you have no religious instruction in your schools?" On my replying in the negative, he suddenly halted in astonishment, and in a voice which I shall not easily forget, he repeated "No religion! How do you impart moral education?" The question stunned me at the time. I could give no ready answer, for the moral precepts I learned in my childhood days were not given in schools; and not until I began to analyse the different elements that formed my notions of right and wrong, did I find that it was Bushido that breathed them into my nostrils.

The direct inception of this little book is due to the frequent queries put by my wife as to the reasons why such and such ideas and customs prevail in Japan.

In my attempts to give satisfactory replies to M. de

うな答えをしようと試みた。そして、わが国の封建制度および武士道とは何であるか、ということを理解しなくては、現在の日本の道徳観念は、結局、封印された秘本のようになってしまうと思ったのである。

　私は長い間病床にあって、止むを得ず無為の日々を送っているのだが、この機会を幸いに、家庭での妻との話し合いの中、私が答えたことを整理したものを発表することにした。その内容は主として、私の少年時代に、わが国の封建制度がなお盛んであったときに教えを受けたものである。

　ラフカディオ・ハーン（小泉八雲）や、ヒュー・フレーザー夫人、さらに、サー・アーネスト・サトウや、チェンバレン教授などがおられるのに、英語をもって日本に関する著述をするのは、全く気のひける仕事である。ただ私が、これらの高名な著述家たちにまさる唯一の長所は、彼らが、つまりは弁護士や検事の立場にあるのに対して、私は自国のために抗弁をする立場をとることができることである。私はしばしば思った。「もし私に、彼らに等しいほどの語学の才能があったならば、もっと雄弁な言葉をもって日本の立場を説明できるであろうに」と。しかし、他国の言葉を借りて語る者は、自分の言うことの意味を、読者に理解されることができさえすれば、それで満足だと思わなければならない。

　この著書の中で、全体を通じて、私の論証しようとする諸点を、私はヨーロッパの歴史や文学から、数例を借りて説明しようと試みた。それによって、これらの問題を外国の読者の理解に近づけることができると思ったからである。

　また、この著書の中で、宗教上の問題や、宣教師についての私の言い方が、万が一侮辱的だと思われるようなことがあっても、私のキリスト教に対する態度は、これによっていさ

Laveleye and to my wife, I found that without understanding feudalism and Bushido, the moral ideas of present Japan are a sealed volume.

Taking advantage of enforced idleness on account of
long illness, I put down in the order now presented to the
public some of the answers given in our household conversation. They consist mainly of what I was taught and
told in my youthful days, when feudalism was still in force.

Between Lafcadio Hearn and Mrs. Hugh Fraser on one
side and Sir Ernest Satow and Professor Chamberlain on
the other, it is indeed discouraging to write anything
Japanese in English. The only advantage I have over them
is that I can assume the attitude of a personal defendant,
while these distinguished writers are at best solicitors and
attorneys. I have often thought,—"Had I their gift of language, I would present the cause of Japan in more eloquent terms!" But one who speaks in a borrowed tongue
should be thankful if he can just make himself intelligible.

All through the discourse I have tried to illustrate
whatever points I have made with parallel examples from
European history and literature, believing that these will
aid in bringing the subject nearer to the comprehension
of foreign readers.

Should any of my allusions to religious subjects and to
religious workers be thought slighting, I trust my attitude
toward Christianity itself will not be questioned. It is with

さかも疑われることがないと信じている。私があまり同情することができないのは、教会のやり方やキリストの教えを暗くする諸形式であって、教えそのものではない。私は、キリストが教え、そして『新約聖書』の中に伝えられている宗教、ならびに心にしるされている律法を信じている。さらに私は、神はすべての民族や国民との間に――異邦人であれユダヤ人であれ、キリスト教徒であれ異教徒であることを問わず――『旧約』と名づけられている契約をもって結ばれたことを信じている。私の神学に対する考え方については、さらに論じて読者の忍耐をわずらわす必要はあるまい。

この序文を終るにあたり、数多くの貴重な注意を与えてくれた友人のアンナ・シー・ハーツホーンに謝意を表したい。

明治32年（1899年）12月 ペンシルヴァニア州マルヴェルンにて

新渡戸 稲造

ecclesiastical methods and with the forms which obscure the teachings of Christ, and not with the teachings themselves, that I have little sympathy. I believe in the religion taught by Him and handed down to us in the New Testament, as well as in the law written in the heart. Further, I believe that God hath made a testament which may be called "old" with every people and nation,—Gentile or Jew, Christian or Heathen. As to the rest of my theology, I need not impose upon the patience of the public.

In concluding this preface, I wish to express my thanks to my friend Anna C. Hartshorne for many valuable suggestions.

Inazo Nitobe

Malvern, Pa., Twelfth Month, 1899.

第 1 章
道徳体系としての 武士道

武士道は、日本を表徴する桜の花と同じように、わが国土の固有の花である。その花は、ひからびた古代道徳の標本となって、わが国の歴史の中に保存されているというわけではない。それは現在でもなお、その力と美をもって、わが民族の心の中に生きつづけている。武士道は明白な形態はとらないが、それにもかかわらず、その道徳的雰囲気の香りは、今なおわれわれに力強い感化をあたえている。武士道を生み育てた社会状態は、すでに消え失せてしまった。しかし、はるかな過去には存在し、現在ではその本体を失った星が、今でもなおわれわれの頭上に光り輝いているように、封建制度の子として生まれた武士道は、その母である制度が滅び去ってしまってもなお生き残り、われわれの道徳を照らしているのである。（英国の政治家であり作家である）エドモンド・バークが、かつて、ヨーロッパにおける騎士道が、滅び

CHAPTER I

BUSHIDO AS AN ETHICAL SYSTEM

CHIVALRY is a flower no less indigenous to the soil of Japan than its emblem, the cherry blossom; nor is it a dried-up specimen of an antique virtue preserved in the herbarium of our history. It is still a living object of power and beauty among us; and if it assumes no tangible shape or form, it not the less scents the moral atmosphere, and makes us aware that we are still under its potent spell. The conditions of society which brought it forth and nourished it have long disappeared; but as those far-off stars which once were and are not, still continue to shed their rays upon us, so the light of chivalry which was a child of feudalism, still illuminates our moral path, surviving its mother institution. It is a pleasure to me to reflect upon this subject in the language of Burke, who uttered the

去って誰にもかえりみられないときに、その柩に騎士道を誉めたたえる有名な言葉をたむけたが、今私は、そのバークの国語である英文でもって、この問題を考究することは、まことに喜ばしいことである。

悲しいのは、極東に関する知識の欠乏により、ジョージ・ミラー博士のような博学の学者でさえも、「騎士道もしくは、それに類似した制度は、古代の諸国においても、現代の東洋においても、かつて存在したことがなかった[注1]」と、ためらいもなく断言していることである。しかし、このような無智は許されてもいいだろう。なぜならば、ミラー博士がその著書（『歴史哲学理解』）の第3版を刊行したのは、ペリー提督が（浦賀の港にきて）わが国の（二百数十年にわたる）鎖国の門戸をたたいたのと同じ年だったからである。それから十余年の後になって、わが国の封建制度がまさに滅び去ろうとしているころ、カール・マルクスは、その著書『資本論』の中で、「封建制の社会制度と政治制度の研究は、現代においてもなお生き残っている日本のその制度を観察するのがもっとも有意義である」と、述べている。私も同じように、ヨーロッパの歴史学者や倫理学者に、現代日本における武士道の研究をお勧めしたい。

ヨーロッパと日本の封建制度、ならびに、騎士道と武士道との歴史的な比較研究をすることは、まことに興味深い問題ではあるが、それを詳述することは、本書の目的ではない。私が述べたいのはむしろ、第一に日本の武士道の起源と淵源、第二にその特性と教え、第三に一般の人々に及ぼした感化、第四にその感化の継続性と永続性である。このうち第一については、簡略に述べるにとどめる。さもないと、読者をわが国の歴史の紆余曲折の小路に連れこむことになる。第二につ

注1 『歴史哲学理解』（1853年、第3版）第2巻2ページ。

well-known touching eulogy over the neglected bier of its European prototype.

It argues a sad defect of information concerning the Far East, when so erudite a scholar as Dr. George Miller did not hesitate to affirm that chivalry, or any other similar institution, has never existed either among the nations of antiquity or among the modern Orientals.[1] Such ignorance, however, is amply excusable, as the third edition of the good Doctor's work appeared the same year that Commodore Perry was knocking at the portals of our exclusivism. More than a decade later, about the time that our feudalism was in the last throes of existence, Carl Marx, writing his *Capital*, called the attention of his readers to the peculiar advantage of studying the social and political institutions of feudalism, as then to be seen in living form only in Japan. I would likewise point the Western historical and ethical student to the study of chivalry in the Japan of the present.

Enticing as is an historical disquisition on the comparison between European and Japanese feudalism and chivalry, it is not the purpose of this paper to enter into it at length. My attempt is rather to relate *firstly*, the origin and sources of our chivalry; *secondly*, its character and teaching; *thirdly*, its influence among the masses; and, *fourthly*, the continuity and permanence of its influence. Of these several points, the first will be only brief and cur-

---

[1] *History Philosophically Illustrated* (3d ed., 1853), vol. II, p. 2.

いてもう少し詳細に論じるのは、われわれの考え方や行動の
仕方は、国際倫理学者や比較性格学者がもっとも関心のある
ところだと思うからである。その他の点については、必要に
応じて論じることにする。

　私は日本語の武士道を、大ざっぱに英語でシヴァリー
（Chivalry）と訳したが、その原語においては、騎士道
（Horsemanship）というよりも、もっと深い意味がある。す
なわち、武士道は文字通り武人あるいは騎士の道であり、武
士がその職分を尽くすときでも、日常生活の言行においても、
守らなければならない道であって、言いかえれば、武士の掟
であり、武士階級の身分に伴う義務なのである。武士道とい
う日本語はこのような意味をもつので、原語のまま武士道
（Bushido）という言葉を用いることを許してもらいたい。原
語を使用することの便利な理由は他にもある。武士道は他に
類のない独特の教えなので、それが固有の考え方と性格を生
み、また、非常に地方性の強い教えなので、特異性を前面に
掲げなければならないのである。次に、言葉には、その国独
特の表現があって、民族の特性があまりにも強くでている言
葉は、最高の翻訳者でもふさわしい訳語を見つけるのは困難
であろう。だから、わざわざふさわしくない訳語をつけて苦
情の種をつくることはないのである。ドイツ語のゲミュート
（Gemüth）の意味をうまく訳せる者がいるだろうか？　英語
のジェントルマン（gentleman）とフランス語のジャンティ
オム（gentilhomme）という、言語的に非常に類似した語の
違いを感じない者がいるだろうか。
　以上に述べたように、武士道は武士の道徳的な掟であって、
武士はこれを守り、行うことを教えられ、かつ要求されるも

sory, or else I should have to take my readers into the devious paths of our national history; the second will be dwelt upon at greater length, as being most likely to interest students of International Ethics and Comparative Ethology in our ways of thought and action; and the rest will be dealt with as corollaries.

The Japanese word which I have roughly rendered Chivalry, is, in the original, more expressive than Horsemanship. *Bu-shi-do* means literally Military–Knight–Ways—the ways which fighting nobles should observe in their daily life as well as in their vocation; in a word, the "Precepts of Knighthood," the *noblesse oblige* of the warrior class. Having thus given its literal significance, I may be allowed henceforth to use the word in the original. The use of the original term is also advisable for this reason, that a teaching so circumscribed and unique, engendering a cast of mind and character so peculiar, so local, must wear the badge of its singularity on its face; then, some words have a national *timbre* so expressive of race characteristics that the best of translators can do them but scant justice, not to say positive injustice and grievance. Who can improve by translation what the German "*Gemüth*" signifies, or who does not feel the difference between the two words verbally so closely allied as the English *gentleman* and the French *gentilhomme*?

Bushido, then, is the code of moral principles which the knights were required or instructed to observe. It is

のである。しかし、それは成文法ではない。あるいは先人の
口伝えに、あるいは数人の名のある武士や学者の筆によって
伝えられた、わずかの格言があるにすぎない。むしろそれは、
語られもしない書かれもしない、（つまり不言不文の）道徳
の掟であって、だからこそ実行を強く求める力があるのであ
り、武士の心に刻みこまれている律法なのである。そしてそ
れは、一人のすぐれた頭脳によって創造されたものでもなく、
一人の高名な人物の生涯を基としてつくられたものでもな
い。それは、（わが国民が武をもって国を建てて以来）数百
年にわたる武士の生活の間に、徐々に発達をとげ、その形態
をつくってきたものである。道徳史上における武士道の地位
は、おそらく政治史上におけるイギリス憲法の地位と同じで
あろう。しかし武士道には、大憲章（マグナ・カルタ）もな
く、人身保護令（ハベアス・コルプス・アクト）に比較する
ものもない。たしかにわが国は、17世紀のはじめに「武家諸
法度」が制定されたが、その十三ヵ条は、主として、婚姻、
居城、徒党などに関することを規定しているだけであって、
道徳上の規制には、わずかに触れているに過ぎない。それ故
に、わが国の武士道が、いつ頃どこにおいて発生したのか、
「ここが淵源だ」と、その時期と場所を明確に示すことはで
きないのである。それは封建時代において、徐々に自覚され
ていったものであるから、時期については、その起源は封建
制の発生と同一であると見てよいであろう。しかし、封建制
そのものは、多くのたて糸とよこ糸によって織りなされてい
るものであり、武士道もまた、その複雑な性質をうけている
のである。イギリスにおける封建制度は、ノルマン征服[訳注1]の
時代に発生したといわれるが、わが国におけるその発生は、
12世紀の末、源頼朝の制覇（鎌倉幕府の成立）と同時だとい
える。しかし、イギリスにおける封建制の社会的要素が、遠

not a written code; at best it consists of a few maxims handed down from mouth to mouth or coming from the pen of some well-known warrior or savant. More frequently it is a code unuttered and unwritten, possessing all the more the powerful sanction of veritable deed, and of a law written on the fleshly tablets of the heart. It was founded not on the creation of one brain, however able, or on the life of a single personage, however renowned. It was an organic growth of decades and centuries of military career. It, perhaps, fills the same position in the history of ethics that the English Constitution does in political history; yet it has had nothing to compare with the Magna Charta or the Habeas Corpus Act. True, early in the seventeenth century Military Statutes (*Buké Hatto*) were promulgated; but their thirteen short articles were taken up mostly with marriages, castles, leagues, etc., and didactic regulations were but meagerly touched upon. We cannot, therefore, point out any definite time and place and say, "Here is its fountainhead." Only as it attains consciousness in the feudal age, its origin, in respect to time, may be identified with feudalism. But feudalism itself is woven of many threads, and Bushido shares its intricate nature. As in England the political institutions of feudalism may be said to date from the Norman Conquest, so we may say that in Japan its rise was simultaneous with the ascendancy of Yoritomo, late in the twelfth century. As, however, in England, we find the social elements of feudalism far back in the period previous to William the Conqueror, so, too, the germs of feudalism in

くウィリアム征服王以前にさかのぼることができるように、わが国における封建制の芽生えも、鎌倉時代よりはるか以前に存在していたのである。

　ヨーロッパと同じように、日本においても封建制度が確立されると、武士階級が自然に勢力をあらわしてきた。彼らは「サムライ」（侍）とよばれ、その言葉の意味からすれば、英語の古語である、クニヒト（cnihtあるいはknecht、knight）と同じで、護衛または従者を言うのであり、カエサルがアクィタニア地方に存在すると記したソルデュリイ（soldurii）や、タキトゥスがゲルマンの首長の配下にいると記したコミタティ（comitati）と性格が似ており、またもっと後世に匹敵するものを求めれば、中世ヨーロッパ史に現れるミリテス・メディイ（milites medii）があげられる。「サムライ」にあたる漢字の「武家」または「武士」という語も一般に使われてきた。彼らは特権階級であって、元来は戦闘を職業とする粗野な素性の者たちであった。この階級は、長い間戦闘がくり返されているうちに、もっとも勇猛果敢な者の中から自然に選び出されたのであり、その間にも淘汰の過程が進み、弱い者や、卑怯な者、臆病な者は自然と排除されていって、（アメリカの思想家）エマーソンの言葉を借りていえば「まったく男性的で、獣のごとき力をもつ粗野な者たち」だけが生き残り、ついには「サムライ」という家族とその階級をつくりあげてきたのである。そして、彼らはこの階級の者としての大きな名誉と特権を受けるようになると、その責任を自覚し、彼らの行動を律する共通の規準の必要を感じてきた。ことに彼らは常に戦闘者の立場にあり、またそれぞれの異なる氏族に属していたので、その必要はさらに大きかった。たとえば、医者が、医者仲間のいたずらな競争を制限するために、その職業的な道義を守り、あるいは弁護士がその道義を

Japan had been long existent before the period I have mentioned.

Again, in Japan as in Europe, when feudalism was formally inaugurated, the professional class of warriors naturally came into prominence. These were known as *samurai*, meaning literally, like the old English *cniht* (knecht, knight), guards or attendants— resembling in character the *soldurii*, whom Cæsar mentioned as existing in Aquitania, or the *comitati*, who, according to Tacitus, followed Germanic chiefs in his time; or, to take a still later parallel, the *milites medii* that one reads about in the history of Mediæval Europe. A Sinico-Japanese word *Bu-ké* or *Bu-shi* (Fighting Knights) was also adopted in common use. They were a privileged class, and must originally have been a rough breed who made fighting their vocation. This class was naturally recruited, in a long period of constant warfare, from the manliest and the most adventurous, and all the while the process of elimination went on, the timid and the feeble being sorted out, and only "a rude race, all masculine, with brutish strength," to borrow Emerson's phrase, surviving to form families and the ranks of the samurai. Coming to profess great honour and great privileges, and correspondingly great responsibilities, they soon felt the need of a common standard of behaviour, especially as they were always on a belligerent footing and belonged to different clans. Just as physicians limit competition among themselves by professional courtesy, just as lawyers sit in courts of hon-

破ったときには、査問会に出なければならないように、武士もまた、不徳義な行為をすれば、その者に厳しい制裁を下すなんらかの規準がなければならなかったのである。

「喧嘩を堂々とやれ！」というフェア・プレイの精神、この野蛮と子供らしさにみちた原始的な感覚の中には、きわめて豊かな道徳の芽生えを見ることができる。これはあらゆる文武の徳の根本ではないか。「小さな子供をいじめず、大きな子供に背を向けなかった者、という名を、私は後世に残したい」と言った、イギリスの小説（トーマス・ヒューズ〈1822–1896〉の『トム・ブラウンズ・スクールデイズ』）の主人公、トム・ブラウンの子供らしい願いをきいて、われわれは微笑する。（あたかもそんな願いをいだく年齢を通り過ぎてしまったかのように！）。けれども、この願いこそ、その上に偉大な道徳的建造物を建てるときの、その一隅におかれた礎石ではなかろうか。

さらに言えば、最も穏健で、平和を愛する宗教でさえ、この少年の願いに賛同しているものではないだろうか。この少年トムの願いが基礎となって、イギリスの偉大な国家が建設されているのである。武士道の根本に立つ礎石もまた、これよりも小さな石でないことが、じきにわかるであろう。（平和をその教義とする）クエーカー教徒は、戦いは攻撃的なものにせよ、防御的なものにせよ、野蛮であり不正であるとしているが、それでも（ドイツの思想家）レッシングが言うように、「欠点がいかに大きくても、その中から徳が興ってくることを、われわれは知っている」と言うことができよう[注2]。

注2 ラスキンは最も温厚で、平和を愛する人間の一人だった。しかし、彼は奮闘の生涯の崇拝者の熱心さで、戦争の価値を確信していた。その著書『野生のオリーヴの王冠』の中で、こう述べている。「私が、戦争はすべての技術の基礎であると言うとき、戦争が人間のすべての高徳と心的能力の基礎であるということも意味している。このことに気付いたときは、まことに奇異
→

our in cases of violated etiquette; so must also warriors possess some resort for final judgment on their misde-meanours.

Fair play in fight! What fertile germs of morality lie in this primitive sense of savagery and childhood. Is it not the root of all military and civic virtue? We smile (as if we had outgrown it!) at the boyish desire of the small Britisher, Tom Brown, "to leave behind him the name of a fellow who never bullied a little boy or turned his back on a big one." And yet, who does not know that this desire is the corner-stone on which moral structures of mighty dimensions can be reared? May I not go even so far as to say that the gentlest and most peace-loving of religions endorses this aspiration? The desire of Tom is the basis on which the greatness of England is largely built, and it will not take us long to discover that *Bushido* does not stand on a lesser pedestal. If fighting in itself, be it offensive or defensive, is, as Quakers rightly testify, brutal and wrong, we can still say with Lessing, "We know from what failings our virtue springs."[2]

---

[2] Ruskin was one of the most gentle-hearted and peace-loving men that ever lived. Yet he believed in war with all the fervor of a worshipper of the strenuous life. "When I tell you," he says in the *Crown of Wild Olive*, "that war is the foundation of all the arts, I mean also that it is the foundation of all the high virtues and faculties of men. It is very strange to me to discover this, and very dreadful, but I saw it to be quite an undeniable fact… I found, in brief, that all great nations learned their truth of word and strength of thought in war; that they were nourished in war and wasted by peace; taught by war and deceived by peace; trained by war and betrayed by peace; in a word, that they were born in war and expired in peace."

　「卑怯」であり「臆病」であることは、健全で質朴な性質の
人間にとっては、最大の侮辱の言葉である。少年は、このよ
うな観念をもってそれからの人生をはじめる。武士も同じこ
とである。しかし、人間は成長するにしたがいその生活は拡
がり、社会との関わりも多くなり、初期の信念を正当化し、
さらに満足し発展してゆくために、より高い権威と、より合
理的な起源を求めようとする。もし、戦闘の利害のみを目的
として、それを支えるより高い道徳の規準がなかったならば、
武士の理想は、武士道とはほど遠いものに堕ちていたであろ
う。ヨーロッパにおけるキリスト教は、騎士道については譲
歩するような解釈をしているが、それにもかかわらず、騎士
道に霊的な要素を入れた。それについては（フランスの詩人）
ラマルティーヌは、「宗教と戦争と名誉は、完全なるキリス
ト教騎士の三つの魂である」と、言っている。日本において
も、武士道の淵源となる要素がいくつかあった。

→
な感じを抱き、恐ろしいとも思ったが、これはまったく否定しがたい事実で
あると思った……要するに私は、すべての偉大な国家は言葉の真実と思考の
力を戦争において学んだことを、また、国家は戦争において養い育てられ、
平和において消耗させられることを、つまり、国家は戦争の中で生まれ、平
和の中で息を引き取ることを知ったのである」。

"Sneaks" and "cowards" are epithets of the worst opprobrium to healthy, simple natures. Childhood begins life with these notions, and knighthood also; but, as life grows larger and its relations many-sided, the early faith seeks sanction from higher authority and more rational sources for its own justification, satisfaction, and development. If military systems had operated alone, without higher moral support, how far short of chivalry would the ideal of knighthood have fallen! In Europe, Christianity, interpreted with concessions convenient to chivalry, infused it nevertheless with spiritual data. "Religion, war, and glory were the three souls of a perfect Christian knight," says Lamartine. In Japan there were several sources of Bushido.

第 2 章

武士道の淵源

武士道の淵源をたずねるにあたって、私はまず、仏教から
はじめようと思う。仏教は、（常に心を安んじて）すべ
てを運命にまかせるという平常の感覚を武士道に与えた。避け
ることができない運命に対しては冷静に服従するという、危険
や災難に直面したときのストイック[訳注2]的な落ちつきと、生を
軽んじて死に親しむ心を与えてきた。剣道の達人（柳生但馬守）
は、その門弟（であった徳川三代将軍家光公）に、剣の奥義を
伝え終ったとき、「これ以上のことを教えることはできません。
あとは禅に学んでください」と言ったという話がある。禅とは、
（古代インド語の）ディヤーナの日本語訳であり、（小泉八雲の
説明にあるように）「言葉による表現の範囲を超えた思想の領
域に、瞑想をもって自ら達しようとする人間の努力をいう[注1]」
という意味である。その方法は瞑想であり、その目的とすると

注1 ラフカディオ・ハーン著『異国的および回顧的』84ページ。

CHAPTER II

SOURCES OF BUSHIDO

I MAY begin with Buddhism. It furnished a sense of calm trust in Fate, a quiet submission to the inevitable, that stoic composure in sight of danger or calamity, that disdain of life and friendliness with death. A foremost teacher of swordsmanship, when he saw his pupil master the utmost of his art, told him, "Beyond this my instruction must give way to Zen teaching." "Zen" is the Japanese equivalent for the Dhyâna, which "represents human effort to reach through meditation zones of thought beyond the range of verbal expression."[1] Its method is contemplation, and its purport, so far as I understand it, to be convinced of a principle that underlies all phenomena, and, if it can, of the Absolute itself, and thus to put

---

[1] Lafcadio Hearn, *Exotics and Retrospectives,* p. 84.

ころは、私の理解するところによれば、（この宇宙の）すべての現象の底に存在する原理を確認し、それによって、自己を絶対的なるものと調和せしむることにある。このように定義すれば、神の教えは一宗一派の教義にとどまらず（それ以上のものであって）、人間は誰でもこの絶対的なるものを認識できれば、俗世間のあらゆる現象を解脱して「新しい天と新しい地」に目覚めることができるのである。

　仏教が武士道に与えることができなかったものを、神道が豊かに充たしてくれた。主君に対する忠節、祖先に対する崇拝、および親に対する孝行がこれである。この三つの教えは、他のいかなる宗教の信条によっても教えられなかったものである。これによって、武士の（ややもすれば陥りやすい）傲慢な性格は抑制されて、服従性が加えられた。神道の教義には、（キリスト教でいう）「原罪訳注3」の観念はない。かえって反対に、人間性の善を信じ、人間の魂は本来神のように清浄であるとして、その神託を聞く所を神の社として崇め尊ぶ。神社に詣でる者は、その礼拝の対象と道具がはなはだ少なく、奥の殿に掲げられている質素な一面の鏡が、礼拝の主なる対象であることがわかるだろう。この鏡の存在する理由は、容易に説明がつく。鏡は人の心を映し、人の心が静穏で澄みきっているときには、神の真の姿を映すからである。それ故に、神殿の前に立って礼拝する者は、鏡の輝く面に映っている自分の姿を見ることになる。このような礼拝の行為は「汝自身を知れ」という、古代（ギリシャ）のデルフィの神託訳注4と同じである。だが、「自分を知る」ということは、ギリシャの宗教でも、日本の神道でも、人間の肉体に関する知識、すなわち解剖学や精神物理学のことではなくて、知識とは道徳に関するもの、つまりわれわれの道徳的性質の内省、ということである。

oneself in harmony with this Absolute. Thus defined, the teaching was more than the dogma of a sect, and whoever attains to the perception of the Absolute raises himself above mundane things and awakes "to a new Heaven and a new Earth."

What Buddhism failed to give, Shintoism offered in abundance. Such loyalty to the sovereign, such reverence for ancestral memory, and such filial piety as are not taught by any other creed, were inculcated by the Shinto doctrines, imparting passivity to the otherwise arrogant character of the samurai. Shinto theology has no place for the dogma of "original sin." On the contrary, it believes in the innate goodness and Godlike purity of the human soul, adoring it as the adytum from which divine oracles are proclaimed. Everybody has observed that the Shinto shrines are conspicuously devoid of objects and instruments of worship, and that a plain mirror hung in the sanctuary forms the essential part of its furnishing. The presence of this article is easy to explain: it typifies the human heart, which, when perfectly placid and clear, reflects the very image of the Deity. When you stand, therefore, in front of the shrine to worship, you see your own image reflected on its shining surface, and the act of worship is tantamount to the old Delphic injunction, "Know Thyself." But self-knowledge does not imply, either in the Greek or Japanese teaching, knowledge of the physical part of man, not his anatomy or his psycho-physics; knowledge was to be of a

（ドイツの歴史学者）モムゼンは、ギリシャ人とローマ人を
比較して、「ギリシャ人の祈りは思索であり天を仰ぐが、ロ
ーマ人の祈りは内省であり頭を垂れて瞑想する」と言ってい
る。日本人の宗教的観念は、本質的にはローマ人と同じで、
個人的な道徳意識より、むしろ国民的な意識をあらわしてい
るといっていいだろう。神道における自然崇拝の観念は、わ
が国土に親しませ愛着させるということであり、祖先崇拝の
観念は、人々の血脈をその源にまでたどってゆき、皇室をも
って全国民の共通の祖となした。つまり、日本人にとって、
わが国土は金を採掘したり、穀物を収穫したりする土地以上
の意味をもっており、そこはわれわれの祖先の霊が宿ってい
る神聖な棲処なのである。われわれにとって、天皇はたんな
る法治国家の治安の長ではなく、文化国家の擁護者でもない。
それはこの地上において肉体をもった天の代表者であり、天
の力とその仁愛の心を兼ねそなえておられる方である。（イ
ギリスの思想家）M・ブートミー[注2]が、イギリス王室につい
て、「それはたんに権威をあらわすものではなくて、イギリ
ス国民統一の創造者であり象徴である」と言っていることが、
真実であるとすれば、私はそう信じるが、日本の皇室におい
ては、このことは二倍にも三倍にも強調されて言うべきであ
ろう。

　神道の教義は、わが民族の感情生活における二つの特質、
すなわち忠君と愛国の道を説いている。アーサー・メイ・ク
ナップが、「ヘブル文学では、著者が述べているのが神のこ
とか、国家のことか、天国のことか、エルサレムのことか、
救世主のことか、国民全体のことなのか、わかりにくいこと
が多い[注3]」と言っているのは至言である。わが民族の信仰の

[注2] ブートミー著『イギリス国民』188ページ。
[注3] クナップ著『封建的および近代的日本』第1巻183ページ。

moral kind, the introspection of our moral nature. Mommsen, comparing the Greek and the Roman, says that when the former worshipped he raised his eyes to Heaven, for his prayer was contemplation, while the latter veiled his head, for his was reflection. Essentially like the Roman conception of religion, our reflection brought into prominence not so much the moral as the national consciousness of the individual. Its nature-worship endeared the country to our inmost souls, while its ancestor-worship, tracing from lineage to lineage, made the Imperial family the fountain-head of the whole nation. To us the country is more than land and soil from which to mine gold or to reap grain—it is the sacred abode of the gods, the spirits of our forefathers: to us the Emperor is more than the Arch Constable of a *Rechtsstaat*, or even the Patron of a *Culturstaat*—he is the bodily representative of Heaven on earth, blending in his person its power and its mercy. If what M. Boutmy[2] says is true of English royalty—that it "is not only the image of authority, but the author and symbol of national unity," as I believe it to be, doubly and trebly may this be affirmed of royalty in Japan.

The tenets of Shintoism cover the two predominating features of the emotional life of our race.—Patriotism and Loyalty. Arthur May Knapp very truly says: "In Hebrew literature it is often difficult to tell whether the writer is speaking of God or of the Commonwealth; of Heaven or of Jerusalem; of the Messiah or of the Nation itself."[3] A

[2] *The English People*, p. 188.
[3] *Feudal and Modern Japan*, vol. I, p. 183.

用語にも、同様の混乱がみられる。私が混乱と言ったのは、論理的な頭脳の持ち主なら、言葉が曖昧であると思うはずだからである。にもかかわらず、国民的な本能と民族感情の制約の中にあるわが国の信仰は、体系的な哲学や合理的神学に装われることは決してない。この宗教は――あるいは、この宗教が表わしているのは民族感情だと言うほうが、より正確なのだろうか?――忠君愛国の観念を、武士道の中に充分に吹き込んだ。これらの観念は、教義としてよりも、(感情の)刺激として作用した。神道は、中世ヨーロッパのキリスト教会とは異なり、その信者に対してほとんど信仰の箇条を規定してはおらず、簡単率直な形式の行為の規準があるのみである。

　厳正な意味における道徳的教養に関しては、孔子の教える道が、武士道のもっとも豊かな淵源であった。孔子が説いた、君臣、父子、夫婦、長幼、朋友の、この五倫の道は、中国よりこの聖人の教義が輸入される以前から、わが国の民族的本能が、これを認め重んじていたことであって、孔子の教えはこれを確認したにすぎない。

　孔子の説く政治道徳は、平静で寛容、その上処世の知恵に富んでおり、民衆の上に立つ武士の意によく適った。また、孔子の説く貴族的で保守的な教えは、政治家としての武士の要件ともよく合致した。

　孔子についで孟子も、武士道の大きな拠り所となった。孟子の、説得力に溢れ、民主的なところの多い教えは、多くの武士に同感されその心を動かした。その説は、既存社会の秩序を乱し、転覆させる危険思想だとして、長い間禁書になっ

similar confusion may be noticed in the nomenclature of our national faith. I said confusion, because it will be so deemed by a logical intellect on account of its verbal ambiguity; still, being a frame work of national instinct and race feelings, it never pretends to systematic philosophy or a rational theology. This religion—or, is it not more correct to say, the race emotions which this religion expressed?—thoroughly imbued Bushido with loyalty to the sovereign and love of country. These acted more as impulses than as doctrines; for Shintoism, unlike the Mediæval Christian Church, prescribed to its votaries scarcely any *credenda*, furnishing them at the same time with *agenda* of a straightforward and simple type.

As to strictly ethical doctrines, the teachings of Confucius were the most prolific source of Bushido. His enunciation of the five moral relations between master and servant (the governing and the governed), father and son, husband and wife, older and younger brother, and between friend and friend, was but a confirmation of what the race instinct had recognised before his writings were introduced from China. The calm, benignant and worldly-wise character of his politico-ethical precepts was particularly well suited to the samurai, who formed the ruling class. His aristocratic and conservative tone was well adapted to the requirements of these warrior statesmen. Next to Confucius, Mencius exercised an immense authority over Bushido. His forcible and often quite democratic theories were exceedingly taking to sympathetic natures, and they were even thought dangerous to,

たこともあった。それにもかかわらず、この賢人の言葉は、
武士の心から永久に離れることはなかった。

　孔子孟子の書物は、（学問に志す）青少年の第一の教科書
であり、また、大人たちが議論し合う場合の最高の権威とな
るものであった。しかしながら、この二聖人が著わした古典
を読み、その言葉を知っているだけの者は、世間から高い尊
敬は払われず、「論語読みの論語知らず」ということわざが
あるくらいで、そのような者はかえってあざけられた。典型
的な一人の武士（西郷南洲）は「文学の物知りは、書物の虫
である」と言い、またある人（江戸時代の学者三浦梅園）は、
「学問は臭い菜のようなものである。よくよくその臭みを洗
い落とさなければ食べることはできない。少し書物を読めば
少し臭くなり、よけい読めばよけい臭くなる。困ったもので
ある」と言った。その意味するところは、知識がもし、それ
を学ぶ者の心に同化せず、その者の品性に表れることがない
ならば、本当の知識とはいえない、ということである。たん
に知識だけの人間は、それ専門の機械と同じことであると思
われた。知力は道徳的な感情の下位におかれた。人間も宇宙
も、霊的であり道徳的であると考えられた。「宇宙の進行に
には道徳性を有しない」と言った、（イギリスの文学者）ハク
スレーの断定を、武士道は容認することはできなかったので
ある。
　武士道は、そのような種類のたんなる知識を軽んじた。知
識は終極の目的ではなく、智恵を獲得するための手段として
追求すべきであるとした。したがって、その域に到達できな
い者は、他人の求めに応じて、詩歌や格言を吐き出すだけの
便利な機械にすぎないとされた。それ故に、知識と、人生に

and subversive of, the existing social order, hence his works were for a long time under censure. Still, the words of this master mind found permanent lodgment in the heart of the samurai.

The writings of Confucius and Mencius formed the principal text-books for youths and the highest authority in discussion among the old. A mere acquaintance with the classics of these two sages was held, however, in no high esteem. A common proverb ridicules one who has only an intellectual knowledge of Confucius, as a man ever studious but ignorant of *Analects.* A typical samurai calls a literary savant a book-smelling sot. Another compares learning to an ill smelling vegetable that must be boiled and boiled before it is fit for use. A man who has read little smells a little pedantic, and a man who has read much smells yet more so; both are alike unpleasant. The writer meant thereby that knowledge becomes really such only when it is assimilated in the mind of the learner and shows in his character. An intellectual specialist was considered a machine. Intellect itself was considered subordinate to ethical emotion. Man and the universe were conceived to be alike spiritual and ethical. Bushido could not accept the judgment of Huxley, that the cosmic process was unmoral.

Bushido made light of knowledge of such. It was not pursued as an end in itself, but as a means to the attainment of wisdom. Hence, he who stopped short of this end was regarded no higher than a convenient machine, which could turn out poems and maxims at bidding.

おける知識の実践は同一視された。このようなソクラテス的な教義の最大の説明者は、（東洋においては）倦むことなく知行合一を唱えた中国の哲学者、王陽明である。

ここで余談に入ることをお許しいただきたいのは、人格高潔な武士の中で、王陽明の教えから深い感化をうけた者は少なくないからである。西洋の読者は、王陽明の著書の中に、『新約聖書』とよく似ている言葉の数々を、容易に見出すことであろう。それぞれに固有な用語の相違にもかかわらず、「まず神の国と神の義を求めよ。そうすればすべてこれらのものは、汝らに加えられるであろう」という言葉は、王陽明の書の中に終始見出される思想である。

王陽明を師とあおぐ日本人[注4]は「天地生々の主宰、人に宿りて心となる。故に心は活物にして、常に照々たり」と言い、また「その本体の霊明は常に照々たり、その霊明人意に渡らず、自然より発現して、よくその善悪を照らすを良知という、かの天神の光明なり」と言っている。この言葉は、アイザック・ペニントンなどの神秘主義の哲学者たちの言葉ときわめて似た響きではないか！

私の考えによれば、神道の簡潔な教義にあらわれているような日本人の心性は、王陽明の説くような教えを受入れるには、とくに適していたと思われるのである。王陽明はその良

注4 三輪執斎

Thus, knowledge was conceived as identical with its practical application in life; and this Socratic doctrine found its greatest exponent in the Chinese philosopher, Wan Yang Ming, who never wearies of repeating, "To know and to act are one and the same."

I beg leave for a moment's digression while I am on this subject, inasmuch as some of the noblest types of *bushi* were strongly influenced by the teachings of this sage. Western readers will easily recognise in his writings many parallels to the New Testament. Making allowance for the terms peculiar to either teaching, the passage, "Seek ye first the kingdom of God and his righteousness; and all these things shall be added unto you," conveys a thought that may be found on almost any page of Wan Yang Ming. A Japanese disciple[4] of his says—"The lord of heaven and earth, of all living beings, dwelling in the heart of man, becomes his mind (*Kokoro*); hence a mind is a living thing, and is ever luminous": and again, "The spiritual light of our essential being is pure, and is not affected by the will of man. Spontaneously springing up in our mind, it shows what is right and wrong: it is then called conscience; it is even the light that proceedeth from the god of heaven." How very much do these words sound like some passages from Isaac Pennington or other philosophic mystics!

I am inclined to think that the Japanese mind, as expressed in the simple tenets of the Shinto religion, was particularly open to the reception of Yang Ming's pre-

---

[4] Miwa Shissai.

心無謬説を極端な超越主義にまで押し進め、正邪の区別だけ
でなく、心的事実と物理的現象の性質をも認知する能力が良
心にあるとした。バークレイやフィヒテを超えているとはい
わないが、その徹底した理想主義は、人間の理解を超える物
事の存在を否定している。その理論体系は、唯我論が非難さ
れている論理的誤りをすべて含んでいたとしても、強固な確
信が力となっており、性格については個性を育て、気性につ
いては運命を甘受する落ち着きを育てるうえで、道徳を重視
する点については、反駁の余地はない。

　これまで述べてきたように、その淵源は何であったにせよ、
武士道が自ら吸収し同化した本質的な原理は、その数は少な
くしかも単純なものであった。しかしわが国の歴史上、戦乱
に明け暮れた最も不安定な時代の、不安な日々においてさえ
も、人生に確固とした不屈の教訓を与えるのに充分だったの
である。われわれの先祖である武士たちの、健全で純朴な性
格は、古代思想の大道、あるいは小道から、平凡で断片的な
教訓の落穂を拾い集め、それを精神の豊かな糧とし、時代の
要求に応じて、その教訓からさらに比類のない人間の道を新
たに形成していったのである。
　鋭敏なるフランスの学者、ド・ラ・マズリエールは、（その
著書『日本史論』の中で）16世紀の日本の印象について次の
ように述べている。
「16世紀の中頃にいたるまで、日本においては政治も社会も
宗教も、すべて混乱に陥っていた。しかし、内乱があいつぎ、
生活の仕方は野蛮な状態に逆戻りし、自分の権利は自分で守
らなければならなくなって、（フランスの哲学者）テーヌが
16世紀のイタリア人について、『旺盛な独創力、すみやかな

cepts. He carried his doctrine of the infallibility of conscience to extreme transcendentalism, attributing to it the
faculty to perceive, not only the distinction between right
and wrong, but also the nature of psychical facts and
physical phenomena. He went as far as, if not farther
than, Berkeley and Fichte, in Idealism, denying the existence of things outside of human ken. If his system had all
the logical errors charged to Solipsism, it had all the efficacy of strong conviction, and its moral import in developing individuality of character and equanimity of
temper cannot be gainsaid.

Thus, whatever the sources, the essential principles
which *Bushido* imbibed from them and assimilated to itself,
were few and simple. Few and simple as these were, they
were sufficient to furnish a safe conduct of life even through
the unsafest days of the most unsettled period of our
nation's history. The wholesome unsophisticated nature
of our warrior ancestors derived ample food for their
spirit from a sheaf of commonplace and fragmentary
teachings, gleaned as it were on the highways and byways of
ancient thought, and, stimulated by the demands of the
age, formed from these gleanings a new and unique type
of manhood. An acute French savant, M. de la Mazelière,
thus sums up his impressions of the sixteenth century:

"Toward the middle of the sixteenth century, all is
confusion in Japan, in the government, in society, in the
church. But the civil wars the manners returning to bar-
barism, the necessity for each to execute justice for himself,—these formed men comparable to those Italians of

決断と着手の習性、偉大なる実行と忍耐の能力』と賞めたた
えた、それと比較できる人間が、日本においても形成されて
きた。イタリアにおけると同様に日本においても、『中世の
粗野なる風習』は人間をして『完全に戦闘的、反抗的な』偉
大なる動物となしたのである。そしてこれこそ日本民族の主
要なる特性、つまり精神と気質のいちじるしい複雑性が、16
世紀において最高度に発揮され、多方面に発展していった理
由である。中国においてもインドにおいても、人間の優劣は、
主としてその人の精力もしくは知力の程度によるとしている
が、日本ではそれと異なり、その人の品性の独自性によって
判断する。個性のある人格は、優秀なる民族と、発達した文
明のしるしである。（ドイツの哲学者）ニーチェが好んだ言
葉を借りていえば、アジア大陸においては、その民族を語る
のは平原を語ることであるが、日本においてはヨーロッパと
同じように、山岳によってその民族を代表せしめているので
ある、と言えよう」

　マズリエールの評論の対象となった、わが民族の共有する
特性について、私はこれから解明を試みようと思う。まず
「義」について次章で述べよう。

the sixteenth century, in whom Taine praises 'the vigorous initiative, the habit of sudden resolutions and desperate undertakings, the grand capacity to do and to suffer.' In Japan as in Italy 'the rude manners of the Middle Ages' made of man a superb animal, 'wholly militant and wholly resistant.' And this is why the sixteenth century displays in the highest degree the principal quality of the Japanese race, that great diversity which one finds there between minds (*esprits*) as well as between temperaments. While in India and even in China men seem to differ chiefly in degree of energy or intelligence, in Japan they differ by originality of character as well. Now, individuality is the sign of superior races and of civilisations already developed. If we make use of an expression dear to Nietzsche, we might say that in Asia, to speak of humanity is to speak of its plains; in Japan as in Europe, one represents it above all by its mountains."

To the pervading characteristics of the men of whom M. de la Mazelière writes, let us now address ourselves. I shall begin with Rectitude.

第 3 章

義または正義

義は、武士道の中でも最も厳しい教訓である。武士にとって、卑劣な行動や不正な行為ほど忌むべきものはない。義の観念には、あるいは誤ったところがあるかもしれないし、狭少なところがあるかもしれない。ある著名な武士（林子平）は、これを定義して、「義とは、勇気を伴って為される決断力である。道理にまかせて決断をし、いささかもためらうことをしない心をいう。死ぬべき場合には死に、討つべき場合には討つことである」と言った。

またある勤王の志士（真木和泉）は、「節義とは、例えていえば、人の体に骨があるようなものである。骨がなければ首も正しく胴体の上に坐っていることができない。それと同じように、人は才能があってもまた学問があっても、節義がなければ世に立つことはできない。節義があれば、不作法、不調法であっても、武士としてあるだけはこと欠かないもの

CHAPTER III

RECTITUDE
OR JUSTICE

HERE we discern the most cogent precept in the code of the samurai. Nothing is more loathsome to him than underhand dealings and crooked undertakings. The conception of Rectitude may be erroneous—it may be narrow. A well-known bushi defines it as a power of resolution;—"Rectitude is the power of deciding upon a certain course of conduct in accordance with reason, without wavering;—to die when it is right to die, to strike when to strike is right." Another speaks of it in the following terms: "Rectitude is the bone that gives firmness and stature. As without bones the head cannot rest on the top of the spine, nor hands move nor feet stand, so without rectitude neither talent nor learning can make of a human frame a samurai. With it the lack of accomplishments is as

である」と言っている。さらに孟子は、「仁は人の心であり、義は人の道である」と言い、かつ嘆いて、「その道を捨ててかえりみず、その心を見失って求めることを知らないのは、哀しいことである。人は鶏や犬を見失っても、再びこれを求めることができるが、心を見失っては、もうこれを求めることはできない」と言った。

　ここで孟子から300年のちに異国で偉大な教師（キリスト）が「鏡に映して見るようにぼんやりとしか見えないが」と言った、つまり自分は義の道であり、自分を通じて見失われたものを見つけることができる、というこの比喩が思い起こされるではないか。やや脱線してしまったが、要するに孟子によれば、義とは、人が見失ってしまった楽園を回復するために歩んでゆかねばならぬ、真直なかつ狭い道である。

　わが国の封建時代の末期には、泰平の時代が長く続いたので、武士の生活に余暇が生じ、あらゆる種類の娯楽と技芸のたしなみが生じた。しかしそのような時代においてさえも、「義士」という言葉は、学問や芸術に長じた者に与えられるいかなる名称よりも、すぐれたものであると考えられていた。わが国の（赤穂浪士）47名の忠臣は、俗に義士と呼ばれ、わが国民教育で大いに取りあげられているのである。

　ややもすれば、陰謀が戦術として通り、欺瞞が戦略として通っていた時代に、義士とよばれるこの正直な率直な男子たちの徳は、宝石のように光り輝き、人々の最も高く賞めたたえたものだったのである。義と勇の二つは双生児であって、共に武士の徳であるとされた。しかし勇について述べる前に、しばらく「義理」について説明しよう。義理は義から出て、はじめはその元の意味から、わずかにしか離れていなかった

nothing." Mencius calls Benevolence man's mind, and Rectitude or Righteousness his path. "How lamentable," he exclaims, "is it to neglect the path and not pursue it, to lose the mind and not know to seek it again! When men's fowls and dogs are lost, they know to seek for them again, but they lose their mind and do not know to seek for it." Have we not here "as in a glass darkly" a parable propounded three hundred years later in another clime and by a greater Teacher, Who called Himself the Way of righteousness, through whom the lost could be found? But I stray from my point. Righteousness, according to Mencius, is a straight and narrow path which a man ought to take to regain the lost paradise.

Even in the latter days of feudalism, when the long continuance of peace brought leisure into the life of the warrior class, and with it dissipations of all kinds and accomplishments of gentle arts, the epithet *Gishi* (a man of rectitude) was considered superior to any name that signified mastery of learning or art. The Forty-seven Faithfuls—of whom so much is made in our popular education—are known in common parlance as the Forty-seven *Gishi.*

In times when cunning artifice was liable to pass for military tact and downright falsehood for *ruse de guerre*, this manly virtue, frank and honest, was a jewel that shone the brightest and was most highly praised. Rectitude is a twin brother to Valour, another martial virtue. But before proceeding to speak of Valour, let me linger a little while on what I may term a derivation from Recti-

が、次第に離れていって、ついには俗世間で誤り用いられるようになり、本来の意味は曲げられてしまった。義理という言葉は、もともと「正義の道理」という意味であったが、時代を経るにしたがい、漠然とした義務の観念を意味するようになって、世論が人々に対し、これを守り行うことを期待する言葉となってしまった。義理という言葉が、本来もっている純粋な意味は、単純で明快な義務のことであった。したがって、両親や目上の者や目下の者からはじまって、一般社会などに義理を負っているという、その義理はすなわち義務という意味であった。なんとなれば、義務とは「正義の道理」がわれわれにそれを要求し、かつ命令するものに外ならないからである。「正義の道理」が、われわれに対する絶対命令でないわけがあったろうか。

　以上述べたように、義理の本来の意味は義務に外ならないのであるが、この義理という言葉が出てきた理由は、次のような事実に由来すると思われる。すなわち、われわれの行為、たとえば父母に仕えるという行為の唯一の動機は、愛であるべきだが、もしそれが欠けた場合、孝行を命ずる何らかの権威が他になくてはならない。そこで人々はこの権威を、義理ということで形成していった。この義理という権威を形成したことは、きわめて正しかった。もし愛が徳行を促さない場合は、人間の知性に頼れば、理性がすぐに働いて、正しい行為をする必要性を納得させるからである。同じことは、他の道徳的な義務についても言い得る。もし人が、義務を重荷と感じ、それを嫌うならば、義理がただちにあらわれてきて介入し、その人が義務を怠ることを妨げるのである。

　義理をこのように理解するとき、それは厳格な教師のようなものであって、鞭を手にして怠け者を打ちすえ、その役目を果たさせるのである。それ故に、義理は道徳における第二

tude, which, at first deviating slightly from its original, became more and more removed from it, until its meaning was perverted in the popular acceptance. I speak of *Gi-ri*, literally the Right Reason, but which came in time to mean a vague sense of duty which public opinion expects an incumbent to fulfil. In its original and unalloyed sense, it meant duty, pure and simple,—hence, we speak of the *Giri* we owe to parents, to superiors, to inferiors, to society at large, and so forth. In these instances *Giri* is duty; for what else is duty than what Right Reason demands and commands us to do? Should not Right Reason be our categorical imperative?

Giri primarily meant no more than duty, and I dare say its etymology was derived from the fact, that in our conduct, say to our parents, though love should be the only motive, lacking that, there must be some other authority to enforce filial piety; and they formulated this authority in *Giri*. Very rightly did they formulate this authority—*Giri*—since if love does not rush to deeds of virtue, recourse must be had to man's intellect and his reason must be quickened to convince him of the necessity of acting aright. The same is true of any other moral obligation. The instant Duty becomes onerous, Right Reason steps in to prevent our shirking it.

Giri thus understood is a severe task master, with a birch-rod in his hand to make sluggards perform their part. It is a secondary power in ethics; as a motive it is

義的な力であるに過ぎず、動機としてはキリスト教における愛の教えと比べると、いちじるしく劣っている。愛は律法なのである。思うに、義理は人為的社会の諸条件から生みだされたものである。どのような社会かといえば、偶然的な生まれや実力に関係のない恩典によって階級的差別が構築され、家族が社会的な単位であり、年長者はなんら才能がなくても重んじられ、自然の愛情はしばしば人間の恣意的につくった習慣に屈服しなければならなかった社会である。このような人為性のために、義理はやがて堕落し、たとえば、母親がその長子を助けるために、必要とあればその弟妹を犠牲にしたり、あるいは父親の放蕩のためにその娘の貞操を売ったりするのは何故であるか、これらの理由を説明したり、是認したりするときに呼びおこされる漠然とした適否の感覚となってしまった。「正義の道理」として出発した義理は、私見では、階級的義務観による決疑論に屈服した場合が多かったのである。さらには、非難をおそれる不安の種にまで堕落してしまった。（イギリスの作家、ウォルター・）スコットが、愛国心について「それは最も美しいものであると同時に、しばしば、以て非なる他の感情の仮面としてあらわれるもっとも疑わしいものである」と言っていることは、義理についても言い得るのではないだろうか。義理は、正しい道理から遠ざかって誤用されるようになると、あらゆる種類の詭弁と偽善の隠れみのとなってしまった。それ故に、武士道においても、もし正しい勇気の信念と、敢為堅忍の精神がなかったならば、義理は一変して、卑怯者の巣と化してしまったであろう。

infinitely inferior to the Christian doctrine of love, which should be *the* law. I deem it a product of the conditions of an artificial society—of a society in which accident of birth and unmerited favour instituted class distinctions, in which the family was the social unit, in which seniority of age was of more account than superiority of talents, in which natural affections had often to succumb before arbitrary man-made customs. Because of this very artificiality, *Giri* in time degenerated into a vague sense of propriety called up to explain this and sanction that,—as, for example, why a mother must, if need be, sacrifice all her other children in order to save the first-born; or why a daughter must sell her chastity to get funds to pay for the father's dissipation, and the like. Starting as Right Reason, *Giri* has, in my opinion, often stooped to casuistry. It has even degenerated into cowardly fear of censure. I might say of *Giri* what Scott wrote of patriotism, that "as it is the fairest, so it is often the most suspicious, mask of other feelings." Carried beyond or below Right Reason, *Giri* became a monstrous misnomer. It harboured under its wings every sort of sophistry and hypocrisy. It would have been easily turned into a nest of cowardice, if Bushido had not a keen and correct sense of courage, the spirit of daring and bearing.

第4章

勇気・敢為堅忍の精神

勇気は、義のために行われるものでなければ、徳としての価値はほとんどない。

孔子は『論語』の中で、いつもの消極的な論法にしたがって、勇気についての定義を下し、「義を見てなさざるは勇なきなり」と説いているが、この格言を積極的に言い直せば「勇気とは義をなすことである」ということになるであろう。

あらゆる危険をおかして命をあやうくし、死に向って飛び込むことは、しばしば勇気と同一に見られた。しかし、このような武人の無謀な行為は、シェークスピアの言う、いわゆる「勇気の私生児」であって、不当に讃美された。しかし、武士道においては、そうではなかった。死に値いしないことのために死ぬのを、「犬死」といって卑しめてきた。（ギリシャの哲人）プラトンは、勇気を定義して「恐るべきものと、恐るべからざるものとを識別することである」と言っている

CHAPTER IV

COURAGE, THE SPIRIT OF DARING AND BEARING

COURAGE was scarcely deemed worthy to be counted among virtues, unless it was exercised in the cause of Righteousness. In his *Analects* Confucius defines Courage by explaining, as is often his wont, what its negative is. "Perceiving what is right," he says, "and doing it not, argues lack of courage." Put this epigram into a positive statement, and it runs "Courage is doing what is right." To run all kinds of hazards, to jeopard one's self, to rush into the jaws of death—these are too often identified with Valour, and in the profession of arms such rashness of conduct—what Shakespeare calls "valour misbegot"—is unjustly applauded; but not so in the Precepts of Knighthood. Death for a cause unworthy of dying for, was called a "dog's death." "To rush into the thick of battle and to be

が、プラトンの名前すら聞いたことがなかった、水戸の義公（徳川光圀）は、次のように言っている。「戦いに臨んで討死することは難しいことではない。それはどのような野人でもできることである。しかし、生きるべきときに生き、死ぬべきときに死ぬことこそ、真の勇気なのである」と。西洋においては、肉体的な勇気と道徳的な勇気とを区別しているが、わが国民の間でも昔からそのことはよく知られており、いやしくも武家に生まれた者は、少年の頃より「大勇」と「匹夫の勇」との違いをわきまえない者はいなかったであろう。

　勇気、我慢、大胆、自若、勇猛などの心性は、少年武士の心に最も強く訴えられ、実例を模範として幼いときから訓練され、励みとされた、いわば最も人気のある徳性であった。彼らは、母親のふところに抱かれた幼児のころから、軍記物語をくり返し聞かされ、もし何か苦痛なことがあって泣き出したりすれば、「これくらいのことで泣くとは、なんて臆病なんでしょう」と、母親に叱られ、「もし戦場に出て、腕を切られるようなことがあったら、どうしますか。もし切腹を命じられたときは、どうしますか」と、励まされた。

　（歌舞伎における）『先代萩』の千松が、「籠に寄りくる親鳥の、餌ばみをすれば小雀の、嘴さしよるありさまに、小鳥を羨む稚心にも、侍の子は、ひもじい目をするのが忠義じゃ」と、けなげにも我慢したといういじらしい話は、人々のよく知っていることである。

　その他にも、勇気と我慢を説いたお伽ばなしは数多くあっ

slain in it," says a Prince of Mito, "is easy enough, and the merest churl is equal to the task; but," he continues, "it is true courage to live when it is right to live, and to die only when it is right to die"—and yet the prince had not even heard of the name of Plato, who defines courage as "the knowledge of things that a man should fear and that he should not fear." A distinction which is made in the West between moral and physical courage has long been recognised among us. What samurai youth has not heard of "Great Valour" and the "Valour of a Villain?"

Valour, Fortitude, Bravery, Fearlessness, Courage, being the qualities of soul which appeal most easily to juvenile minds, and which can be trained by exercise and example, were, so to speak, the most popular virtues, early emulated among the youth. Stories of military exploits were repeated almost before boys left their mother's breast. Does a little booby cry for any ache? The mother scolds him in this fashion: "What a coward to cry for a trifling pain! What will you do when your arm is cut off in battle? What when you are called upon to commit *hara-kiri*?" We all know the pathetic fortitude of a famished little boy-prince of Sendai, who in the drama is made to say to his little page, "Seest thou those tiny sparrows in the nest, how their yellow bills are opened wide, and now see! There comes their mother with worms to feed them. How eagerly and happily the little ones eat! But for a samurai, when his stomach is empty, it is a disgrace to feel hungry." Anecdotes of fortitude and bravery abound in nursery tales, though stories of this kind are

たが、幼少時に敢為自若の精神を養成する方法は、このような物語だけではなかった。ときには残酷にも思われる厳しさでもって、親はその子の胆力（たんりょく）をきたえ、「獅子はその児を千仞（せんじん）の谷底に落とす」というようなことさえした。こうして武士の子は、艱難（かんなん）の谷底に落とされ、（ギリシャ神話の中の）シジフォス[訳注5]的苦役にかり立てられた。ときとしては寒気にさらされ、食物も与えられず、それが忍耐の精神を養うための大事な試練だと考えられた。

　さらに武士の子は、幼少のころより、遠い未知の場所へ使いにやらせられたり、厳寒の日の出前に起こされ、朝食の前に素足で先生の家に通って、素読の勉強をさせられることもあった。また月に一度か二度、天満宮の祭日などには、数人の少年が集まって、夜を徹して順番に大きな声で素読をすることもあった。あるいは、刑場や墓場や化物屋敷などのような、こわくてさびしい場所に出かけることは、少年たちが好んでした遊びであった。斬首（ざんしゅ）の刑が行われた時は、少年たちはその気味のわるい光景を見にやらせられただけでなく、夜暗くなってから、ひとりでその刑場をおとずれ、さらし首に印をつけて帰ってくるように命じられることもあった。

　このような超[訳注6]スパルタ式[補注]の、（胆力をきたえる）訓練の方法は、現代の教育者を驚かせ、そんなやり方では、かえって人の心のやさしい情緒を、つぼみのうちに摘みとってしまうのではないかと、疑問と恐れを抱かせるかもしれない。ここで、武士道における勇気の他の概念を考察してみよう。

not by any means the only method of early imbuing the spirit with daring and fearlessness. Parents, with sternness sometimes verging on cruelty, set their children to tasks that called forth all the pluck that was in them. "Bears hurl their cubs down the gorge," they said. Samurai's sons were let down to steep valleys of hardship, and spurred to Sisyphus-like tasks. Occasional deprivation of food or exposure to cold, was considered a highly efficacious test for inuring them to endurance. Children of tender age were sent among utter strangers with some message to deliver, were made to rise before the sun, and before breakfast attend to their reading exercises, walking to their teachers with bare feet in the cold of winter; they frequently—once or twice a month, as on the festival of a god of learning,—came together in small groups and passed the night without sleep in reading aloud by turns. Pilgrimages to all sorts of uncanny places—to execution grounds, to graveyards, to houses reputed of being haunted, were favourite pastimes of the young. In the days when decapitation was public, not only were small boys sent to witness the ghastly scene, but they were made to visit alone the place in the darkness of night and there to leave a mark of their visit on the trunkless head.

Does this ultra-Spartan system[1] of "drilling the nerves" strike the modern pedagogist with horror and doubt—doubt whether the tendency would not be brutalising, nipping in the bud the tender emotions of the heart? Let us see in another chapter what other concepts Bushido had of Valour.

(補注) 勇気が、人の精神に宿っている姿は、沈着、すなわち心の落ち着きとしてあらわれる。平静は静止状態の勇気である。平静が勇気の静的な表明であるのに対し、敢為の行為は動的な表現である。真に勇敢な人は、常に沈着であって、決して驚かず、何者によってもその精神の平静さを乱さない。激しい戦闘のただなかでも冷静であり、自然の災害に出会っても、驚かずあわてない。地震に動揺せず、嵐をものともしない。このような真の勇者は、さしせまった危険に際しても、あるいは死に直面しても、詩を吟じ歌を詠むなど、その音声も筆蹟も平生と少しも変わりなく、人々はこれを賞めたたえた。そのようなことができるのは、その人の心の中に大きな余裕があったことを示す、何よりの証拠であり、それは、あわてず、困らず、常にゆとりを残している広い心のことをいう。

　史実として伝えられるところによると、江戸城を創建した太田道灌が敵の槍に刺されたとき、彼が歌を好むことを知っていた刺客は、刺しながら次のような上の句をよんだ。

　　　かかる時さこそ命の惜しからめ

　これを聞いて、息をひきとろうとしている英雄は、脇腹の致命傷に少しもひるまず、下の句をつづけた。

　　　かねて無き身と思い知らずば

　勇気には、明るく陽気な要素もある。凡人にとっては深刻なことであっても、勇者にとっては遊戯に過ぎないことがある。昔戦場にのぞんで相戦う同士が、戯言のやりとりをしたり、歌合戦をした例はまれではない。合戦は暴力による争いだけではなく、知的な競技でもあった。

[1] The spiritual aspect of valour is evidenced by composure—calm presence of mind. Tranquillity is courage in repose. It is a statical manifestation of valour, as daring deeds are a dynamical. A truly brave man is ever serene; he is never taken by surprise; nothing ruffles the equanimity of his spirit. In the heat of battle he remains cool; in the midst of catastrophes he keeps level his mind. Earthquakes do not shake him, he laughs at storms. We admire him as truly great, who, in the menacing presence of danger or death, retains his self-possession; who, for instance, can compose a poem under impending peril, or hum a strain in the face of death. Such indulgence betraying no tremor in the writing or in the voice is taken as an infallible index of a large nature—of what we call a capacious mind (*yoyu*), which, far from being pressed or crowded, has always room for something more.

It passes current among us as a piece of authentic history, that as Ota Dokan, the great builder of the castle of Tokyo, was pierced through with a spear, his assassin, knowing the poetical predilection of his victim, accompanied his thrust with this couplet:

> "Ah! how in moments like these
> Our heart doth grudge the light of life";

whereupon the expiring hero, not one whit daunted by the mortal wound in his side, added the lines:

> "Had not in hours of peace,
> It learned to lightly look on life."

There is even a sportive element in a courageous nature. Things which are serious to ordinary people, may be but play to the valiant. Hence in old warfare it was not at all rare for the parties to a conflict to exchange repartee or to begin a rhetorical contest. Combat was not solely a matter of brute force; it was, as well, an intellectual engagement.

　11世紀の末（におこった前九年の役）の、衣川の戦いのとき、東軍方は敗れ、その大将安倍貞任が逃れた。そのとき追手の大将、源義家が、貞任にせまって声高く、「きたなくも敵に後を見するものかな、しばし返せや」と、呼ばった。すると貞任が馬を止めたので義家は、

　　　　衣のたてはほころびにけり

と、大声で詠みかけると、その声が終らないうちに、敗軍の将貞任は従容として、

　　　　年を経し糸のみだれの苦しさに

と、詠み返した。義家は引きしぼった弓をゆるめ、つがえていた矢を捨てて貞任が逃げるのにまかせた。家来の者はあやしんでその理由をたずねたところ、義家は、「敵に激しく追われながらも、心の平静を失わない貞任のような剛胆な勇士を、恥かしめるに忍びない」と、答えたという。

　ブルータスの死に際して、アントニウスとオクタヴィウスが感じた悲哀は、勇者が一般に経験するものであった。上杉謙信は、14年もの間武田信玄と戦いつづけたが、信玄が病気で亡くなったときくと、「敵の中の最もよき者」と、信玄の死をいたみ慟哭したという。信玄への対し方に、常に立派な模範を示したのもこの謙信だった。信玄の領地は、山国で海に臨んでいなかった。それで必要な塩はいつも東海道の北条氏に頼っていた。北条氏は信玄と交戦状態ではなかったが、信玄を弱らせるために、この必需品の交易路を断った。謙信は、敵の窮状を聞き、塩は自分の領地の海岸で自給できたので、信玄に書状を書いて、北条氏はきわめて卑劣な手段をとったこと、彼（謙信）は彼（信玄）と交戦中であるが、十分な塩を提供するように命じたことを知らせ、「我の貴公と争うところは、弓箭にありて米塩にあらず」とつけ加えた。この言葉は、「ローマ人は金をも

Of such character was the battle fought on the banks of the Koromo River, late in the eleventh century. The eastern army routed, its leader, Sadato, took to flight. When the pursuing general pressed him hard and called about, "It is a disgrace for a warrior to show his back to the enemy," Sadato reined his horse; upon this the conquering chief shouted an impromptu verse:

"Torn into shreds is the warp of the cloth (*koromo*)."

Scarcely had the words escaped his lips when the defeated warrior, undismayed, completed the couplet:

"Since age has worn its threads by use."

Yoshiie, whose bow had all the while been bent, suddenly unstrung it and turned away, leaving his prospective victim to do as he pleased. When asked the reason of his strange behaviour, he replied that he could not bear to put to shame one who had kept his presence of mind while hotly pursued by his enemy.

The sorrow which overtook Antony and Octavius at the death of Brutus, has been the general experience of brave men. Kenshin, who fought for fourteen years with Shingen, when he heard of the latter's death, wept aloud at the loss of "the best of enemies." It was this same Kenshin who had set a noble example for all time in his treatment of Shingen, whose provinces lay in a mountainous region quite away from the sea, and who had consequently depended upon the Hôjô provinces of the Tokaido for salt. The Hôjô prince wishing to weaken him, although not openly at war with him, had cut off from Shingen all traffic in this important article. Kenshin, hearing of his enemy's dilemma and able to obtain his salt from the coast of his own dominions, wrote Shingen that in his opinion the Hôjô lord had committed a very mean act, and that although he (Kenshin) was at war with him (Shingen) he had ordered his subjects

って戦わず、鉄をもって戦う」と言ったカミラスの言葉に
匹敵することあまりある。

　また、（ドイツの哲学者）ニーチェが、「汝はその敵を誇
りとすべきである。しからば敵の成功は、また汝の成功で
ある」と言ったのは、よくわが国の武士の心情を語るもの
である。

　実際、勇気と名誉はともに、平時において友人とする価
値のある者だけを、戦時における敵とするべきことを要求
する。勇気がこの高みに達したときに、それは仁に近づく。

to furnish him with plenty of salt—adding, "I do not fight with salt, but with the sword," affording more than a parallel to the words of Camillus, "We Romans do not fight with gold, but with iron." Nietzsche spoke for the Samurai heart when he wrote, "You are to be proud of your enemy; then the success of your enemy is your success also." Indeed, valour and honour alike required that we should own as enemies in war only such as prove worthy of being friends in peace. When valour attains this height, it be comes akin to Benevolence.

第 5 章

仁・惻隠の心

　愛情、寛容、同情、憐憫は、昔から最高の徳とされ、人の霊魂の属性の中で、最も高貴なるものと認められてきた。

　それは、二通りの意味において、王者の徳と考えられた。すなわち、高貴な精神に伴う多くの属性のなかで王位を占めるものとして王者的であり、王者としての道に特にふさわしい徳として王者的であるとみなされた。慈悲は王冠よりも王者に似合い、王笏（権力の象徴）をもってする支配よりも強い影響力があるということを、言葉で表現するにはシェークスピアを必要としたが、これを心に感じるには、われわれは全世界の人々と同様に、あえて彼を必要としなかった。

　孔子や孟子も人を治める者の最高の必要条件は、仁にあると繰り返している。孔子は、「君子はまず徳を慎しむ、徳有

CHAPTER V

BENEVOLENCE, THE FEELING OF DISTRESS

L OVE, magnanimity, affection for others, sympathy and pity, were ever recognised to be supreme virtues, the highest of all the attributes of the human soul. It was deemed a princely virtue in a twofold sense: princely among the manifold attributes of a noble spirit; princely as particularly befitting a princely profession. We needed no Shakespeare to feel—though, perhaps, like the rest of the world, we needed him to express it—that mercy became a monarch better than his crown, that it was above his sceptered sway. How often both Confucius and Mencius repeat the highest requirement of a ruler of men to consist in benevolence. Confucius would say—"Let but a prince cultivate virtue, people will flock to him; with people will come to him lands; lands will bring forth for

ればこれ人有り、人有ればこれ土有り、土有ればこれ財有り、財有ればこれ用有り、徳は本也(もと)、利は末也」と言った。そして、「仁を好む王者の下には、義を好まない民はいない」と言った。

　孟子はこれらのことを、さらに詳しく「不仁にして一国を得る者はいるが、不仁にして、天下を得るものはいない」と言い、さらに、「民を心服させないで王となった者はいない」と言った。孔子孟子ともに、王者として欠かせない要件を定義して「仁は人なり」と言った。

　封建制度の下における政治は、武力をもって制圧する、つまり武断政治に陥りやすい。そのような状態における最悪の専制から、われわれを救うものは、仁の徳であった。人民がその身体と生命を主君に捧げ、主君がそれをほしいままにするとき、絶対専制政治が生まれる。これはしばしば「東洋的専制政治」と呼ばれる。あたかも西洋の歴史には、一人の専制者も存在しなかったかのように！

　私はいかなる専制政治をも、断じて支持しない。しかし、専制政治と封建政治とを同一視するのは誤りである。フレデリック大王は、「王は国家の第一の召し使いである」と言ったが、この言葉に対して、ある法学者が「それは自由主義発達の一新時代を迎える声である」と、評したことは正しい。ところが偶然にも、これとほとんど時を同じくして、東北日本の僻地(へきち)において、米沢の藩主、上杉鷹山公(ようざん)は、これとまさしく同一のことを言って、封建制がまったくの武断専制では

him wealth; wealth will give him the benefit of right uses. Virtue is the root, and wealth an outcome." Again, "Never has there been a case of a sovereign loving benevolence, and the people not loving righteousness." Mencius follows close at his heels and says, "Instances are on record where individuals attained to supreme power in a single state, without benevolence, but never have I heard of a whole empire falling into the hands of one who lacked this virtue. Also,—It is impossible that anyone should become ruler of the people to whom they have not yielded the subjection of their hearts. Both defined this indispensable requirement in a ruler by saying, "Benevolence—benevolence is Man."

Under the regime of feudalism, which could easily degenerate into militarism it was to benevolence that we owed our deliverance from despotism of the worst kind. An utter surrender of "life and limb" on the part of the governed would have left nothing for the governing but self-will, and this has for its natural consequence the growth of that absolutism so often called "oriental despotism," as though there were no despots of occidental history!

Let it be far from me to uphold despotism of any sort; but it is a mistake to identify feudalism with it. When Frederick the Great wrote that "Kings are the first servants of the State," jurists thought rightly that a new era was reached in the development of freedom. Strangely coinciding in time, in the backwoods of North-western Japan, Yozan of Yonézawa made exactly the same declaration, showing that feudalism was not all tyranny and

なかったことを示している。封建制下の主君は、臣下に対して相互的な義務を負うということは悟らなかったが、自分の先祖ならびに天に対し高い責任感をもっていた。すなわち、「臣民は天よりゆだねられた子であり、主君はその父である」という思想である。中国の古典『詩経』によれば、「殷のいまだ師を喪わざるとき、克く上帝に配せり」とある。また、孔子は『大学』において、「民の好むところ、これを好み、民の悪むところ、これを悪む、これをこれ民の父母という」と教えた。こうして民衆の世論と君主の意思、あるいは民主主義と絶対主義は融合した。武士道も、これと同じように、通常与えられているのとは異なる意味において、父権政治を受け入れ、確認した。それは、あまり関心のない叔父政治（すなわちアンクル・サムの政治！）に対して父親的であった。

　専制政治と父権政治との違いは、次の点である。すなわち、前者にあっては、人民はいやいやながら服従するのに反し、後者にあっては（イギリスの歴史学者）バークが言っているように「誇りをもってする帰順、品位を保てる従順、臣下でありながら、高い自由の精神の中に生きる服従[注1]」なのである。イギリス国王のことを「臣下がしばしば謀反を起こし、退位させるから、悪魔の王」と呼び、フランスの王を「租税公課を無限に負わすから、驢馬の王」と呼び、スペイン王には「人民が喜んで服従しているから、人間の王」という称号を与えるという古い諺は、まったくの間違いではない。だが、もうこのくらいにしよう。

[注1] バーク著『フランス革命史』。

oppression. A feudal prince, although unmindful of owing reciprocal obligations to his vassals, felt a higher sense of responsibility to his ancestors and to Heaven. He was a father to his subjects, whom Heaven entrusted to his care. According to the ancient Chinese *Book of Poetry*, "Until the house of Yin lost the hearts of the people, they could appear before Heaven." And Confucius in his *Great Learning* taught: "When the prince loves what the people love and hates what the people hate, then is he what is called the parent of the people." Thus are public opinion and monarchical will or democracy and absolutism merged one in the other. Thus also, in a sense not usually assigned to the term, Bushido accepted and corroborated paternal government—paternal also as opposed to the less interested avuncular government. (Uncle Sam's, to wit!) The difference between a despotic and a paternal government lies in this, that in the one the people obey reluctantly, while in the other they do so with "that proud submission, that dignified obedience, that subordination of heart which kept alive, even in servitude itself, the spirit of exalted freedom."[1] The old saying is not entirely false which called the king of England the "king of devils, because of his subjects' often insurrections against, and depositions of, their princes," and which made the French monarch the "king of asses, because of their infinite taxes and impositions," but which gave the title of the "king of men to the sovereign of Spain, because of his subjects' willing obedience." But enough!

---

[1] Burke, *French Revolution.*

　アングロ・サクソン人にとっては、道徳と絶対権力とは相容れないものだと思うかもしれない。ロシアの政治家ポベドノスツェフは、イギリス社会の基盤と、他のヨーロッパ社会の基盤との違いを明らかにして、「ヨーロッパ大陸諸国の社会は、人民の共通の利害を基盤にしているが、これに反し、イギリスの社会の特色は、強大に発達した個人の人格を重んずることにある」と言った。さらに彼は、「ヨーロッパ大陸の諸国、ことにスラブ系民族の間においては、個人の人格はその集団社会に依存し、そして究極においては国家に依存する」と言っている。このことは日本人については特に然りと言っていいであろう。わが国民にあっては、主君の権力の自由な行使は、ヨーロッパにおけるような重圧を感ずる心配はなく、しかも主君は、人民の感情に対し、父親的感情をもって接してきた。（ドイツの政治家）ビスマルクも、次のように言っている。「絶対政治の第一の要件は、統治者が無私正直であって、義務を重んじ、自らの精力と、謙譲な心を保っていることである」と。この問題について、もう一つ引用することを許していただけるなら、ドイツ皇帝がコブレンツで行った演説の一節をあげたい。「王位は神の恩寵により与えられたもので、神のみに負う重い責務と巨大な責任を伴い、いかなる人も、大臣も、議会も、国王をそれから解放しえない」。

　仁は、やさしくなごやかな徳である。たとえていえば母の心である。誠実なる義と、厳格なる正義とが男性的であるとすれば、仁愛は女性的なやさしさと説得力をもつ。しかしながら仁愛を行うのに、正義と義をもってしなければ、みだりに愛に溺れることがあるので、これはいましめなければならない。伊達政宗の「義に過ぎれば固くなる。仁に過ぎれば弱

Virtue and absolute power may strike the Anglo-Saxon mind as terms which it is impossible to harmonise. Pobyedonostseff has clearly set forth before us the contrast in the foundations of English and other European communities; namely, that these were organised on the basis of common interest, while that was distinguished by a strongly developed independent personality. What this Russian statesman says of the personal dependence of individuals on some social alliance and in the end of ends on the State, among the continental nations of Europe and particularly among Slavonic peoples, is doubly true of the Japanese. Hence not only is a free exercise of monarchical power not felt as heavily by us as in Europe, but it is generally moderated by paternal consideration for the feelings of the people. "Absolutism," says Bismarck, "primarily demands in the ruler impartiality, honesty, devotion to duty, energy and inward humility." If I may be allowed to make one more quotation on this subject, I will cite from the speech of the German Emperor at Coblenz, in which he spoke of "Kingship, by the grace of God, with its heavy duties, its tremendous responsibilities to the Creator alone, from which no man, no minister, no parliament, can release the monarch."

We knew benevolence was a tender virtue and mother-like. If upright Rectitude and stern Justice were peculiarly masculine, Mercy had the gentleness and the persuasiveness of a feminine nature. We were warned against indulging in indiscriminate charity, without seasoning it with justice and rectitude. Masamuné expressed

くなる」という、しばしば引用される格言は、そのことをよく表わしている。

　幸いにも仁は美しく、稀有ではない。「最も剛毅なる者は最もやさしくなごやかで、最も愛のある者は最も勇敢である」とは、古今東西を通じての真理である。「武士の情」とは、人々の心に美しい響をもって訴える高貴な感情を表わす言葉であった。武士の仁愛は他の者の仁愛と、その種類が異なるわけではない。しかし武士の場合においては、それが漠然とした感情から生まれたものではなく、その心には正義を忘れない仁愛があり、それはまた衝動的な発現ではなく、その背後に、相手に対する生殺与奪の権力を有した愛なのである。経済学者が有効である需要と、有効でない需要の区別を明らかにしているように、武士の愛は、それを受ける相手に、利益もしくは損害を加えることができる実行力をもっていた。

　武士は武力を持ち、それを用いる特権をもっていることを誇りとした。しかしながら同時に、孟子の説く仁の力にも同意した。孟子は、「仁は必ず不仁に勝つ、それは水が火に勝つようなものであり、今の仁をなす者はなお一杯の水をもって一車の薪の火を救うがごときである」、さらにまた、「思いやりの心は、仁という大道のはじまりである」と言っている。したがって、仁の心をもつ人間はつねに苦しみ悩んでいる人を思いやる、と言っているのである。道徳哲学の基礎を同情においたアダム・スミスよりはるか以前に、孟子はこのように説いていたのである。

it well in his oft-quoted aphorism—"Rectitude carried to excess hardens into stiffness; benevolence indulged beyond measure sinks into weakness."

Fortunately mercy was not so rare as it was beautiful, for it is universally true that "The bravest are the tenderest, the loving are the daring." "*Bushi no nasaké*"—the tenderness of a warrior—had a sound which appealed at once to whatever was noble in us; not that the mercy of a samurai was generically different from the mercy of any other being, but because it implied mercy where mercy was not a blind impulse, but where it recognised due regard to justice, and where mercy did not remain merely a certain state of mind, but where it was backed with power to save or kill. As economists speak of demand as being effectual or ineffectual, similarly we may call the mercy of Bushi effectual, since it implied the power of acting for the good or detriment of the recipient.

Priding themselves as they did in their brute strength and privileges to turn it into account, the samurai gave full consent to what Mencius taught concerning the power of love. "Benevolence," he says, "brings under its sway whatever hinders its power, just as water subdues fire: they only doubt the power of water to quench flames who try to extinguish with a cupful a whole burning waggon-load of fagots." He also says that "the feeling of distress is the root of benevolence," therefore a benevolent man is ever mindful of those who are suffering and in distress. Thus did Mencius long anticipate Adam Smith who founds his ethical philosophy on sympathy.

　およそ国の東西を問わず、一国の武士の名誉の掟が、他国のそれといかに一致するかは実に驚くべきものがある。言い換えれば、多くの非難を浴びた東洋の道徳観念の中に、ヨーロッパ文学における最も高貴な格言と一致する部分はずいぶんと多いのである。たとえば、ローマの詩人ヴェルギリウスが、ローマ建国の精神を次のように歌った。

　　敗れたる者を安んじ
　　逆らう者をくじいて
　　平和の道を立てることこそ
　　汝の業なれ

　この詩を日本の紳士が読めば、あるいはわが国文学の中から、ひそかに盗んできた語句であると思うかもしれない。

　弱者、劣者、敗者に対する仁愛は、武士の美徳として特に賞賛された。日本美術の愛好家であれば、一人の僧がうしろ向きになって牛に乗っている絵を見たことがあるだろう。この僧こそ、かつてその名を聞くだけで、人々に恐れられた勇猛な武士（源氏の熊谷次郎直実）であった。

　1184年、わが国の歴史上、最も決定的な合戦の一つ、源氏と平家が須磨の浦で戦ったときのことである。この猛将は、敵を追いかけ、そのたくましい腕で組み伏せた。このような場合には、相手が名高い武将か、自分と力量が劣らぬ剛の者でなければ、血を流さないことが戦場での作法であったので、彼は自分の名を名乗り、相手の名を知ろうとした。しかし相手はそれを拒んだので、その兜をおしあげて見ると、まだ髭もない顔立ちの美しい若武者であった。彼は驚いて腕をゆる

It is indeed striking how closely the code of knightly honour of one country coincides with that of others; in other words, how the much abused oriental ideas of morals find their counterparts in the noblest maxims of European literature. If the well-known lines,

> Hæ tibi erunt artes—pacisque imponere morem,
> Parcere subjectis, et debellare superbos,

were shown a Japanese gentleman, he might readily accuse the Mantuan bard of plagiarising from the literature of his own country.

Benevolence to the weak, the down-trodden or the vanquished, was ever extolled as peculiarly becoming to a samurai. Lovers of Japanese art must be familiar with the representation of a priest riding backwards on a cow. The rider was once a warrior who in his day made his name a by-word of terror. In that terrible battle of Sumano–ura, (1184 A.D.) which was one of the most decisive in our history, he overtook an enemy and in single combat had him in the clutch of his gigantic arms. Now the etiquette of war required that on such occasions no blood should be spilt, unless the weaker party proved to be a man of rank or ability equal to that of the stronger. The grim combatant would have the name of the man under him; but he refusing to make it known, his helmet was ruthlessly torn

め、抱き起こして、「助けてまいらせよう。そなたの母のもとへ行け、熊谷の刃は、そなたのような者の血に染めたくない。敵に見とがめられぬ間に、早く逃げのびたまえ」と言った。

　しかしこの若武者は逃げるのをこばみ、双方の名誉のため、この場で自分の首をはねるよう熊谷に頼んだ。熊谷は、幾人もの敵の生命を断った刀を白髪頭の上にふりかざしたが、今日の初陣に先駆けしていったわが子小次郎の姿が目の前に浮かび、勇猛の心もくだけて、この平家の若武者平敦盛に逃げるようにすすめたが、どうしてもきかず、そのうちに味方の軍勢の足音が近づいてきたので、「もうこうなっては、名もない者の手によって討たれるよりは、この熊谷の手にかけたてまつり、後の御供養もいたしましょうぞ」と言って、念仏を唱え、ふりおとした大刀はその若武者の血で朱に染まったのであった。

　（平家は敗れて）戦いは終わり、熊谷は凱旋したが、彼はもう勲功も名誉も思わず、武士を捨てて出家し、頭をまるめて僧衣を着て、西方浄土を念じ、西方に背を向けまいと誓い、諸国を行脚しながらその余生を送ったという。

　批評家は、この物語を読んで、あるいはこの物語の欠点を指摘するかもしれないが、いずれにしろ、優しさ、憐み、愛、が武士の最も激烈なる武功を美化する特質であることを、こ

off, when the sight of a juvenile face, fair and beardless, made the astonished knight relax his hold. Helping the youth to his feet, in paternal tones he bade the stripling go: "Off, young prince, to thy mother's side! The sword of Kumagayé shall never be tarnished by a drop of thy blood. Haste and flee o'er yon pass before thine enemies come in sight!" The young warrior refused to go and begged Kumagayé, for the honour of both, to dispatch him on the spot. Above the hoary head of the veteran gleams the cold blade, which many a time before has sundered the chords of life, but his stout heart quails; there flashes athwart his mental eye the vision of his own boy, who this self-same day marched to the sound of bugle to try his maiden arms; the strong hand of the warrior quivers; again he begs his victim to flee for his life. Finding all his entreaties vain and hearing the approaching steps of his comrades, he exclaims: "If thou art overtaken, thou mayst fall at a more ignoble hand than mine. O thou Infinite! receive his soul!" In an instant the sword flashes in the air, and when it falls it is red with adolescent blood. When the war is ended, we find our soldier returning in triumph, but little cares he now for honour or fame; he renounces his war-like career, shaves his head, dons a priestly garb, devotes the rest of his days to holy pilgrimage, never turning his back to the West where lies the Paradise whence salvation comes and whither the sun hastes daily for his rest.

Critics may point out flaws in this story, which is casu-istically vulnerable. Let it be: all the same it shows that Tenderness, Pity and Love were traits which adorned the

の物語が示すことにはかわりがない。古いことわざにも「窮鳥懐に入れば猟師も殺さず」と言っているが、この格言は、とくにキリスト教的であると考えられている赤十字運動が、わが国においてはすでにその根を張っていた理由をあらわすものではあるまいか。われわれは、ジュネーブにおける万国赤十字条約を耳にする数十年前に、わが国最大の小説家、滝沢馬琴の筆によって、敵の負傷者に医療を加える物語に親しんでいた。昔から尚武の精神が盛んで、青年武士の訓育に著名であった薩摩藩においては、青年たちの間に音楽をたしなむ風習があった。その音楽とは、（シェークスピアの言う）「血と死との騒々しい前触れ」である、喇叭を吹き太鼓を打つ進軍の音楽などではなくて、哀れにも優しい琵琶[注2]の曲で、それを弾じては猛き心を和らげ、その思いを血なまぐさい戦いの外へといたらしめるものであった。（ギリシャの歴史家）ポリビウスの伝えるところによれば、（古代ギリシャの）アルカディアの憲法においては、30歳以下の青年すべてに、音楽を習得することを課したという。それによって、アルカディア山脈に住む人々は過酷な風土からくる厳格な性格を和らげたといい、ポリビウスは、この地方の人々に残忍性が見られない理由を、この音楽の影響だとしている。

　日本において、武士階級の間にこのような優雅な風習があったのは、ひとり薩摩藩だけではない。白河の藩主松平楽翁（定信）公が、心に浮かぶままに書き記した随筆の中に、次のような言葉がある。「枕に通うとも、罪のないものは、花の香り、遠い寺の鐘の音、霜の夜の虫の音は、ことにあわれである」。また、こうも言っている。「憎くとも宥すことができるのは、花に吹く風、月にかかる雲、考えもなく浅はかに

注2 琵琶。ギターに似ている。

most sanguinary exploits of a samurai. It was an old maxim among them that "It becomes not the fowler to slay the bird which takes refuge in his bosom." This in a large measure explains why the Red Cross movement, considered so peculiarly Christian, so readily found a firm footing among us. Decades before we heard of the Geneva Convention, Bakin, our greatest novelist, had familiarised us with the medical treatment of a fallen foe. In the principality of Satsuma, noted for its martial spirit and education, the custom prevailed for young men to practise music; not the blast of trumpets or the beat of drums,— "those clamorous harbingers of blood and death"—stirring us to imitate the actions of a tiger, but sad and tender melodies on the *biwa*,[2] soothing our fiery spirits, drawing our thoughts away from scent of blood and scenes of carnage. Polybius tells us of the Constitution of Arcadia, which required all youths under thirty to practise music, in order that this gentle art might alleviate the rigours of the inclement region. It is to its influence that he attributes the absence of cruelty in that part of the Arcadian mountains.

Nor was Satsuma the only place in Japan where gentleness was inculcated among the warrior class. A Prince of Shirakawa jots down his random thoughts, and among them is the following: "Though they come stealing to your bedside in the silent watches of the night, drive not away, but rather cherish these—the fragrance of flowers, the sound of distant bells, the insect hummings of a frosty

---

[2] A musical instrument, resembling the guitar.

争う人は、宥すことはできない」。

このような優美な感情を表現し、それによって自分の内面を修養しようとする武士の間には、詩歌が奨励された。それゆえ、わが国の詩歌には悲壮と優雅とがその底に強く流れている。有名なある田舎侍（大鷲文吾）の話がこれをよくあらわしている。彼は俳諧を勧められ、「鶯[注3]の音」という題で生まれて初めて俳句をつくろうとしたが、猛々しい心が出てしまい、次のような句を師に差し出した。

　　　鶯の初音をきく耳は別にしておく武士かな

彼の師（大星由良之助）は、この粗野な感情にも驚かず、この若侍を励ましつづけたところ、ある日彼の魂の音楽が目覚め、鶯の妙なる音に感じてこう書いた。

　　　武士の鶯きいて立ちにけり

ドイツの詩人ケルナーは、戦場で傷つき倒れたとき「生命

注3 ウグイス、さえずり鳥、日本のナイチンゲールとも呼ばれる。

night." And again, "Though they may wound your feel-ings, these three you have only to forgive, the breeze that scatters your flowers, the cloud that hides your moon, and the man who tries to pick quarrels with you."

It was ostensibly to express, but actually to cultivate, these gentler emotions that the writing of verses was encouraged. Our poetry has therefore a strong undercur-rent of pathos and tenderness. A well-known anecdote of a rustic samurai illustrates the case in point. When he was told to learn versification, and "The Warbler's Notes"[3] was given him for the subject of his first attempt, his fiery spirit rebelled and he flung at the feet of his master this uncouth production, which ran

> "The brave warrior keeps apart
> The ear that might listen
> To the warbler's song."

His master, undaunted by the crude sentiment, con-tinued to encourage the youth, until one day the music of his soul was awakened to respond to the sweet notes of the *uguisu*, and he wrote

> "Stands the warrior, mailed and strong,
> To hear the uguisu's song,
> Warbled sweet the trees among."

We admire and enjoy the heroic incident in Körner's

---

[3] The *uguisu* or warbler, sometimes called the nightingale of Japan.

の告別」という有名な詩を書いた。若くして戦死したこの壮烈な詩人の生涯を、われわれは讃美する。しかし、同じようなことは、わが国古来の戦いには、決してまれではなかった。ことに、わが国の簡潔な詩形は、ものに触れ、事に感じて、とっさの感情を表現するには最も適している。少しでも教養のある者は、和歌や俳諧をたしなんだ。戦場を行進する武士が、しばしば馬をとめて、腰の矢立から筆をとり出して歌を詠み、戦場の露と消えたのち、兜の中や鎧の胸当の中に、彼の詠んだ歌がおさめられていることもあった。この優しさこそ、わが国の武士の風習だったのである。

　激しい戦闘の恐怖の真只中においても、愛と憐れみの感情をよびおこすことを、ヨーロッパではキリスト教が教えた。それをわが国では、音楽と詩歌の愛好がこれを果したのである。優雅な感情を養うと、他人の苦痛を察する思いやりを生む。他人の感情を尊敬することから生まれた、謙譲、丁寧の心は、礼儀の根本を成すものである。

short life when, as he lay wounded, on the battle-field, he scribbled his famous *Farewell to Life*. Incidents of a similar kind were not at all unusual in our warfare. Our pithy, epigrammatic poems were particularly well suited to the improvisation of a single sentiment. Everybody of any education was either a poet or a poetaster. Not infrequently a marching soldier might be seen to halt, take his writing utensils from his belt, and compose an ode,—and such papers were found afterward in the helmets or the breastplates when these were removed from their lifeless wearers.

What Christianity has done in Europe toward rousing compassion in the midst of belligerent horrors, love of music and letters has done in Japan. The cultivation of tender feelings breeds considerate regard for the sufferings of others. Modesty and complaisance, actuated by respect for others' feelings, are at the root of politeness.

礼儀

外国人が、観光客としてわが国を訪れると、誰でも日本人の丁重な礼節に注目し、これが日本人の特性だと思うようである。礼儀がもし上品でないと思われることを恐れるだけで実行されるならば、それは徳とはいえない。まことの礼儀は、他人の感情を察する同情的な思いやりが外にあらわれたもので、正当なるものに対する尊敬、ひいては社会的地位に対する公正なる尊敬を意味する。なぜなら、社会的地位とは、貧富の差に基づくものではなく、実際の価値に基づくものだからである。

礼儀の最高の形はほとんど愛に近い。われわれは敬愛なる気持ちをもって、（聖句の愛を礼の一字にかえて）「礼は寛容であって人の利をはかる。礼は妬まず、誇らず、たかぶらず、非礼を行わず、自分の利を求めず、軽々しく怒らず、人の悪を思わない」と、言えるだろう。ディーン教授は、人間性に

CHAPTER VI

POLITENESS

COURTESY and urbanity of manners have been noticed by every foreign tourist as a marked Japanese trait. Politeness is a poor virtue, if it is actuated only by a fear of offending good taste, whereas it should be the outward manifestation of a sympathetic regard for the feelings of others. It also implies a due regard for the fitness of things, therefore due respect to social positions; for these latter express no plutocratic distinctions, but were originally distinctions for actual merit.

In its highest form, politeness almost approaches love. We may reverently say, politeness "suffereth long, and is kind; envieth not, vaunteth not itself, is not puffed up; doth not behave itself unseemly, seeketh not her own, is not easily provoked, taketh not account of evil." Is it any wonder

六つの要素をあげた中で、礼をもって最も高い地位を与え、これをもって社交の最も成熟した結果であるとしたことは、なにもあやしむにたりない。

　私はこのように礼儀を尊ぶが、これを諸徳の第一位に置こうとするものではない。礼を解明してみれば、ほかのさらに高貴な道徳と相関関係にあることを見出すであろう。どのような徳でも孤立しては存在しえない。礼は武人特有の徳として賞賛され、それが賞すべき価値以上に尊重されるようになり、いやむしろ、それほど高く尊重されたがために、その偽物が生まれてしまった。孔子も繰り返し教えている。「虚礼がまことの礼ではないことは、ただ音を響かすことが音楽ではないのと同じである」と。

　礼が重視されて社交の必須条件にまでなると、当然、若者に社交上の正しいふるまい方を教えるための詳細な行儀作法の体系が広まった。挨拶のときの頭の下げ方、歩き方や坐り方が細心の注意をもって教えられ、学ばれた。食事の作法は学問にまで発展し、茶を点じて喫むことも礼式まで高められ、教養のある者は、当然、すべての作法に通じていると思われるまでになった。（アメリカの社会学者）ヴェブレンが、その著書[注1]の中で礼儀は、「有閑階級の生活の産物であり、表徴である」と言っているのは、まことに適切である。

　ヨーロッパ人が、日本人の繊細で技巧的な礼式を軽視して、「あまりにも人間の思考を無駄に費やすものであって、それを固苦しく守ることはばかげたことである」と批評するのを、しばしば耳にしたことがある。礼式の中には、たしかに不必要な末節の規定があることは、私も知っている。しかし、絶

[注1] ヴェブレン著『有閑階級論』ニューヨーク、1899年、46ページ。

that Professor Dean, in speaking of the six elements of humanity, accords to politeness an exalted position, inasmuch as it is the ripest fruit of social intercourse?

While thus extolling politeness, far be it from me to put it in the front rank of virtues. If we analyze it, we shall find it correlated with other virtues of a higher order; for what virtue stands alone? While—or rather because—it was exalted as peculiar to the profession of arms, and as such esteemed in a degree higher than its deserts, there came into existence its counterfeits. Confucius himself has repeatedly taught that external appurtenances are as little a part of propriety as sounds are of music.

When propriety was elevated to the *sine qua non* of social intercourse, it was only to be expected that an elaborate system of etiquette should come into vogue to train youth in correct social behaviour. How one must bow in accosting others, how he must walk and sit, were taught and learned with utmost care. Table manners grew to be a science. Tea serving and drinking were raised to ceremony. A man of education is, of course, expected to be master of all these. Very fitly does Mr. Veblen, in his interesting book,[1] call decorum "a product and an exponent of the leisure-class life."

I have heard slighting remarks made by Europeans upon our elaborate discipline of politeness. It has been criticised as absorbing too much of our thought and in so far a folly to observe strict obedience to it. I admit that there may be unnecessary niceties in ceremonious eti-

---

[1] *Theory of the Leisure Class*, N. Y., 1899, p. 46.

えず変化してゆく流行を追う西洋人と、どちらがばかげているか、その判断はなかなか難しい。流行でさえも私は、たんなる虚栄の移り気だとは考えない。かえって、それは美に対する絶えざる探究心だとみる。まして細かい規定の礼式を、全然つまらぬものだとは思わない。礼式は、一定の結果を達成するための長年の体験から生まれた、最も適切な方式であって、何かを為そうとするには、必ず最良の方法があるはずである。その最良の方法は、最も経済的であると同時に、最も優美なる方法である。（イギリスの社会学者）スペンサーは、優美ということについてその定義を下し、動作の最も経済的な方法であるとした。茶道の作法は、茶碗、茶杓、茶帛などを取り扱うのに、一つの方式を定めている。その方式は、初心者にとっては、あるいは退屈にみえるかもしれないが、しばらく経つと、その方式が結局、時間と労力を最も節約するものであり、言い換えれば、力の利用の最も経済的なものであって、スペンサーの定義に従えば、最も優美なるものであることがわかる。

　社交的な礼法の精神的な意義は、（イギリスの思想家）カーライルの『衣裳哲学』の用語を借りていえば、「礼儀作法は、精神的な規律のたんなる外衣にすぎない」となるが、その意義は外見的なものにくらべて、はるかに大きい。私はスペンサー氏の例にならって、わが国の礼法の起源と、その成立の道徳的動機の跡を尋ねることができるであろうが、それは本書の目的とするところではない。私が言おうとするところは、礼法の厳密な遵守の中に含まれている道徳的な訓練のことである。

quette, but whether it partakes as much of folly as the adherence to ever-changing fashions of the West, is a question not very clear to my mind. Even fashions I do not consider solely as freaks of vanity; on the contrary, I look upon these as a ceaseless search of the human mind for the beautiful. Much less do I consider elaborate ceremony as altogether trivial; for it denotes the result of long observation as to the most appropriate method of achieving a certain result. If there is anything to do, there is certainly a best way to do it, and the best way is both the most economical and the most graceful. Mr. Spencer defines grace as the most economical manner of motion. The tea ceremony presents certain definite ways of manipulating a bowl, a spoon, a napkin, etc. To a novice it looks tedious. But one soon discovers that the way prescribed is, after all, the most saving of time and labour; in other words, the most economical use of force,—hence, according to Spencer's dictum, the most graceful.

The spiritual significance of social decorum—or, I might say, to borrow from the vocabulary of the "Philosophy of Clothes," the spiritual discipline of which etiquette and ceremony are mere outward garments—is out of all proportion to what their appearance warrants us in believing. I might follow the example of Mr. Spencer and trace in our ceremonial institutions their origins and the moral motives that gave rise to them; but that is not what I shall endeavour to do in this book. It is the moral training involved in strict observance of propriety, that I wish to emphasise.

　今まで述べてきたように、礼儀作法はまことに精細なところまで規定され、それゆえに流儀の異なる多くの流派が生まれたが、本質においてはすべて揆を一にする。最も著名な流派である小笠原流宗家（の、小笠原清務）の言葉によれば、「礼道の要は、心を訓練するにある。礼をもって正坐すれば、凶人が剣をとって立ち向ってきても、害を加えることができない」と言うことにある。言い換えれば、絶えず正しい礼法を修めることによって、人の身体のすべての部分と機能は完全に整えられ、身体とそれをとりまく外部の環境とがまったく調和し、肉体に対する精神の支配を表現するに至る、ということである。フランス語の（礼儀を意味する）ビアンセアンス（bienséance[注2]）、この意味は深く、なんと新鮮ではないか。

　優美は力の経済的な方法であるということが、はたして真であれば、その論理的な結果として、優美なる作法を常に実践すれば、力が蓄えられ、保持される。ゆえに、洗練された作法は休息状態の力を意味する。蛮族のゴール人がローマを略奪して、会議中の元老院に乱入し、敬うべき元老たちの髭を引っ張る無礼を働いたという話に、われわれは責められるべきは、礼儀作法の威厳と強さに欠けた元老たちではないかと考える。礼儀から本当に高邁な精神的境地に到達できるのだろうか？　できないはずがあろうか、すべての道はローマに通ずるのだ！

　最も簡単なことでも一つの芸術となり、かつ精神修養の道となる一例として、茶の湯をあげよう。茶を飲むことが芸術になるのか？　いや、ありうるのではないか。子供が砂の上

[注2] 語源は、正坐ということ。

I have said that etiquette was elaborated into the finest niceties, so much so that different schools, advocating different systems, came into existence. But they all united in the ultimate essential, and this was put by a great exponent of the best known school of etiquette, the Ogasawara, in the following terms: "The end of all etiquette is to so cultivate your mind that even when you are quietly seated, not the roughest ruffian can dare make onset on your person." It means, in other words, that by constant exercise in correct manners, one brings all the parts and faculties of his body into perfect order and into such harmony with itself and its environment as to express the mastery of spirit over the flesh. What a new and deep significance the French word *bienséance*[2] comes to contain.

If the promise is true that gracefulness means economy of force, then it follows as a logical sequence that a constant practice of graceful deportment must bring with it a reserve and storage of force. Fine manners, therefore, mean power in repose. When the barbarian Gauls, during the sack of Rome, burst into the assembled Senate and dared pull the beards of the venerable Fathers, we think the old gentlemen were to blame, inasmuch as they lacked dignity and strength of manners. Is lofty spiritual attainment really possible through etiquette? Why not?—All roads lead to Rome!

As an example of how the simplest thing can be made into an art and then become spiritual culture, I may take *Cha-no-yu*, the tea ceremony. Tea-sipping as a fine art!

---

[2] Etymologically, well-seatedness.

に絵を描き、未開人が岩石に絵を刻む。そこから、ラファエロやミケランジェロの芸術が芽生えていったのである。まして、（インドの）ヒンズー教の隠者の瞑想と共にはじまった茶の飲用が、宗教および道徳の補助的な役割をになうまでに発展しても当然のことではなかろうか。

　茶の湯の道の第一義は、心の平静と感情の明澄、立居振舞いの静穏であって、それは正しい思索と感情を生み出す第一の要件である。騒々しい俗世間の光景と音から遮断された、あくまでも清らかな小さな部屋自体が、人の思考を俗世間から離脱させる。室内には、西洋の客間に見られるような、人の目を魅惑するような数多い絵画や美術品などはなく、壁間の「掛物[注3]」は、色彩の美しさよりもむしろ、構図の優美さで人の目を惹く。それは極限まで洗練された趣味を求めるのが目的であって、いささかの虚飾も、宗教的な畏怖の念からも、そこでは遠ざけられる。

　戦乱の時代にあっても、茶の湯の道が、一人の瞑想的隠者（千利休）によって工夫されたという事実は、この作法がたんなる遊びでないことをはっきりと証明している。茶の湯の席に列なる人々は、茶室の静寂境に入るに先立って、まず腰の刀と共に、戦場の荒々しい心を、あるいは政治の煩わしい心を置き去って、この室内に平和と友情を見出したのである。

[注3] 掛物、掛軸。床飾りに用いられる水墨画や書。

Why should it not be? In the children drawing pictures on the sand, or in the savage carving on a rock, was the promise of a Raphael or a Michael Angelo. How much more is the drinking of a beverage, which began with the transcendental contemplation of a Hindoo anchorite, entitled to develop into a handmaid of Religion and Morality? That calmness of mind, that serenity of temper, that composure and quietness of demeanour which are the first essentials of *Cha-no-yu*, are without doubt the first conditions of right thinking and right feeling. The scrupulous cleanliness of the little room, shut off from sight and sound of the madding crowd, is in itself conducive to direct one's thoughts from the world. The bare interior does not engross one's attention like the innumerable pictures and bric-a-brac of a Western parlour; the presence of *kakémono*[3] calls our attention more to grace of design than to beauty of colour. The utmost refinement of taste is the object aimed at; whereas anything like display is banished with religious horror. The very fact that it was invented by a contemplative recluse, in a time when wars and the rumours of wars were incessant, is well calculated to show that this institution was more than a pastime. Before entering the quiet precincts of the tea-room, the company assembling to partake of the ceremony laid aside, together with their swords, the ferocity of battle-field or the cares of government, there to find peace and friendship.

---

[3] Hanging scrolls, which may be either paintings or ideograms, used for decorative purposes.

　茶の湯の道は、礼法以上のもので、それは芸術であり、律動的な動作をリズムとする詩である。つまり、茶の湯の道は、精神的修養の実行方式にほかならなかった。茶の湯の最大の価値は、この最後の点にある。しかし茶道を学ぶ者の中には、他の枝葉末節のことばかりにその心を注いでいる者も少なくない。だからといって、茶道の本質が精神的なものではない、ということにはならない。

　礼儀は、たとい、その人の動作に優美さを与えるにすぎないものだとしても、その修得は大いに意義のあるものであるが、その機能はそれだけにとどまらない。礼儀は仁愛と謙譲の動機より発して、他人の感情を洞察するやさしい感情によって働く、同情の優美な表現である。礼が要求することは、悲しむ者と共に悲しみ、喜ぶ者と共に喜ぶことである。

　このような教訓的な要求が、日常生活の細やかな点に及ぶときは、ほとんど他人の注意をひかない小さな行為としてあらわれる。たとい注意をひいたとしても、二十余年も日本に在住していたある外国人の婦人宣教師が、かつて私に語ったように、それは「はなはだおかしい」ように見えるのである。たとえば日照りの暑い日に、日傘を持たないで戸外を歩いていると、たまたま日本人の知人と出会って挨拶をしたら、その知人はすぐに帽子を脱いだ。そこまではきわめて自然であるとしても、立ち話をするあいだ、知人は自分の持っていた日傘を閉じて日照りの中に立ちつくしている。このような動作は、「はなはだおかしい」ことなのである。なんとばかげたことか！　もちろん、この知人のこうした動作が、「私は日照りにさらされているあなたに同情する。私の日傘が大きいか、あるいはあなたと旧知の間柄であるならば、私はあなたをこの日傘の中に入れてあげたい。しかし私の日傘はあなたを入れるほど大きくはないから、私はせめてあなたと不快

Cha-no-yu is more than a ceremony—it is a fine art; it is poetry, with articulate gestures for rhythms: it is a *modus operandi* of soul discipline. Its greatest value lies in this last phase. Not infrequently the other phases preponderated in the mind of its votaries, but that does not prove that its essence was not of a spiritual nature.

Politeness will be a great acquisition, if it does no more than impart grace to manners; but its function does not stop here. For propriety, springing as it does from motives of benevolence and modesty, and actuated by tender feelings toward the sensibilities of others, is ever a graceful expression of sympathy. Its requirement is that we should weep with those that weep and rejoice with those that rejoice. Such didactic requirement, when reduced into small everyday details of life, expresses itself in little acts scarcely noticeable, or, if noticed, is, as one missionary lady of twenty years' residence once said to me, "awfully funny." You are out in the hot, glaring sun with no shade over you; a Japanese acquaintance passes by; you accost him, and instantly his hat is off—well, that is perfectly natural, but the "awfully funny" performance is, that all the while he talks with you his parasol is down and he stands in the glaring sun also. How foolish!—Yes, exactly so, provided the motive were less than this: "You are in the sun; I sympathise with you; I would willingly take you under my parasol if it were large enough, or if we were familiarly acquainted; as I cannot shade you, I will share your discomforts." Little acts of this kind, equally or more amusing, are not mere gestures or conventionalities. They

を共にしたい」ということでなければ、それは「はなはだお
かしい」ことであろう。これと同じように、いやこれ以上お
かしなちょっとした行為は、たんなる動作や習慣ではなく、
他人を思いやる思慮深い感情の「体現」なのである。

　わが国の礼法によって定められている習慣の中で「はなは
だおかしい」例をもう一つあげよう。その表面だけの観察に
よって、日本のことを批評する外国人は、わが国民の一般的
な習慣は、なんでも「さかさま」に考えることだと、簡単に
片付けている。そのような習慣に接した外国人は、その場で
適当な返答をするのに当惑を感ずることを告白するであろ
う。ほかでもない、贈り物をするとき、それがアメリカ人で
あれば、受け取る人に向かってその品物を賞めそやすが、日
本ではこれを控えめに、あるいは軽んじて言う。アメリカ人
の気持ちはこうである。「これはたいへん良い物です。良い
物でなければあなたに贈りはしないでしょう。良くない物を
贈るのは、あなたを侮辱することになるのですから」。これ
に対し、日本人の論法はこうである。「あなたは良い方です。
どんな良い贈り物でも、あなたにはふさわしくありません。
この贈り物は、品物に価値があるのではなくて、私の誠意の
しるしとしてお受けとり下さい。どんな最良の品物でもあな
たにふさわしい贈り物だというのは、あなたを侮辱すること
になります」。この二つの考え方をくらべてみれば、帰する
ところは同じであって、どちらも「はなはだおかしい」もの
ではない。ただアメリカ人は贈り物にした品物の価値につい
て言い、日本人は贈り物をする人の精神について言っている
のである。

　日本人の礼儀の感覚が、その動作のきわめて細かいところ
まで現われているため、その最も些細なものだけを取りあげ
てそれを典型とし、礼儀の本質を批判するのは、それこそ

are the "bodying forth" of thoughtful feelings for the comfort of others.

Another "awfully funny" custom is dictated by our canons of Politeness; but many superficial writers on Japan have dismissed it by simply attributing it to the general topsy-turvyness of the nation. Every foreigner who has observed it will confess the awkwardness he felt in making proper reply upon the occasion. In America, when you make a gift, you sing its praises to the recipient; in Japan we depreciate or slander it. The underlying idea with you is, "This is a nice gift: if it were not nice I would not dare give it to you; for it will be an insult to give you anything but what is nice." In contrast to this, our logic runs: "You are a nice person, and no gift is nice enough for you. You will not accept anything I can lay at your feet except as a token of my good will; so accept this, not for its intrinsic value, but as a token. It will be an insult to your worth to call the best gift good enough for you." Place the two ideas side by side, and we see that the ultimate idea is one and the same. Neither is "awfully funny." The American speaks of the material which makes the gift; the Japanese speaks of the spirit which prompts the gift.

It is perverse reasoning to conclude, because our sense of propriety shows itself in all the smallest ramifications of our deportment, to take the least important of them

「さかさま」な論法であろう。食事と、食事の礼法を守ることと、どちらが重要だろうか。中国の賢人（孟子）は、「食事が重要な者と、礼を軽視する者を比較すれば、ただたんに食事の方が重要だと言うのみである」と答えている。「金属は羽より重い」というが、これはひとかけらの金属と車一杯の羽を比べて言っているのだろうか？　一片の木を取ってこれを高楼の上に置いても、これをもって高楼より高いと言う者はいないであろう。「真実を語ることと、礼儀を守ることと、いずれがより重要であるか」と、質問したならば、日本人は全くアメリカ人と正反対の答え方をするであろう、と言われている。この説はしばらくおき、私は次の章で「誠実」について述べることにしよう。

and uphold it as the type, and pass judgment upon the principle itself. Which is more important, to eat or to observe rules of propriety about eating? A Chinese sage answers, "If you take a case where the eating is all-important, and the observing the rules of propriety is of little importance, and compare them together, why not merely say that the eating is of the more importance?" "Metal is heavier than feathers," but does that saying have reference to a single clasp of metal and a waggon-load of feathers? Take a piece of wood a foot thick and raise it above the pinnacle of a temple, none would call it taller than the temple. To the question, "Which is the more important, to tell the truth or to be polite?" the Japanese are said to give an answer diametrically opposite to what the American will say,—but I forbear any comment until I come to speak of veracity and sincerity.

真実および誠実

礼儀を行うのに、真実と誠実の心が欠けていたならば、それは茶番になりお芝居となってしまう。伊達政宗は「礼儀も過ぎれば、へつらいとなる」と、言っている。「心だに誠の道にかないなば、祈らずとても神や守らん」といましめた昔の詩人（菅原道真）は、ポロニウスを超えるものがあった。孔子は、その著『中庸』の中で、誠実を神聖視して、これに超越的な力があるとし、その力をほとんど神と同一視して、「この世のあらゆるものは、誠に始まり誠に終わる。誠はあらゆるものの根元であり、誠がないとすれば、そこにはもう何ものもあり得ない」と、述べている。さらに、誠実がもつ遠大で不朽の性質と、動かずして相手を変化させ、存在するだけでおのずから目的を遂げる力について、とうとうと述べている。誠という漢字は、「言」と「成」との結合によってできており、これは新プラトン学派の説く「ロゴス」

CHAPTER VII

VERACITY
AND
SINCERITY

WITHOUT veracity and sincerity, politeness is a farce and a show. "Propriety carried beyond right bounds," says Masamuné, "becomes a lie." An ancient poet has outdone Polonius in the advice he gives: "To thyself be faithful: if in thy heart thou strayest not from truth, without prayer of thine the Gods will keep thee whole." The apotheosis of Sincerity to which Confucius gives expression in the *Doctrine of the Mean*, attributes to it transcendental powers, almost identifying them with the Divine. "Sincerity is the end and the beginning of all things; without Sincerity there would be nothing." He then dwells with eloquence on its far-reaching and long-enduring nature, its power to produce changes without movement and by its mere presence to accomplish its

（言葉を通じて実体化された理性的な活動）との類似を思わせるものがある。孔子はこのような非凡な精神的な飛翔をもって、これほどまでの高みに到達しているのである。

　嘘の言葉と逃げ言葉は、ともに卑怯なものとされてきた。武士は社会的な地位が高いのだから、農民や商人よりも誠実であることが要求された。「武士の一言」というのは、侍の言葉という意味で、ドイツ語のリッターヴォルト（Ritter-wort）がまさにこれに当たるが、それだけで、言われたことの内容の真実性は十分に保証された。武士の言葉は、証文がなくとも約束が果たされるという重みを持ち、証文を書くことは武士の威厳にかかわるものとされた。「二言」すなわち二枚舌を使ったことを、死をもってその罪を償った多くの壮烈な逸話が語られた。

　真実はこれほど重んじられていたので、一般のキリスト教徒が、主の、誓うなかれという明白な考えを、絶えず破っているのとは異なり、真の侍は、誓うことは自分の名誉を傷つけることだと思っていた。武士がさまざまな神や、刀にかけて誓ったことは承知しているが、彼等の誓いが、不謹慎な形式や、その責任を問うような不敬なことにまで堕落したことは決してなかった。言葉を強調するために、文字どおり血判が押されることもあった。このようなことが行われていた説明としては、ゲーテの『ファウスト』をあげるだけで十分だろう。

　最近アメリカのピーリー博士が、その著書の中で、「もし、ふつうの日本人に向かって、嘘を言うことと、礼を失することと、いずれをとるかと質問したならば、必ず『嘘を言う方

purpose without effort. From the Chinese ideogram for Sincerity, which is a combination of "Word" and "Perfect," one is tempted to draw a parallel between it and the Neo-Platonic doctrine of *Logos*—to such height does the sage soar in his unwonted mystic flight.

Lying or equivocation were deemed equally cowardly. The bushi held that his high social position demanded a loftier standard of veracity than that of the tradesman and peasant. *Bushi no ichi-gon*—the word of a samurai, or in exact German equivalent, *Ritterwort*—was sufficient guaranty for the truthfulness of an assertion. His word carried such weight with it that promises were generally made and fulfilled without a written pledge, which would have been deemed quite beneath his dignity. Many thrilling anecdotes were told of those who atoned by death for *ni-gon*, a double tongue.

The regard for veracity was so high that, unlike the generality of Christians who persistently violate the plain commands of the Teacher not to swear, the best of samurai looked upon an oath as derogatory to their honour. I am well aware that they did swear by different deities or upon their swords; but never has swearing degenerated into wanton form and irreverent interjection. To emphasise our words a practice was sometimes resorted to of literally sealing with blood. For the explanation of such a practice, I need only refer my readers to Goethe's *Faust*.

A recent American writer is responsible for this statement, that if you ask an ordinary Japanese which is better, to tell a falsehood or be impolite, he will not hesitate to

がよい』と答えるであろう[注1]」と、述べているが、この説は、一部分は当っているが一部分は間違っている。ふつうの日本人ばかりでなく、武士でさえもそう答えるであろうが、ピーリー博士が、ウソという言葉を、falsehood（虚偽）と英語に訳して、この言葉に過当な重みをおいた点に大きな誤りがある。日本語では、ウソとはマコト（真実）でないこと、あるいはホントウ（事実）でないことを示す言葉である。ローウェルによれば、ワーズワースは真実と事実を識別することができなかった、というが、この点においては、ふつうの日本人はワーズワースと同じである。

　日本人あるいは、いくらか教養のあるアメリカ人に「あなたは私が嫌いですか」とか、あるいは「吐き気がしますか」と質問してみたならば、彼は内心は不快に思っていても、ただちに「いや、私はあなたを大変好きです」とか、「ありがとう、私は大丈夫です」と、ウソの答えをするであろう。しかし礼儀のためだけに真実を犠牲にすることは「虚礼」であり、「甘言は人を欺くもの」とされた。

　私は今、武士道の真実観を言っているのだが、さらにこれをひろげて、日本の商業道徳について、しばらく言っておきたい。外国人の著書や新聞などでは、日本人の商業道徳について不平を訴えているものが少なくない。たしかに日本人の商業道徳は、これまでおざなりな点が多く、これはわが国の体面上においても最悪の汚点であった。しかし、そのような悪口を言うことによって、わが国民の全般を非難する前に、冷静に考えてみよう。そうすれば、将来の慰めが得られるであろう。

　人の世の中における多くの職業の中でも、武士と商人ほど遠く隔たったものはなかった。商人は、士農工商の階級の中で最下位におかれた。武士は土地よりその所得をえて、やる

[注1] ピーリー著『日本の真相』86ページ。

answer, "To tell a falsehood!" Dr. Peery[1] is partly right and partly wrong; right in that an ordinary Japanese, even a samurai, may answer in the way ascribed to him, but wrong in attributing too much weight to the term he translates "falsehood." This word (in Japanese, *uso*) is employed to denote anything which is not a truth (*makoto*) or fact (*honto*). Lowell tells us that Wordsworth could not distinguish between truth and fact, and an ordinary Japanese is in this respect as good as Wordsworth. Ask a Japanese, or even an American of any refinement, to tell you whether he dislikes you or whether he is sick at his stomach, and he will not hesitate long to tell falsehoods and answer "I like you much," or, "I am quite well, thank you." To sacrifice truth merely for the sake of politeness was regarded as an "empty form" (*kyo-rei*) and "deception by sweet words."

I own I am speaking now of the Bushido idea of veracity: but it may not be amiss to devote a few words to our commercial integrity, of which I have heard much complaint in foreign books and journals. A loose business morality has indeed been the worst blot on our national reputation; but before abusing it or hastily condemning the whole race for it, let us calmly study it and we shall be rewarded with consolation for the future.

Of all the great occupations of life, none was farther removed from the profession of arms than commerce. The merchant was placed lowest in the category of voca-

---

[1] Peery, *The Gist of Japan*, p. 86.

気さえあれば自ら農業を楽しむこともできたが、算盤をもって商売をすることは嫌った。この社会的階級の中にある取りきめの知恵をわれわれは知っている。（フランスの思想家）モンテスキューは、貴族に商業を禁じたのは、それによって権力に富を集中させることを防止した、すぐれた社会政策である、と言っている。富と権力との分離は、富の分配を均等に近づける。

『西ローマ帝国最後の時代』の著者ディル教授は、ローマ帝国衰亡の一原因は、貴族が商業に従事することを許し、その結果、少数の元老とその家族による富と権力の独占が生じたからである、と述べている。

　封建時代における日本の商業は、自由な状況であれば到達していたはずの段階までは発達しなかった。この職業は世間からさげすまれたため、自然と、世間の評判などを気にしない人々が集まった。（西洋でも）「人を泥棒とよべば、その人は盗むであろう」というが、ある職業に汚名を着せれば、その職業に従事する者も、その汚名にふさわしい行為をするようになる。ヒュー・ブラックの言うように、「正常な良心は、要求された高さまで上り、期待される標準の限界にまで、たやすく下がる」のは当然だからである。商業であれ他の職業であれ、道徳の規範なしには行われないことは言うまでもない。封建時代のわが国の商人でも、彼らの間には道徳の規範があって、それがなければ、同業組合、銀行、取引所、保険、手形、為替などの基本的な制度を発展させることはできなか

tions,—the knight, the tiller of the soil, the mechanic, the merchant. The samurai derived his income from land and could even indulge, if he had a mind to, in amateur farming; but the counter and abacus were abhorred. We know the wisdom of this social arrangement. Montesquieu has made it clear that the debarring of the nobility from mercantile pursuits was an admirable social policy, in that it prevented wealth from accumulating in the hands of the powerful. The separation of power and riches kept the distribution of the latter more nearly equable. Professor Dill, the author of *Roman Society in the Last Century of the Western Empire*, has brought afresh to our mind that one cause of the decadence of the Roman Empire, was the permission given to the nobility to engage in trade, and the consequent monopoly of wealth and power by a minority of the senatorial families.

Commerce, therefore, in feudal Japan did not reach that degree of development which it would have attained under freer conditions. The obloquy attached to the calling naturally brought within its pale such as cared little for social repute. "Call one a thief and he will steal." Put a stigma on a calling and its followers adjust their morals to it, for it is natural that "the normal conscience," as Hugh Black says, "rises to the demands made on it, and easily falls to the limit of the standard expected from it." It is unnecessary to add that no business, commercial or otherwise, can be transacted without a code of morals. Our merchants of the feudal period had one among themselves, without which they could never have developed, as

った。しかし職業を異にする者たちとの関係においては、商人の生活は評判どおりよくなかったのである。

　このような事情であったために、ひとたびわが国が開港して、諸外国と通商することになると、冒険的で無節操な商人だけがまず開港場に突進してゆき、昔からの信用ある商家は、政府から支店開設を再三要請されても、しばらくの間はこれを拒否しつづけた。それでは、武士道は、このような商業上の不名誉な流れをせきとめる力がなかったであろうか。その点について考えてみよう。

　わが国の歴史に通じている者は、わが国が開港してから数年足らずで、封建制度が廃止されたことを憶えているだろう。それと同時に武士はその家禄を失い、その代わり公債を与えられ、その公債を商業に投資する自由も与えられた。そこで諸君は、こう質問するであろう。「なぜ彼ら武士は、その誇りとする誠実をもって新しい事業関係に応用し、これまでの商業の悪い習慣を一掃することができなかったのか」と。彼らの多くは、高潔で正直な武士であった。彼らは不慣れな新しい商工業の分野で、利にさとい商人と対抗し競争しても、商売のかけ引きも知らず、回復しがたい大失敗を招いた。その運命には、いくら同情しても同情し足りない。アメリカのような実業国においてさえ、実業家の80パーセントは失敗するということであるから、士族の商法でようやく成功した者が、100人の中で一人しかなくても、驚くにはあたらない。要するに、武士道を商取引に応用しようとして、どれほどの資産が破滅していったことか、その額が判明するには、しばらく時間がかかるだろう。しかし、注意深い者ならば、富の

they did in embryo, such fundamental mercantile institutions as the guild, the bank, the bourse, insurance, checks, bills of exchange, etc.; but in their relations with people outside their vocation, the tradesmen lived too true to the reputation of their order.

This being the case, when the country was opened to foreign trade, only the most adventurous and unscrupulous rushed to the ports, while the respectable business houses declined for some time the repeated requests of the authorities to establish branch houses. Was Bushido powerless to stay the current of commercial dishonour? Let us see.

Those who are well acquainted with our history will remember that only a few years after our treaty ports were opened to foreign trade, feudalism was abolished, and when with it the samurai's fiefs were taken and bonds issued to them in compensation, they were given liberty to invest them in mercantile transactions. Now you may ask, "Why could they not bring their much boasted veracity into their new business relations and so reform the old abuses?" Those who had eyes to see could not weep enough, those who had hearts to feel could not sympathise enough, with the fate of many a noble and honest samurai who signally and irrevocably failed in his new and unfamiliar field of trade and industry, through sheer lack of shrewdness in coping with his artful plebeian rival. When we know that eighty percent of the business houses fail in so industrial a country as America, is it any wonder that scarcely one among a hundred samurai who went

道は名誉の道でないことはすぐにわかったであろう。では、両者の違いはどこにあるのだろうか。

（アイルランドの歴史学者）レッキーは、人間に誠実をもたらすものとして、「経済的なるもの、政治的なるもの、哲学的なるもの」の三つを挙げたが、その中で、第一のものは武士道には全く欠けていた。第二のものも、封建制度下の政治社会においては、ほとんど発達することができなかった。正直がわが国民の道徳の中で、高い地位を得たのは、その第三の哲学的なものによってであり、レッキーが言うように、それを最高の表現としていたのである。

私はアングロ・サクソン民族が、すぐれた商業道徳をもっていることを見て、深く尊敬しているのだが、そのよってきたる原因を問うと「正直は最良の政策である」つまり「正直は引き合う」という答である。では、この正直という徳自体が報酬ではないのか。虚偽をするよりも多くの収入を得るから、正直という徳を行うということであれば、武士道はむしろ虚偽に味方してしまうであろう。

武士道が「あるものに対してあるもの」という報酬の原理を拒否すれば、抜け目のない商人はすぐにそれを受け容れるだろう。レッキーが、誠実は、主として商工業によって発展してゆくと、言っているのは、きわめて正しい。また（ドイツの哲学者）ニーチェが、正直は、諸徳の中で最も幼いと、述べているが、言い換えれば、誠実は、近代産業の養子であって、この養母がいなかったならば、誠実は、貴族的な孤児として、最も教養ある者の心の中でしか養い育てることがで

into trade could succeed in his new vocation? It will be long before it will be recognised how many fortunes were wrecked in the attempt to apply Bushido ethics to business methods; but it was soon patent to every observing mind that the ways of wealth were not the ways of honour. In what respects, then, were they different?

Of the three incentives to veracity that Lecky enumerates, viz., the industrial, the political, and the philosophical, the first was altogether lacking in Bushido. As to the second, it could develop little in a political community under a feudal system. It is in its philosophical and, as Lecky says, in its highest aspect, that honesty attained elevated rank in our catalogue of virtues. With all my sincere regard for the high commercial integrity of the Anglo-Saxon race, when I ask for the ultimate ground, I am told that "honesty is the best policy,"—that it *pays* to be honest. Is not this virtue, then, its own reward? If it is followed because it brings in more cash than falsehood, I am afraid Bushido would rather indulge in lies!

If Bushido rejects a doctrine of *quid pro quo* rewards, the shrewder tradesman will readily accept it. Lecky has very truly remarked that veracity owes its growth largely to commerce and manufacture; as Nietzsche puts it, honesty is the youngest of the virtues—in other words, it is the foster-child of modern industy. Without this mother, veracity was like a blue-blood orphan whom only the most cultivated mind could adopt and nourish. Such

きなかったであろう。このような心は、武士の間では一般的であった。しかし、平民的で実利的な近代産業という養母がいなかった故に、この世慣れない幼児は、発育をとげることができなかったのである。もし、産業が発達すれば、誠実はこれを実行するに容易となり、しかも、有利な徳であることがわかってくるであろう。（ドイツの宰相）ビスマルクが、ドイツ帝国の領事に訓令を発して、「わがドイツ船に積んだ貨物が、その数量、品質共に、いちじるしく信用を欠くのは、まことに嘆かわしい」と、警告を発したのは、1880年（明治13年）10月のことであった。しかし、現代においては、商業上のことでドイツ人の不正直や不注意を耳にすることは比較的少なくなった。20年の間に、ドイツ商人は、結局正直が引き合うことを学んだのである。わが国の商人も、すでにこの道理をわきまえている。以上のことに関しては、アメリカの思想家クナップの『封建的および近代的日本』およびランサムの『転換期における日本』の二つの近著を読んで的確な判断をしていただきたい[注2]。これらの日本に関する記述の中で、とくに興味深いことは、商人であっても、その債務をおこすに当たって、正直と名誉を重んずることを証書の中に記入し、それをもって最も確実なる保証としていることである。

　その証文の中に、「お借りした金子（きんす）の返済を怠ったときには、衆人満座の前で、お笑いなされても宜（よろ）しゅうございます」とか、あるいは、「お借りした金子を返済できなくなったときには、ばかと嘲（あざけ）りくださいますように」などという文句を記入するのが、ふつうに行われていたことである。

　私は、武士道における誠実が、勇気以上の高い動機をもっているかどうか、しばしば疑ってみた。日本には「偽りの証（あかし）

[注2] クナップ著『封建的および近代的日本』第1巻第4章。ランサム著『転換期における日本』第8章。

minds were general among the samurai, but, for want of a more democratic and utilitarian foster-mother, the tender child failed to thrive. Industries advancing, veracity will prove an easy, nay a profitable virtue to practise. Just think—as late as November, 1880, Bismarck sent a circular to the professional consuls of the German Empire, warning them of "a lamentable lack of reliability with regard to German shipments *inter alia*, apparent both as to quality and quantity." Nowadays we hear comparatively little of German carelessness and dishonesty in trade. In twenty years her merchants have learned that in the end honesty pays. Already our merchants have found that out. For the rest I recommend the reader to two recent writers for well-weighed judgment on this point.[2] It is interesting to remark in this connection that integrity and honour were the surest guaranties which even a merchant debtor could present in the form of promissory notes. It was quite a usual thing to insert such clauses as these: "In default of the repayment of the sum lent to me, I shall say nothing against being ridiculed in public"; or, "In case I fail to pay you back, you may call me a fool," and the like.

Often have I wondered whether the veracity of Bushido had any motive higher than courage. In the absence of

---

[2] Knapp, *Feudal and Modern Japan*, Vol. I., ch. iv; Ransome, *Japan in Transition*, ch. viii.

をたてることなかれ」という、積極的ないましめの言葉がな
いため、虚言をしても罪として裁かれず、たんにこれを弱さ
として排斥し、はなはだ不名誉なるものとされてきた。たし
かに、正直の観念は名誉と密接な関係をもっており、ラテン
語でもドイツ語でも、その語源は名誉と同一なのである。

　さていよいよ、武士道の「名誉」について述べることにし
よう。

any positive commandment against bearing false witness, lying was not condemned as sin, but simply denounced as weakness, and, as such, highly dishonourable. As a matter of fact, the idea of honesty is so intimately blended, and its Latin and its German etymology so identified with honour, that it is high time I should pause a few moments for the consideration of this feature of the Precepts of Knighthood.

第 8 章

名誉

名誉の感覚は、人格の尊厳とその価値にかかわる明白な自覚から生まれる。したがって自分の生まれながらにもっている身分に伴う、義務と特権を重んずることを知り、そのような教養を受けた武士の特色とならねばならなかった。

　今日honourの訳語として用いられる名誉という言葉は、よく使われていたわけではないが、その観念は、「名」「面目」「外聞」などという言葉であらわされてきた。これらの言葉は、聖書で用いられているname（名）、ギリシャ語で仮面をあらわす言葉から出てきたpersonality（人格）、およびfame（名声）を連想させるものである。名声は人の体面であり、「自分に備わった不滅のものであり、これがなかったならば、人は馬やけものと同じである」とされた。したがって、名声を侵されることは、最も恥とされた。そして「恥を知る心」

CHAPTER VIII

HONOUR

THE sense of honour, implying a vivid consciousness of personal dignity and worth, could not fail to characterise the samurai, born and bred to value the duties and privileges of their profession. Though the word ordinarily given nowadays as the translation of honour was not used freely, yet the idea was conveyed by such terms as *na* (name), *menmoku* (countenance), *guaibun* (outside hearing), reminding us respectively of the biblical use of "name," of the evolution of the term "personality" from the Greek mask, and of "fame." A good name—one's reputation, "the immortal part of one's self, what remains being bestial"—assumed as a matter of course, any infringement upon its integrity was felt as shame, and the sense of shame (*Renchishin*) was one of the earliest to be

（廉恥心）は、少年の教育において第一の徳目であり、「笑われるぞ」「体面を汚すぞ」「恥かしくないか」などの言葉は、少年に対して、正しい行動を促すときの最後のいましめであった。このように、少年の名誉心に訴えることは、あたかも母親の胎内にいたときから名誉で養われていたかのように、彼のハートの最も敏感なところに触れたのである。名誉の感覚は、胎児のときからの感化であり、家庭的な自覚と強く結びついていたといえよう。

　（フランスの文学者）バルザックは、「社会は家族の団結を失ったことにより、モンテスキューが言ったところの『名誉』という根本的な力を失ってしまった」と言ったが、実に「恥を知る心」は人類の道徳的自覚の最も早い徴候であると私は思う。（『旧約聖書』では）人類（の先祖イヴ）が禁断の果実を味わったがため、神より罰を下された、というが、私の考えによれば、最初のそして最悪の罰は、子を産む苦しみでもなく、いばらとあざみのトゲの痛みでもなく、羞恥の感覚を自覚したことではなかったろうか。つまり、最初の母イヴが、その指に粗末な針をもち、夫アダムが摘んできた無花果の葉を、ふるえながら縫っている姿ほど、哀れでしかも悲しいできごとが歴史上にあったろうか。この最初の不服従の果実は、他に類のない執拗さでわれわれから離れない。人類の裁縫の技を尽くしても、いまだにこの「羞恥心」をおおい隠すエプロンを縫うことはできないのである。ある武人（新井白石）がその少年時代に、軽い屈辱に妥協して品性を落とすことを拒んだのは正しかった。彼はその理由を、「不名誉は樹の切り傷のように、時がたてば消えるどころか、かえって大きくなる」と言った。

　カーライルは「恥はすべての徳、立派な行為、そしてすぐ

cherished in juvenile education. "You will be laughed at," "It will disgrace you," "Are, you not ashamed?" were the last appeal to correct behaviour on the part of a youthful delinquent. Such a recourse to his honour touched the most sensitive spot in the child's heart, as though it had been nursed on honour while he was in his mother's womb; for most truly is honour a pre-natal influence, being closely bound up with strong family consciousness. "In losing the solidarity of families," says Balzac, "society has lost the fundamental force which Montesquieu named Honour." Indeed, the sense of shame seems to me to be the earliest indication of the moral consciousness of the race. The first and worst punishment which befell humanity in consequence of tasting "the fruit of that forbidden tree" was, to my mind, not the sorrow of childbirth, nor the thorns and thistles, but the awakening of the sense of shame. Few incidents in history excel in pathos the scene of the first mother plying, with heaving breast and tremulous fingers, her crude needle on the few fig leaves which her dejected husband plucked for her. This first fruit of disobedience clings to us with a tenacity that nothing else does. All the sartorial ingenuity of mankind has not yet succeeded in sewing an apron that will efficaciously hide our sense of shame. That samurai was right who refused to compromise his character by a slight humiliation in his youth; "because," he said, "dishonour is like a scar on a tree, which time, instead of effacing, only helps to enlarge."

Mencius had taught centuries before, in almost the

れた道徳の土壌である」と言ったが、彼に先立つおよそ2千年前に孟子は、ほとんど同じような言葉で（恥を知る心は、義のはじまりであると言って）教えている。

武士は、はなはだ不名誉を恐れた。わが国の文学には、シェークスピアがノーフォークの口で言わしめたような雄弁さはないが、不名誉は武士の頭上にかけられたダモクレス^{訳注7}の剣のようであって、その恐れがしばしば病的な性質を帯びることさえあった。武士道の掟において、少しも許されそうもない行為でも、名誉の名において行われることがあった。きわめて小さな侮辱を受けたがために、いやそれを過大に想像してしまって、短気な高慢者が立腹し、刀を抜いて無用の闘争を引きおこし、無実の人を殺すことも少なくなかった。ある町人が、一人の武士の背中に蚤がはねているのを見て、善意をもって注意したところ、たちどころに斬られてしまったという話がある。なぜなら、蚤は畜生にたかる虫であるから「貴い武士と畜生とを同一視するのは許されない侮辱である」という単純にして奇怪な理由によるというのである。

このような話は、あまりばかげていて信じられないだろう。しかし、このような話の流布には、三つの意味がある。一つは、平民を畏怖させるために作られたこと。二つは、武士に与えられた名誉ある身分的特権が実際に乱用されたこと。三つは、武士の間に、恥を知る心が強大に発達していたこと、である。異常な一例をあげて、ただちに武士道を非難するのは明らかに不公平であって、たとえばキリストの真の教えが、狂信や妄信の果実である、中世の宗教裁判や偽善で判断されるのと同じことである。しかし、このような狂信といえども、酔っぱらいの狂態にくらべれば、その中に何か人を動かす高貴なものがあるように、武士が極端に名誉を重んずる敏感な

identical phrase, what Carlyle has latterly expressed,—namely, that "Shame is the soil of all Virtue, of good manners and good morals."

The fear of disgrace was so great that if our literature lacks such eloquence as Shakespeare puts into the mouth of Norfolk, it nevertheless hung like Damocles' sword over the head of every samurai and often assumed a morbid character. In the name of honour, deeds were perpetrated which can find no justification in the code of Bushido. At the slightest, nay—imaginary insult—the quick-tempered braggart took offence, resorted to the use of the sword, and many an unnecessary strife was raised and many an innocent life lost. The story of a well-meaning citizen who called the attention of a bushi to a flea jumping on his back, and who was forthwith cut in two, for the simple and questionable reason, that inasmuch as fleas are parasites which feed on animals, it was an unpardonable insult to identify a noble warrior with a beast—I say, stories like these are too frivolous to believe. Yet, the circulation of such stories implies three things: (1) that they were invented to overawe common people, (2) that abuses were really made of the samurai's profession of honour; and (3) that a very strong sense of shame was developed among them. It is plainly unfair to take an abnormal case to cast blame upon the precepts, any more than to judge of the true teachings of Christ from the fruits of religious fanaticism and extravagance,—inquisitions and hypocrisy. But, as in religious monomania there is something touchingly noble as compared with the

心の中に、純粋な徳性の基層を認めることができないであろうか。

　繊細な名誉の規範が、病的な行き過ぎに陥りやすいのを未然に防ぐために、寛容と忍耐の教えがあった。ささいな刺激で怒るのは「短気」として笑われた。ことわざにも「ならぬ堪忍するが堪忍」といい、かの偉大なる武士徳川家康の遺訓にも、「人の一生は、重い荷物を背負って遠い道を行くようなものである。急いではいけない……堪忍は無事長久の基である……おのれを責めて人を責めるな」と、述べており、彼は自分でそう説いたことを、自分の生涯で、これを実証した人である。

　ある狂歌師は、わが国の歴史上有名な三人の武士の口に、それぞれの性格をあらわす句を言わせた。信長は「鳴かざれば殺してしまえほととぎす」、秀吉は「鳴かざれば鳴かしてみようほととぎす」であり、家康は「鳴かざれば鳴くまで待とうほととぎす」ということであった。

　孟子も、忍耐や我慢を、大いに人にすすめ、「自分のそばに、肌をぬいだり裸になったりする無作法な人間がいても、おまえはおまえ、私は私である。おまえはなにも私を汚すことはできない」と言い、さらに「小事に怒るのは、君子の恥とするところであって、大事のために怒るのは義憤である」と、教えている。

　武士道が、どれほど非戦闘的で非抵抗的である柔和の高みにまで到達しようとしたかは、武士たちの発言からもわかる

delirium tremens of a drunkard, so in that extreme sensitiveness of the samurai about their honour do we not recognise the substratum of a genuine virtue?

The morbid excess into which the delicate code of honour was inclined to run was strongly counterbalanced by preaching magnanimity and patience. To take offence at slight provocation was ridiculed as "short-tempered." The popular adage said: "To bear what you think you cannot bear is really to bear." The great Iyéyasu left to posterity a few maxims, among which are the following:—"The life of man is like going a long distance with a heavy load upon the shoulders. Haste not... Reproach none, but be forever watchful of thine own short-comings... Forbearance is the basis of length of days." He proved in his life what he preached. A literary wit put a characteristic epigram into the mouths of three well-known personages in our history: to Nobunaga he attributed, "I will kill her, if the nightingale sings not in time"; to Hidéyoshi, "I will force her to sing for me"; and to Iyéyasu, "I will wait till she opens her lips."

Patience and long-suffering were also highly commended by Mencius. In one place he writes to this effect: "Though you denude yourself and insult me, what is that to me? You cannot defile my soul by your outrage. Elsewhere he teaches that anger at a petty offence is unworthy a superior man, but indignation for a great cause is righteous wrath.

To what height of unmartial and unresisting meekness Bushido could reach in some of its votaries, may be seen

だろう。たとえば、小河（立所）は、「人からどんなに悪く言われようと、悪口を返すのではなく、自分の義務の遂行にもっと忠実でいられたかどうかを反省することだ」と言っている。また（江戸時代の儒者）熊沢（蕃山）は、「人が自分を咎（とが）めても、自分は咎めまい。人が自分を怒っても、自分は怒るまい。怒りと欲とを棄ててこそ、常に心は楽しめるものである」と、言っている。もう一つの例として、その高い額（ひたい）の上には「恥も坐するを恥ずる」と言われた西郷（南洲）の遺訓をあげよう。「道というものは、天地自然の道に外ならない。ゆえに人はこの道を行うものであるから、天を敬うことを目的とするべきである。天は人をも自分をも同一に愛し給うゆえに、自分を愛する心をもって人を愛するべきである。人を相手とせず、天を相手として力を尽くし、人を咎めず、自分の誠が足りないことをいつも反省しなければならない」。これらの言葉は、キリスト教の教訓を想起させ、実践的な道徳においては、自然宗教もいかに深く天啓宗教に近づき得るか、ということをわれわれに示すものである。さらに、このような言葉は、たんに言葉としてあるだけではなく、現実の多くの人々によって実行されたものである。

　寛容、忍耐、寛恕（かんじょ）などの、高い徳にまで到達した者は、たしかにごく少数の者に過ぎなかった。ことに武士の名誉を形成するものとして、明白なそして一般的な教えを述べたものが何一つなかったのは、まことに悲しむべきことである。ただ少数の智徳のすぐれた人々だけが、名誉は「境遇から生まれるものではなく」、各人がその分を守り尽くすことである、ということを知っていたのである。なぜなら、青年はまだ幼い穏やかな時期に学んだ孟子の教えを、行動するときの勢い

in their utterances. Take, for instance, this saying of Ogawa: "When others speak all manner of evil things against thee, return not evil for evil, but rather reflect that thou wast not more faithful in the discharge of thy duties." Take another of Kumazawa:—"When others blame thee, blame them not; when others are angry at thee, return not anger. Joy cometh only as Passion and Desire part." Still another instance I may cite from Saigo, upon whose overhanging brows "Shame is ashamed to sit":—"The Way is the way of Heaven and Earth; Man's place is to follow it; therefore make it the object of thy life to reverence Heaven. Heaven loves me and others with equal love; therefore with the love wherewith thou lovest thyself, love others. Make not Man thy partner but Heaven, and making Heaven thy partner do the best. Never condemn others; but see to it that thou comest not short of thine own mark." Some of these sayings remind us of Christian expostulations, and show us how far in practical morality natural religion can approach the revealed. Not only did these sayings remain as utterances, but they were really embodied in acts.

It must be admitted that very few attained this sublime height of magnanimity, patience and forgiveness. It was a great pity that nothing clear and general was expressed as to what constitutes honour, only a few enlightened minds being aware that it "from no condition rises," but that it lies in each acting well his part; for nothing was easier than for youths to forget in the heat of action what they had learned in Mencius in their calmer moments. Said

で簡単に忘れてしまったからである。この賢人は、「貴きを欲するは人の同じき心也。人々己に貴き者あり、思わざるのみ。人の貴くするところの者は良貴に非ざるなり。趙孟の貴くする所は、趙孟能くこれを賤しくす」と、このように教えている。たいていの場合、侮辱に対しては直ちに怒りが向けられ、死をもって報いられた。これに反して、後で述べるように、名誉は、しばしば虚栄、あるいは俗世間的な評判にすぎなかったとしても、人生における最高の善として貴ばれた。

多くの少年の目標は、富でもなければ知識でもなく、名誉であった。少年は志を立てて家を出るときは、世にもし名を成さなかったならば、死んでも帰らぬと誓い、功名心のある彼らの母たちは、わが子がもし「錦を着て故郷に帰る」のでなければ、再び会うことを拒んだ。少年たちは、恥をまぬがれ、名を立てるためには、どんなに不自由な暮しもいとわず、肉体的あるいは精神的な苦痛にも耐えた。少年の時に得た名誉は、年齢と共に成長してゆくことを、彼らは知っていたのである。

大阪冬の陣の戦いのとき、徳川家康の若い息子（頼宣）は、先鋒隊に加えられるように熱心に願ったが、後陣に入れられた。敵の城が落ちたとき、彼は激しく泣いた。一人の老臣は彼を慰め、励まそうと思い、「今日の合戦に出られなくても、何もお急ぎになることはありません。これからこのような合戦は何度もありましょうぞ」と、言うと、頼宣はその老臣に怒りの目を向けて、「われらに13歳の時がまたあるか」と、言ったという。もし名誉と名声が得られるならば、生命を捨

this sage: " 'T is in every man's mind to love honour; but little doth he dream that what is truly honourable lies within himself and not elsewhere. The honour which men confer is not good honour. Those whom Châo the Great ennobles, he can make mean again." For the most part, an insult was quickly resented and repaid by death, as we shall see later, while honour—too often nothing higher than vainglory or worldly approbation—was prized as the *summum bonum* of earthly existence. Fame, and not wealth or knowledge, was the goal toward which youths had to strive. Many a lad swore within himself as he crossed the threshold of his paternal home, that he would not recross it until he had made a name in the world; and many an ambitious mother refused to see her sons again unless they could "return home," as the expression is, "caparisoned in brocade." To shun shame or win a name, samurai boys would submit to any privations and undergo severest ordeals of bodily or mental suffering. They knew that honour won in youth grows with age. In the memorable siege of Osaka, a young son of Iyéyasu, in spite of his earnest entreaties to be put in the vanguard, was placed at the rear of the army. When the castle fell, he was so chagrined and wept so bitterly that an old councillor tried to console him with all the resources at his command; "Take comfort, Sire," said he, "at the thought of the long future before you. In the many years that you may live, there will come diverse occasions to distinguish yourself." The boy fixed his indignant gaze upon the man and said—"How foolishly you talk! Can ever my fourteenth

てても惜しくないと思われていた。それ故に、生命よりも大事であると思われる事態が起これば、きわめて平静に、そして即座に一命が投げうたれた。

　生命をも犠牲にしてもかまわない、と思う理由の中には、主君に対する忠義があった。忠節の義務こそ、封建道徳を均整のとれた形に構築している土台石であった。

year come round again?" Life itself was thought cheap if honour and fame could be attained therewith: hence, whenever a cause presented itself which was considered dearer than life, with utmost serenity and celerity was life laid down.

Of the causes in comparison with which no life was too dear to sacrifice, was the duty of loyalty, which was the key-stone making feudal virtues a symmetrical arch.

第 9 章

忠義

封建道徳には、他の道徳体系や、武士以外の階級にも共通しているものも多くあった。しかし、この目上の者に対する服従と忠誠の徳は、封建道徳の中ではっきりとその特色を示すものである。あらゆる種類や境遇における人間の間に、忠誠が重んじられたことは、私もよく知っている。例えば掏摸の一団がその親分に対して忠誠を負うということがある。しかし、忠誠が徳として最も重んじられたのは、武士の名誉にかかわる規範においてのみであった。

（ドイツの哲学者）ヘーゲル[注1]は、（その著書の中で）封建的な臣下の忠誠を批評して、それは個人に対する義務であって、国家に対する義務ではないから、全然不当な原理の上に立てられた規範である、と言ったが、ヘーゲルと同国の英雄ビスマルクは、「個人の忠誠は、ドイツ国民の美徳である」と言

[注1] ヘーゲル著『歴史哲学』（シブリー英訳）第4部第2篇第1章。

CHAPTER IX

THE DUTY OF LOYALTY

FEUDAL morality shares other virtues in common with other systems of ethics, with other classes of people, but this virtue—homage and fealty to a superior—is its distinctive feature. I am aware that personal fidelity is a moral adhesion existing among all sorts and conditions of men,—a gang of pickpockets owe allegiance to a Fagin; but it is only in the code of chivalrous honour that loyalty assumes paramount importance.

In spite of Hegel's criticism[1] that the fidelity of feudal vassals, being an obligation to an individual and not to a commonwealth, is a bond established on totally unjust principles, a great compatriot of his made it his boast that personal loyalty was a German virtue. Bismarck had good

[1] *Philosophy of History* (Eng. trans. by Sibree), Pt. IV, sec. ii., ch. i.

って誇った。ビスマルクがこのように言ったのには理由がある。それは、彼の誇った忠誠が、祖国、あるいはどこかの一国民一民族だけに存在するものだからではなくて、この騎士道が生んだ徳が封建制度の最も長く続いた国民の間に、最も長く留（とど）まっていたが故である。アメリカのように「すべての者は他の者と同等であり」、なおこれにアイルランド人がつけ加えたように、「同時に他の者より勝（まさ）ってもいる」という国より見れば、日本人の主君に対するきわめて高い忠誠の観念は「ある一定の範囲内において優れたもの」ではあっても、われわれ国民の間にみられるようなことは、「まこと不合理である」と考えられるかもしれない。かつて、モンテスキューは、フランス国境のピレネー山脈の一方の側において、正しいと考えられたことが、他の側においては誤りであると言って嘆いたが、最近起こったドレフュス事件[訳注8]の裁判は、彼の言葉の正しいことを証明し、しかもフランスの正義が通用しない境界線はピレネー山脈だけではないことを示した。これと同じように、われわれ日本人の抱く忠義の観念は、他の国の人には、讃美されないかもしれない。しかしこれはわれわれの観念が誤りである故ではなくて、おそらく他国の人々が、それを忘れ去ったからであり、また、われわれが他のいかなる国においても到達できなかった程度の高さまでこの観念を発達せしめたが故であろう。（アメリカの牧師）グリッフィス[注2]は、（その著書の中で）「中国においては、儒教が親に対する服従をもって、人間第一の義務としているのに対し、日本においては、主君に対する忠誠をその第一義に置いている」と、述べていることは、全くその通りである。ここで、読者を驚かし、あるいは嫌悪を感じさせるかもしれない危険をも顧みず、シェークスピアが言っているように「零落（れいらく）した主君に仕

注2 グリッフィス著『日本の宗教』。

reasons to do so, not because the *Treue* he boasts of was the monopoly of his Fatherland or of any single nation or race, but because this favoured fruit of chivalry lingers latest among the people where feudalism has lasted longest. In America, where "everybody is as good as anybody else," and, as the Irishman added, "better too," such exalted ideas of loyalty as we feel for our sovereign may be deemed "excellent within certain bounds," but preposterous as encouraged among us. Montesquieu complained long ago that right on one side of the Pyrenees was wrong on the other, and the recent Dreyfus trial proved the truth of his remark, save that the Pyrenees were not the sole boundary beyond which French justice finds no accord. Similarly, loyalty as we conceive it may find few admirers elsewhere, not because our conception is wrong, but because it is, I am afraid, forgotten, and also because we carry it to a degree not reached in any other country. Griffis[2] was quite right in stating that whereas in China Confucian ethics made obedience to parents the primary human duty, in Japan precedence was given to loyalty. At the risk of shocking some of my good readers, I will relate of one "who could endure to follow a fall'n lord" and who thus, as Shakespeare assures, "earned a place i' the story."

---

[2] *Religions of Japan.*

えて艱難（かんなん）を共にし」、これによって「物語に名を残した」ある一人の忠臣の物語を述べよう。

　その物語は、わが国の歴史的人物の一人、菅原道真に関する話である。菅原道真は、政敵の嫉妬讒言（ざんげん）によって都を追われ、流罪（るざい）の身になったが、敵はその一族をも全て亡ぼそうと、幼い道真の子供（菅　秀才）をさがし求めた。そしてついに道真の旧臣武部源蔵が、その子供を里の寺子屋にかくまっていることを知り、源蔵に「子供の首を打って差し出せ」と厳命した。

　命令を受けた源蔵がまず思いついたのは、適当な身代わりを見つけることだった。寺子屋で学ぶ子供の名簿を開いて、そこにやってきた少年たちを注意深く見ていたが、田舎育ちの子供らは、かくまっている若君に少しも似ていない。だが、彼の絶望もほんの一瞬だった。寺子屋入りを頼んできた母と子があった。その子は幼君と年格好も同じ、その面ざしもよく似ていたのである。

　幼い主君とこの幼い家臣とがよく似ていることは、この母子自身もよく知っていたのである。この母子は、自分の家の祭壇の前で祈り、密かに自分の身を捧げる決心をしていたのである。息子は自分の命を、そして母親は自分の心を。だが、そのことは少しも顔色にも出さなかった。そのようなことを知らない源蔵は、二人の思う通りになったのである。

　これはつまり、スケープゴートである！　物語の後半を簡単に述べよう。定められた日に、検視の役人が首を確認し、受け取りのためにやってきた。役人は偽の首にだまされるだろうか？（実はこの役人松王丸はこの母親の夫であり、この子の父親であり、その妻にわが子を連れて寺子屋にゆかせた

The story is of one of the greatest characters of our history, Michizané, who, falling a victim to jealousy and calumny, is exiled from the capital. Not content with this, his unrelenting enemies are now bent upon the extinction of his family. Strict search for his son—not yet grown—reveals the fact of his being secreted in a village school kept by one Genzo, a former vassal of Michizané. When orders are dispatched to the schoolmaster to deliver the head of the juvenile offender on a certain day, his first idea is to find a suitable substitute for it. He ponders over his school list, scrutinises with careful eyes all the boys, as they stroll into the class-room, but none among the children born of the soil bears the least resemblance to his protégé. His despair, however, is but for a moment; for, behold, a new scholar is announced—a comely boy of the same age as his master's son, escorted by a mother of noble mien.

No less conscious of the resemblance between infant lord and infant retainer, were the mother and the boy himself. In the privacy of home both had laid themselves upon the altar; the one his life—the other her heart, yet without sign to the outer world. Unwitting of what had passed between them, it is the teacher from whom comes the suggestion.

Here, then, is the scapegoat!—The rest of the narrative may be briefly told.—On the day appointed, arrives the officer commissioned to identify and receive the head of the youth. Will he be deceived by the false head? The poor Genzo's hand is on the hilt of the sword, ready to strike a

のは彼だったのである。）さて、あわれな源蔵は刀の柄に手をかけ、もし計略が見破られたならば、検視の役人を斬るか、自刃しようと身構えていた。検視の役人（松王丸）は無残な首を引き寄せて、その特徴を仔細にあらため、落ちついた事務的な口調で本物であると言い放った。その夜、人里離れた一軒家では、寺子屋を訪れた母親が待っていた。彼女は子供の運命を知っているのだろうか？　彼女が戸の開くのを熱心に見つめているのは、子供の帰りを待っているからではない。彼女の舅は長い間、道真の恩顧を受けていたが、道真がいなくなって、彼女の夫の松王丸はやむをえず一家の恩人の敵に仕えていた。彼自身は残酷な主君に不忠を働くことはできなかったが、自分の息子は祖父の主君のお役に立つことができた。流刑になった道真の家族を知る者として、少年の首の確認する役目を命じられたのは、彼であった。そして、その日の、いや人生の、つらい仕事を終えて、彼は家に戻ってきた。家の敷居をまたいだとたん、妻に呼びかけた。「女房喜べ、倅はお役に立ったわ、やい！」

「なんという残酷な物語！」と叫ぶ人がきっとあるであろう。「他人の生命を救うために、親がなんの罪もない吾子を犠牲にするとは！」。しかしこの少年は、自分でもそのことをよく知って、甘んじて犠牲になったのである。この物語は身代わりとなって死ぬ話であり、（『旧約聖書』の中の）アブラハム[訳注9]がその子イサクを、犠牲に供しようとした物語となんら異なるものではなく、それ以上に嫌悪すべきものでもない。この二つの場合は共に、義務に対する従順、上からくる声に命じられるままの行為なのである。目に見える天使か、目に見えない天使に告げられたか、肉体の耳で聞いた声か、心の

blow either at the man or at himself, should the examination defeat his scheme. The officer takes up the gruesome object before him, goes calmly over each feature, and in a deliberate, business-like tone, pronounces it genuine.— That evening in a lonely home awaits the mother we saw in the school. Does she know the fate of her child? It is not for his return that she watches with eagerness for the opening of the wicket. Her father-in-law has been for a long time a recipient of Michizané's bounties, but since his banishment, circumstances have forced her husband to follow the service of the enemy of his family's benefactor. He himself could not be untrue to his own cruel master; but his son could serve the cause of the grandsire's lord. As one acquainted with the exile's family, it was he who had been entrusted with the task of identifying the boy's head. Now the day's—yea, the life's—hard work is done, he returns home and as he crosses its threshold, he accosts his wife, saying: "Rejoice, my wife, our darling son has proved of service to his lord!"

"What an atrocious story!" I hear my readers exclaim. "Parents deliberately sacrificing their own innocent child to save the life of another man's!" But this child was a conscious and willing victim: it is a story of vicarious death— as significant as, and not more revolting than, the story of Abraham's intended sacrifice of Isaac. In both cases was obedience to the call of duty, utter submission to the command of a higher voice, whether given by a visible or an invisible angel, or heard by an outward or an inward ear;—but I abstain from preaching.

耳で聞いた声か、いずれにしろそれだけの差であろう。しかし、これ以上論ずるのはさしひかえよう。

　西洋の個人主義は、父と子、夫と妻に対しても、それぞれの利害を認めているので、人の他に対して負う義務は必然的に相当軽くなる。だが武士道は、一家とその家族の利害は一体であって分けることはできず、その利害は愛情と結びついており、自然でかつ本能的なもので、これに抵抗することができない。われわれはこの自然の愛（動物さえももっているところの）によって、愛する者のために死ぬことができるとしたら、それはどういうことなのか？　「なぜなら、あなたがたは自分の愛する者を愛したとしても、なんの報いがあるだろうか？　収税史であったとしても同じことをするだろうか？」

　頼山陽は、彼の大著『日本外史』のなかで、平重盛の、父（清盛）の（法皇に対する）反逆に関する苦衷を切々と述べている。「忠ならんと欲すれば孝ならず、孝ならんと欲すれば忠ならず」と。哀れむべきは重盛である。その後彼は、死をもって天に祈り、純潔と正義の住みがたいこの世より離脱することを願っているのである。

　この重盛のように、義務と人情の衝突によって、心を引き裂かれた者は昔から少くなかった。実際、シェークスピアにも『旧約聖書』にも、わが国の子として親を敬う概念である「孝」に当たる適当な表現は見あたらないが、一度このような衝突がおこると、武士道は忠をとることに、いささかもためらわなかった。婦人もまた、主君のためにそのすべてを犠牲にするよう子供を励ましたのである。（イギリスのチャールズ1世が、清教徒と戦って敗れたとき、忠臣ウィンダムとその3人の子供も戦死した。ある人が、未亡人ウィンダムのために悲しむ

The individualism of the West, which recognises separate interests for father and son, husband and wife, necessarily brings into strong relief the duties owed by one to the other; but Bushido held that the interest of the family and of the members thereof is intact,—one and inseparable. This interest is bound up with affection—natural, instinctive, irresistible; hence, if we die for one we love with natural love (which animals themselves possess), what is that? "For if ye love them that love you, what reward have ye? Do not even the publicans the same?"

In his great history, Sanyo relates in touching language the heart struggle of Shigemori concerning his father's rebellious conduct. "If I be loyal, my father must be undone; if I obey my father, my duty to my sovereign must go amiss." Poor Shigemori! We see him afterward praying with all his soul that kind Heaven may visit him with death, that he may be released from this world where it is hard for purity and righteousness to dwell.

Many a Shigemori has his heart torn by the conflict between duty and affection. Indeed, neither Shakespeare nor the Old Testament itself contains an adequate rendering of *ko*, our conception of filial piety, and yet in such conflicts Bushido never wavered in its choice of loyalty. Women, too, encouraged their offspring to sacrifice all for the king. Even as resolute as Widow Windham and her illustrious consort, the samurai matron stood ready to give up her boys for the cause of loyalty.

と、彼女は毅然として、「わが一門は王のためにあります。三児を王のために捧げたことは少しも惜しくありません。ほかに子供があれば、きっと王のために捧げたことでしょう」と、答えたというが）この未亡人ウィンダムとその有名な配偶者に劣らず、武士の妻もわが子を忠義のために捧げることに、少しもためらわなかったのである。

武士道においては、（古代ギリシャの哲学者）アリストテレスおよび、近世の二、三の社会学者が言っているように、国家は個人に先んじて存在し、個人は国家の部分および分子として生まれたものであるから、個人は、国家のためあるいは正当な権威の掌握者のために生き、また死ぬべきであるとした。（同じくギリシャの哲学者プラトンは、その著書）『クリトン』の中では、（獄中の）ソクラテスが彼の逃走の問題について、個人と国家を擬人化してアテネの法律と論争し、次のように言わせている。「お前（ソクラテス）は、私（法律または国家）の下に生まれ養われ、教育されてきたのに、お前もまたお前の祖先も、私の生んだ子供でも従者でもない、とあえて言うつもりなのか」。われわれはこの言葉を聞いて、少しも異常を感じない。このようなことは、武士道では昔から当り前のことであった。ただ、国法と国家は、わが国においては、人格によって表現されているということにすぎない。忠義はこのような政治理論によって生まれてきた道徳である。

スペンサー氏が、政治的な服従、すなわち忠義は、ただ過渡的な職能を与えられたものにすぎない[注3]と言ったことを、私も知らないわけではない。その通りかもしれない。「その日の徳はその一日で足りる」。われわれはこの言葉に満足して、何度も繰り返すだろう。それは、われわれは「その」日というのが長い期間であって、わが国の国歌が「さざれ石の

注3 スペンサー著『倫理学原理』第1巻第2部第10章。

Since Bushido, like Aristotle and some modern sociologists, conceived the state as antedating the individual,—the latter being born into the former as part and parcel thereof,—he must live and die for it or for the incumbent of its legitimate authority. Readers of Crito will remember the argument with which Socrates represents the laws of the city as pleading with him on the subject of his escape. Among others he makes them (the laws or the state) say: "Since you were begotten and nurtured and educated under us, dare you once to say you are not our offspring and servant, you and your fathers before you?" These are words which do not impress us as any thing extraordinary; for the same thing has long been on the lips of Bushido, with this modification, that the laws and the state were represented with us by a personal being. Loyalty is an ethical outcome of this political theory.

I am not entirely ignorant of Mr. Spencer's view according to which political obedience—loyalty—is accredited with only a transitional function.[3] It may be so. Sufficient unto the day is the virtue thereof. We may complacently repeat it, especially as we believe *that* day to be a long space of time, during which, so our national anthem

---

[3] *Principles of Ethics*, Vol. I, pt. ii., ch. x.

巌となりて苔のむすまで」とうたっているほど長いものだと
信じているからである。

このことに関連して、イギリス人のような民主的な国民の
間においてさえ、ブートミー氏が最近「一人の人間ならびに
その子孫に対する個人的忠誠の感情は、彼らの祖先であるゲ
ルマン民族がその首領に対して抱いていたものであって、そ
れが多かれ少なかれ伝わって、彼らの主君の血統に対する深
い忠誠の念となり、王室に対する異常な愛着となってあらわ
れている」と言ったことを思い出す。

スペンサーは、さらに予言して、政治的な服従は、やがて
良心の命令に対する忠誠によって代えられるであろう」と言
ったが、いつの日か彼の言う通りになったとしても、忠義と
それに伴う尊敬の本能は、永久に消滅するであろうか。われ
われは、われわれの服従する主君に対する忠誠を、他の主君
に移しても、両者に不誠実であることはなく、この地上の王
権をつかさどる統治者の臣民であることから、心の最奥部に
坐したもう王のしもべとなるのである。数年前、心得ちがい
のスペンサー学徒が始めた、きわめてばかばかしい論争が、
日本の読書家の間に恐慌をひき起こした。彼らは君主に対す
る不可分の忠誠を擁護するのに熱心なあまり、キリスト教徒
はその主に忠実を誓うものであるから反逆の傾向があると非
難した。彼らはソフィストの機知なくしてソフィスト的詭弁
で議論をかまえ、スコラ学徒の洗練に欠けるスコラ的煩瑣で
無用な曲論をならべたてた。彼らは、われわれが、ある意味
で、「これを親しみかれを疎んずることなくして二主に仕え
る」ことができ、「カエサルの物はカエサルに、神のものは
神に納める」ことができるのを知らなかったのである。ソク
ラテスは、彼の良心に対する忠誠の一片すらもゆずることを
拒否しながら、同じ忠実さと平静さで、彼の国家の命令に服

says, "tiny pebbles grow into mighty rocks draped with moss."

We may remember at this juncture that even among so democratic a people as the English, "the sentiment of personal fidelity to a man and his posterity which their Germanic ancestors felt for their chiefs, has," as Monsieur Boutmy recently said, "only passed more or less into their profound loyalty to the race and blood of their princes, as evidenced in their extraordinary attachment to the dynasty."

Political subordination, Mr. Spencer predicts, will give place to loyalty, to the dictates of conscience. Suppose his induction is realised—will loyalty and its concomitant instinct of reverence disappear forever? We transfer our allegiance from one master to another, without being unfaithful to either: from being subjects of a ruler that wields the temporal sceptre we become servants of the monarch who sits enthroned in the penetralia of our hearts. A few years ago a very stupid controversy, started by the misguided disciples of Spencer, made havoc among the reading class of Japan. In their zeal to uphold the claim of the throne to undivided loyalty, they charged Christians with treasonable propensity in that they avow fidelity to their Lord and Master. They arrayed forth sophistical arguments without the wit of Sophists, and scholastic tortuosities minus the niceties of the School-men. Little did they know that we can, in a sense, "serve two masters without holding to the one or despising the other," "rendering unto Cæsar the things that are Cæsar's and unto God the things that are God's." Did not Socrates,

従したのではなかったか。彼は生きては良心に従い、死して
彼の国家に仕えたのである。もし、国家の権力が強大となっ
て、その人民に対して良心の命令権まで要求する日がくると
すれば、それこそ悲しいことではないか！

　武士道は、われわれの良心が、主君の奴隷となることを要
求しなかった。トマス・モーブレーの詩はわれわれの代弁を
している。

> 畏（おそ）るべき君よ、我が身はみもとにささぐ
> 我が生命は君の命のままなり、わが恥は然らず
> 生命を捨つるは我が義務なり、されど死すとも
> 墓に生くる我が芳（かんば）しき名を
> 暗き不名誉の用に供するを得ず

　主君の気まぐれや、酔狂や、妄念のために、自分の良心を
犠牲にするような者たちに、武士道はきわめて低い評価を与
えた。そのような者は、無節操なへつらいで気に入られよう
とする「佞臣（ねい）」、あるいは卑屈な追従（ついしょう）で主君の愛を盗む「寵（ちょう）
臣」と呼ばれ、さげすまれた。これら二種類の臣下はイアゴ
ーの語る臣下と正確に一致している。一方は、「わが身をつ
なぐ首の綱を押しいただき、主君の厩（うまや）の驢馬（ろば）同然、むざむざ
一生を仇（あだ）に過ごす、正直な、はいつくばりの愚者」であり、
もう一方は、「表では忠義らしき身ぶりやしぐさを作り立て、
心の底ではわが身のためにばかりを図っている愚か者」であ
る。臣下がもし、主君と意見が異なる場合には、彼のとるべ
き忠義の道は、（シェークスピアの）リア王に仕えたケント
のように、あらゆる手段を尽くして主君の非を正すことであっ

all the while he unflinchingly refused to concede one iota of loyalty to his *dæmon*, obey with equal fidelity and equanimity the command of his earthly master, the State? His conscience he followed, alive; his country he served, dying. Alack the day when a state grows so powerful as to demand of its citizens the dictates of their conscience!

Bushido did not require us to make our conscience the slave of any lord or king. Thomas Mowbray was a veritable spokesman for us when he said:

> "Myself I throw, dread sovereign, at thy foot.
>   My life thou shall command, but not my shame.
>   The one my duty owes; but my fair name,
>   Despite of death, that lives upon my grave,
>   To dark dishonour's use, thou shall not have."

A man who sacrificed his own conscience to the capricious will or freak or fancy of a sovereign was accorded a low place in the estimate of the Precepts. Such an one was despised as *nei-sin*, a cringeling, who makes court by unscrupulous fawning, or as *chô-shin*, a favourite who steals his master's affections by means of servile compliance; these two species of subjects corresponding exactly to those which Iago describes,—the one, a duteous and knee-crooking knave, doting on his own obsequious bondage, wearing out his time much like his master's ass; the other trimming in forms and visages of duty, keeping yet his heart attending on himself. When a subject differed from his master, the loyal path for him to pursue

た。もしそれが受け入れられないときは、主君の欲するまま
に自分を処置させた。このような場合になったときは、自ら
の血を流し、それによって自分の言葉の誠実をあらわし、主
君の明智と良心に対し、最後の訴えをするのは、武士の常と
したところであった。

　生命は、これをもって主君に仕える手段であると考えられ、
その理想は名誉におかれた。武士の教育はすべてこれに基づ
いて行われたのである。

was to use every available means to persuade him of his error, as Kent did to King Lear. Failing in this, let the master deal with him as he wills. In cases of this kind, it was quite a usual course for the samurai to make the last appeal to the intelligence and conscience of his lord by demonstrating the sincerity of his words with the shedding of his own blood.

Life being regarded as the means whereby to serve his master, and its ideal being set upon honour, the whole education and training of a samurai were conducted accordingly.

武士の教育
および訓練

　武士の教育において、最も重んじられたのは、品性を確立することであって、思慮、知識、弁説などの知的な才能は第二義的なものであった。美的な芸能のたしなみもまた、武士の教育上重要な役割を占めていた。それは教養ある人にとっては欠くべからざるものであったが、武士の教育にとっては本質的なものというより、むしろ付属的なものに過ぎなかった。学問に秀でることはもちろん尊ばれたが、知という言葉は、主として智恵を意味するものであって、知識はやはり第二義的なものとして考えられていた。

　智、仁、勇は、武士道を支える三つの柱であった。要するに武士は行動の人で、学問はその行動の範囲外にあって、武士の職分に関係する限りにおいてこれを利用した。宗教と神学とは僧侶にまかされ、武士はただ自分の勇気を養うのに役

CHAPTER X

THE EDUCATION AND TRAINING OF A SAMURAI

THE first point to observe in knightly pedagogics was to build up character, leaving in the shade the subtler faculties of prudence, intelligence and dialectics. We have seen the important part æsthetic accomplishments played in his education. Indispensable as they were to a man of culture, they were accessories rather than essentials of samurai training. Intellectual superiority was, of course, esteemed; but the word *Chi*, which was employed to denote intellectuality, meant wisdom in the first instance and gave knowledge only a very subordinate place. The tripod which supported the framework of Bushido was said to be *Chi*, *Jin*, *Yu*, respectively, Wisdom, Benevolence, and Courage. A samurai was essentially a man of action. Science was without the pale of his activity. He took

立つ場合においてのみ、宗教や神学を学んだ。あるイギリス
の詩人が歌ったように、武士は「人を救うのは宗教上の信条
ではないが、信条を正当化するのは人である」ということを
信じていた。

　哲学と文学の二つは、武士の知的な教育の主要な部分を占
めていたが、その目標とするところは客観的な真理ではなか
った。要するに、文学は閑つぶしの娯楽としてこれを修め、
哲学は軍事的なあるいは政治的な問題を解明するためか、そ
うでなければ自分の品性をつくる上の、実際的な助けとして
学ばれた。

　以上述べたように、武士教育の課程が、剣術、弓術、柔術[注1]、
馬術、槍術、兵法、書道、道徳、文学、歴史などから成り立
っているのをみても、べつに驚くに足りない。これらの中で、
柔術および書道を必須としている理由について、多少説明し
なければ、あるいはわかりがたいかもしれない。

　武士が、能書良筆を重んじた理由は、わが国の表現文字が
もともと絵画的な性質をもち、美術的な価値があるためと、
筆蹟は人の性格をあらわすものだと認められていたからであ
る。柔術は、これに簡単な定義を下せば、攻撃および防御の
技に、人体の解剖学的な知識を利用したものと言ってよいだ
ろう。相撲とは異なって筋肉の力に頼らないのである。また
他の攻撃法とも異なって武器を用いず、その特色は、敵の身体
のある個所を掴み、あるいは打って麻痺せしめ、再び抵抗す
ることをできなくし、その目的は敵を殺すことではなく、一

注1　jiu-jitsuと誤って綴られる。穏健な武術。「武器は用いない」（ウィリアム・
E. グリッフィス）

advantage of it in so far as it concerned his profession of arms. Religion and theology were relegated to the priests; he concerned himself with them in so far as they helped to nourish courage. Like an English poet the samurai believed "'t is not the creed that saves the man; but it is the man that justifies the creed." Philosophy and literature formed the chief part of his intellectual training; but even in the pursuit of these, it was not objective truth that he strove after,—literature was pursued mainly as a pastime, and philosophy as a practical aid in the formation of character, if not for the exposition of some military or political problem.

From what has been said, it will not be surprising to note that the curriculum of studies, according to the pedagogics of Bushido, consisted mainly of the following:—fencing, archery, *jiujutsu*[1] or *yawara*, horsemanship, the use of the spear, tactics, calligraphy, ethics, literature, and history. Of these, *jiujutsu* and calligraphy may require a few words of explanation. Great stress was laid on good writing, probably because our logograms, partaking as they do of the nature of pictures, possess artistic value, and also because chirography was accepted as indicative of one's personal character. *Jiujutsu* may be briefly defined as an application of anatomical knowledge to the purpose of offence or defence. It differs from wrestling, in that it does not depend upon muscular strength. It differs from other forms of attack in that it uses no weapons. Its feat

---

[1] The same word as that misspelled jiu-jitsu in common English parlance. It is the gentle art. It "uses no weapon." (W. E. G.)

時的に敵の力を奪って活動できなくさせることにあった。

　軍事教育上、当然必要であるべきなのに、武士教育に欠け
ているものは数学であった。しかしこれは、封建時代におけ
る戦争が科学的な精確さをもって行われることがなかったた
めであり、それにまた、武士の教育は数学的な観念を養うの
に適しなかったからである。

　（シェークスピアの『アゼンスとタイモン』の中に）「武士の徳
である名誉心は、利益を得て恥辱をこうむるよりは、むしろ
損失をえらぶ」というヴェンティディウスのせりふがあるが、
武士道は非経済的であって、貧困をもって誇りとした。ド
ン・キホーテは、金銀や領地よりも、錆びた槍、やせた馬を
誇りとしたのである。日本の武士は、誇大妄想にとりつかれ
たこのラ・マンチャの騎士に、深い同情を寄せるであろう。
武士は金銭そのものを——儲けたり蓄えたりすることをいや
しんだ。それは武士にとってまことに汚れた利益だった。世
の中の退廃をあらわす言葉に、「文臣は銭を愛し、武臣は生
命を惜しむ」とい古語がよく用いられ、黄金と生命を惜しむ
者はいやしめられ、それを捨てる者が讃えられた。ことわざ
にも「金銀の欲を思ってはならない。富は智を害する」とい
う言葉があるほどである。これまで述べてきたような理由か
ら、武士の子供は、まったく経済を無視するように養育され
てきた。経済のことを口にすることは悪趣味だとされ、貨幣
の価値を知らないことは、よい教育を受けたしるしだとされ
た。軍勢を集めたり、恩賞や知行を分配したりするには、ど

consists in clutching or striking such part of the enemy's body as will make him numb and incapable of resistance. Its object is not to kill, but to incapacitate one for action for the time being.

A subject of study which one would expect to find in military education and which is rather conspicuous by its absence in the Bushido course of instruction, is mathematics. This, however, can be readily explained in part by the fact that feudal warfare was not carried on with scientific precision. Not only that, but the whole training of the samurai was unfavourable to fostering numerical notions.

Chivalry is uneconomical: it boasts of penury. It says with Ventidius that "ambition, the soldier's virtue, rather makes choice of loss, than gain which darkens him." Don Quixote takes more pride in his rusty spear and skin-and-bone horse than in gold and lands, and a samurai is in hearty sympathy with his exaggerated confrére of La Mancha. He disdains money itself,—the art of making or hoarding it. It was to him veritably filthy lucre. The hackneyed expression to describe the decadence of an age was "that the civilians loved money and the soldiers feared death." Niggardliness of gold and of life excited as much disapprobation as their lavish use was panegyrised. "Less than all things," says a current precept, "men must grudge money: it is by riches that wisdom is hindered." Hence children were brought up with utter disregard of economy. It was considered bad taste to speak of it, and ignorance of the value of different coins was a token of good breeding. Knowledge of numbers was indispensable in

うしても数学の知識が必要であるにもかかわらず、金銭の出納は身分の低い下役人にまかせられ、一藩の財政は、すべてこれら下級武士や御坊主によってまかなわれた。考えのある武士は、金銭が軍備にはどうしても欠かせないものであることを知っていながら、金銭の尊重を、徳にまで高めることは考えなかったのである。武士道において、節約が教えられたのは事実であるが、これも経済上の理由に基づくものではなくて、自分の欲望をおさえる克己の訓練のためであった。ぜいたくは、人間にとって最もおそるべきものであって、武士は常に質素な生活をしなければならぬと考えられ、諸藩においては、ぜいたくを禁ずる法令がしばしば出された。

ローマの古代史を読むと、収税吏など国家の財政をとり扱う人々は、次第にその地位が武士の階級にまで高められ、国家はこれらの人々の職務と金銭とを重要視するようになった、と記されている。そしてこのことが、ローマ人のぜいたくや金銭欲などと、いかに密接に関係していたかは想像に余りある。これに反し、武士道においては、理財の道を一貫して低いものに見た。つまり、道徳的、知的な職務にくらべ、劣等なものとみなしてきたのである。

このように、金銭を軽んじ、蓄財をいやしめたことが、武士道のそれに関わるいろんな弊害からまぬがれてきた理由である。またそのために、わが国の公吏が、長い間、腐敗や汚職から遠ざかることができたのである。だが、悲しいことに、現代における金権思想の、なんとすみやかに増大してきたことか！

現代においては、主に数学によって行なわれている知的訓練は、昔はそれを、文学の解釈と、道徳的義務の討論によっ

the mustering of forces as well as in distribution of benefices and fiefs; but the counting of money was left to meaner hands. In many feudatories, public finance was administered by a lower kind of samurai or by priests. Every thinking bushi knew well enough that money formed the sinews of war; but he did not think of raising the appreciation of money to a virtue. It is true that thrift was enjoined by Bushido, but not for economical reasons so much as for the exercise of abstinence. Luxury was thought the greatest menace to manhood and severest simplicity of living was required of the warrior class, sumptuary laws being enforced in many of the clans.

We read that in ancient Rome the farmers of revenue and other financial agents were gradually raised to the rank of knights, the State thereby showing its appreciation of their service and of the importance of money itself. How closely this is connected with the luxury and avarice of the Romans may be imagined. Not so with the Precepts of Knighthood. It persisted in systematically regarding finance as something low—low as compared with moral and intellectual vocations.

Money and the love of it being thus diligently ignored, Bushido itself could long remain free from a thousand and one evils of which money is the root. This is sufficient reason for the fact that our public men have long been free from corruption; but alas! how fast plutocracy is making its way in our time and generation.

The mental discipline which would nowadays be chiefly aided by the study of mathematics, was supplied

て与えられてきた。したがって、抽象的な問題が青少年の心を悩ますことはまれであった。武士教育の最大の目的は、前にも述べたように、品性を確立することにあった。それ故に、たんに博学だからという理由で尊敬されることはなかったのである。(イギリスの哲学者) ベーコンは、学問の三つの効用をあげて、快楽と、装飾と、能力であると言ったが、武士道はこの中で、能力をもって最優先とした。それは判断と事務の処理に必要だったからである。公務を処理するにせよ、克己の心を訓練するにせよ、武士が教育の目的としたのはこのような実際的な能力であった。孔子も言っているではないか。「いくら学問をしても、深く考えることがなければ、その学問は身につかない。しかし考えるだけで学問をしなかったならば、それは危険である」と。

　知識よりも品性を、知性よりも霊魂をみがくことを教育の任務の主眼とすると、教師の職業は実に神聖な性質をおびるようになった。「私を生んだのは父母であるが、私を人たらしめたのは教師である」。武士はこのような観念をもっていたので、師に対する弟子の尊敬と信頼はきわめて厚く、青少年からこれほど信頼と尊敬をよせられる師は、すぐれた人格と学識を兼ねそなえている人物であらねばならなかった。そのような師は、父なきあとの父であり、迷える者の助言者であった。(当時幼少年の教科書として用いられた『実語教』にも)「父母は天地のようであり、師は日月のようである」と教えているのである。

　あらゆる仕事の報酬に金銭をもってする現代の制度は、武士道の信奉者の間では、広く行われたことはなかった。武士道では、金銭にもよらずその価格をも考えないで他人に尽す仕事があることを信じていた。すなわち、僧侶にせよ教師に

by literary exegesis and deontological discussions. Very few abstract subjects troubled the mind of the young, the chief aim of their education being, as I have said, decision of character. People whose minds were simply stored with information found no great admirers. Of the three services of studies that Bacon gives,—for delight, ornament, and ability,—Bushido had decided preference for the last, where their use was "in judgment and the disposition of business." Whether it was for the disposition of public business or for the exercise of self-control, it was with a practical end in view that education was conducted. "Learning without thought," said Confucius, "is labour lost; thought without learning is perilous."

When character and not intelligence, when the soul and not the head, is chosen by a teacher for the material to work upon and to develop, his vocation partakes of a sacred character. "It is the parent who has borne me: it is the teacher who makes me man." With this idea, therefore, the esteem in which one's preceptor was held was very high. A man to evoke such confidence and respect from the young, must necessarily be endowed with superior personality, without lacking erudition. He was a father to the fatherless, and an adviser to the erring. "Thy father and thy mother."—so runs our maxim—"are like heaven and earth; thy teacher and thy lord are like the sun and moon."

The present system of paying for every sort of service was not in vogue among the adherents of Bushido. It believed in a service which can be rendered only without money and without price. Spiritual service, be it of priest

せよ、その精神的な仕事は、価値がないためではなく、その価値が評価できないほど大きい故に、金銭でもって報酬とすることができないものだとした。こういう点からみれば、実に数学的ではない武士道の名誉あるいは本能は、近世政治経済学を超越して、まことの教訓を与えたといってよいであろう。賃金や俸給は、その仕事の結果が、明白に具体的に計ることができるもののみに対して支払うことができる。しかし、教育における最善の仕事は、人の霊魂の啓発（僧侶の仕事を含む）であって、明白に具体的に掴むことはできず、計ることもできない。それ故に、外見的なものの価値を計る金銭を用いることには適していないのである。昔は、弟子が一年間のある季節を定めて、師に金品を贈る習慣が認められていた。しかし、これは報酬として贈ったのではなく御進物であった。したがって、その性行が厳正で、清貧を誇り、労働をするにはあまりにも威厳があり、物乞いをするにはあまりに自尊心が強い師でも、喜んで弟子のささげる金品を受け取ったのである。そのような師は、逆境に屈しない高邁な精神をもち威厳のある権化で、学問の目的と考えられていたものの模範的な具現者であった。そのような師は、武士道には欠くことができない厳しい鍛練、つまり克己の生きたお手本だったのである。

or teacher, was not to be repaid in gold or silver, not because it was valueless but because it was invaluable. Here the non-arithemetical honour-instinct of Bushido taught a truer lesson than modern Political Economy; for wages and salaries can be paid only for services whose results are definite, tangible, and measurable, whereas the best service done in education,—namely, in soul development (and this includes the services of a pastor), is not definite, tangible, or measurable. Being immeasurable, money, the ostensible measure of value, is of inadequate use. Usage sanctioned that pupils brought to their teachers money or goods at different seasons of the year; but these were not payments but offerings, which indeed were welcome to the recipients as they were usually men of stern calibre, boasting of honourable penury, too dignified to work with their hands and too proud to beg. They were grave personifications of high spirits undaunted by adversity. They were an embodiment of what was considered as an end of all learning, and were thus a living example of that discipline of disciplines, self-control, which was universally required of samurai.

第11章

克己

　勇気の鍛練は、どんな事に対しても、ぐちを言わない忍
耐の精神を養い、礼の教訓は、自分の悲哀や苦痛をあ
らわして、他人の快楽や安静を妨害しないようにすることで
ある。この二つが相合して、ストイック的な心性を生み出し、
ついには外見的ストイック主義といってもよいわが国民性を
形成した。私が外見的ストイック主義といったのは、真のス
トイック主義は国民性となることはでき得ないことを信じて
いるからであり、また、わが国民の作法や習慣が、外国人の
眼には、しばしば冷酷とも映ずることがあるかもしれないか
らである。しかしわれわれは、実際にはこの広い世界に住む
すべての人類と同じように、やさしい情緒に対して敏感に応
ずることができるのである。

　ある意味においては、われわれ日本人は、他民族以上に感
情が細やかで、自然に発する感情を押さえることに、かえっ

CHAPTER XI

SELF-CONTROL

THE discipline of fortitude on the one hand, inculcating endurance without a groan, and the teaching of politeness on the other, requiring us not to mar the pleasure or serenity of another by expressions of our own sorrow or pain, combined to engender a stoical turn of mind, and eventually to confirm it into a national trait of apparent stoicism. I say apparent stoicism, because I do not believe that true stoicism can ever become the characteristic of a whole nation, and also because some of our national manners and customs may seem to a foreign observer hard-hearted. Yet we are really as susceptible to tender emotion as any race under the sky.

I am inclined to think that in one sense we have to feel more than others—yes, doubly more—since the very

て苦痛を感ずるほどである。たとえば、わが国の少年少女は、幼い時から、自分の感情を押さえて、いたずらに涙を流したり、苦痛の声をだしたりしないように教育されてきた。このような努力は、神経をにぶくするものなのか、それともかえって敏感にするものなのか、まさに生理学上の一問題であろう。

　武士が、感情を顔にあらわすのは男らしくないと考えられ、「喜怒を色に現わさず」とは、強い性格を評価する言葉であって、最も自然な愛情をも抑制されてきた。たとえば、父がその子を抱くのは、父の威厳を害うことであり、夫は、私室においてはともかく、人前では妻にキスをしなかった。ある青年が「アメリカ人は人前で妻にキスをし、私室では妻をなぐる。日本人はこれと反対に、人前では妻をなぐり、私室では妻にキスをする」と、たわむれに言った言葉の中にも、いくらかの真理はあるだろう。

　その動作が沈着で、精神が平静であれば、どのような感情にも、たやすく乱されはしない。中国との戦争（日清戦争）の当時、ある連隊が故郷の町から出発するとき、多くの人々が隊長以下の兵士を駅頭に見送りに行った。あるアメリカ人が見に行って、これらの見送りの人々は兵士たちとの別れに際し、きっと大声をあげ、感情を爆発させるだろうと予想していた。それらの人々の中には、兵士たちの父もおり母もおり、妻もおり恋人もいたからである。ところがそのアメリカ人は、奇異の感にうたれて失望してしまった。なぜならば、汽笛がなって列車が進行しはじめると、数千のそれらの人々は黙って帽子を脱ぎ、うやうやしく別れの礼をし、ハンカチーフを振る者もなく、声をあげる者もなく、ただ深い沈黙の

attempt to restrain natural promptings entails suffering. Imagine boys—and girls, too—brought up not to resort to the shedding of a tear or the uttering of a groan for the relief of their feelings,—and there is a physiological problem whether such effort steels their nerves or makes them more sensitive.

It was considered unmanly for a samurai to betray his emotions on his face. "He shows no sign of joy or anger," was a phrase used, in describing a great character. The most natural affections were kept under control. A father could embrace his son only at the expense of his dignity; a husband would not kiss his wife,—no, not in the presence of other people, whatever he might do in private! There may be some truth in the remark of a witty youth when he said, "American husbands kiss their wives in public and beat them in private; Japanese husbands beat theirs in public and kiss them in private."

Calmness of behaviour, composure of mind, should not be disturbed by passion of any kind. I remember when, during the late war with China, a regiment left a certain town, a large concourse of people flocked to the station to bid farewell to the general and his army. On this occasion an American resident resorted to the place, expecting to witness loud demonstrations, as the nation itself was highly excited and there were fathers, mothers, wives, and sweethearts of the soldiers in the crowd. The American was strangely disappointed; for as the whistle blew and the train began to move, the hats of thousands of people were silently taken off and their heads bowed in

なかで、わずかにすすり泣きがもれてくるのが聞こえるだけ
だったのである。家庭においても同じことが言える。たとえ
ば子供が病気で寝ているとする。親心の弱さをさとられまい
と、ふすまの陰に立って一晩中病む子の呼吸を数えている父
親がいる！　また、臨終に際して、他郷にいるわが子の勉強
の妨げにならないように、これを呼び返すことを拒んだ母親
がいる！　わが国の歴史と日常には、プルタークの最も感動
的なページに匹敵する英雄的婦人のこのような実例に充ちて
いる。わが国の農民の中に、イアン・マクラレンは、多くの
マーゲット・ホウを見いだすにちがいない。

　日本のキリスト教会において、信仰が熱狂的なかたちで現
われることが少ないのは、日本人のこの自制の鍛練で説明でき
るかもしれない。男子でも女子でも、おのれの霊魂に感激を
おぼえるところがあれば、まず自分の本能を静かに抑え、外
へあらわさないように努める。たまたま誠実と情熱につき動
かされることがあっても、心を抑えきれずに、思いつくまま
に話すことはまれである。軽々しく霊的な体験を口にするこ
とは、十戒の（神の名をみだりに口にしてはならないという）
第三の戒めを破ることにつながる。日本人の耳には、烏合の
衆に向って、最も神聖な言葉や、最も秘めやかな心の体験が、
語られるのを聞くのはまことに耳ざわりなのである。ある青
年武士は、日記に次のようなことを書いている。「おまえは、
おまえの霊魂の土壌の中から、秘めやかな思想が、かすかに
動き出してくるのを感じないか。それは種子が芽生えてくる
ときである。よけいな言葉でもってそれを妨げるな。静かに
そしてひそかに動くままにさせよ」と。

reverential farewell; no waving of handkerchiefs, no word uttered, but deep silence in which only an attentive ear could catch a few broken sobs. In domestic life, too, I know of a father who spent whole nights listening to the breathing of a sick child, standing behind the door that he might not be caught in such an act of parental weakness! I know of a mother who, in her last moments, refrained from sending for her son, that he might not be disturbed in his studies. Our history and everyday life are replete with examples of heroic matrons who can well bear comparison with some of the most touching pages of Plutarch. Among our peasantry an Ian Maclaren would be sure to find many a Market Howe.

It is the same discipline of self-restraint which is accountable for the absence of more frequent revivals in the Christian churches of Japan. When a man or woman feels his or her soul stirred, the first instinct is quietly to suppress the manifestation of it. In rare instances is the tongue set free by an irresistible spirit, when we have eloquence of sincerity and fervour. It is putting a premium upon a breach of the third commandment to encourage speaking lightly of spiritual experience. It is truly jarring to Japanese ears to hear the most sacred words, the most secret heart experiences, thrown out in promiscuous audiences. "Dost thou feel the soil of thy soul stirred with tender thoughts? It is time for seeds to sprout. Disturb it not with speech; but let it work alone in quietness and secrecy,"—writes a young samurai in his diary.

　多くの巧みな言葉をついやして、自分の内心にあるもの、ことに宗教的な思想や感情を発表することは、われわれの間にあっては、その思想や感情は深遠でもなく誠実でもないことの証拠であるとされた。ことわざにも「口開いてはらわた見ゆる柘榴かな」という言葉が（あり、多言巧言の者は、口を大きく開いて自分の心情を暴露するようなものだ、というので）ある。

　われわれが、感情に動かされたとき、これを隠そうとし口を閉じるのは、決して東洋人の心がひねくれている故ではない。日本人にとって、話すことはしばしば、あるフランス人（の政治家タレーラン）の言ったように「思想を隠す技術」だったからである。

　試みに日本人の友人が、最も深い悲しみと苦痛にあっているときに訪問してみたらよい。その友人は、赤い眼をし、濡れた頬に微笑みを浮かべて君を迎えるであろう。君はそんな友人を一見して、あるいはヒステリーをおこしたのかと思うかもしれない。強いてその理由を尋ねてみるならば、友人は「人生には悲哀が多いものです」とか、「会う者は別れるのが常です」とか、「生きる者は必ず死ぬものです」とか、「死んだ子供の年齢を数えるのはおろかなことですが、女はそのようなおろかなことに流されるものです」とか、ありふれたいくつかの言葉で答えるであろう。このように、「口に出さないで耐えることを学べ」という、ホーエンツォレルンの高貴な言葉に共鳴する心が、この言葉が言われるはるか以前からわが国には多くあったのである。

　実際に、日本人は人間性の弱さが激しい試練に会ったとき、常に笑いに頼る傾きがある。われわれ国民のこのような笑いの習慣には、（笑いの哲人といわれた古代ギリシャの）デモクリトスより以上の理由があると私は思っている。つまり、

To give in so many articulate words one's inmost thoughts and feelings—notably the religious—is taken among us as an unmistakable sign that they are neither very profound nor very sincere. "Only a pomegranate is he"—so runs a saying "who, when he gapes his mouth, displays the contents of his heart."

It is not altogether perverseness of oriental minds that the instant our emotions are moved, we try to guard our lips in order to hide them. Speech is very often with us, as the Frenchman defines it, "the art of concealing thought."

Call upon a Japanese friend in time of deepest affliction and he will invariably receive you laughing, with red eyes or moist cheeks. At first you may think him hysterical. Press him for explanation and you will get a few broken commonplaces—"Human life has sorrow"; "They who meet must part"; "He that is born must die"; "It is foolish to count the years of a child that is gone, but a woman's heart will indulge in follies"; and the like. So the noble words of a noble Hohenzollern—"Lerne zu leiden ohne klagen"—had found many responsive minds among us long before they were uttered.

Indeed, the Japanese have recourse to risibility whenever the frailties of human nature are put to severest test. I think we possess a better reason than Democritus himself for our Abderian tendency, for laughter with us oftenest

日本人が逆境にあって心を乱され、苦しみと悲しみにうちひしがれたとき、しばしば笑うのは、その心の平静を保とうとする努力を、人前で隠そうとするためであって、笑いは、悲しみやあるいは怒りのバランスをとるためのものであった。

　このような感情を押さえることが常に求められたために、その感情を簡潔な詩歌などの安全弁を通してあらわすようになった。10世紀の一歌人（紀貫之）は、次のように言っている。「中国でもわが国でも、歌は心に思うだけでは耐えられぬ時に出てくるわざである」と。死んだわが子のことを思い悲しみ、その子が生きていたころのように、蜻蛉つりに出かけていると想像し、自分のやるせない悲しみを慰めようとしたひとりの母親（加賀の千代女）は、次のように詠んだ。

　　　蜻蛉つり今日はどこまで行ったやら

　私はこれ以上ほかの例をあげることをやめよう。なぜならば、一滴一滴血を吐くようにしてしぼり出されてつづられたわが国の珠玉の文学を、外国語に訳そうとすれば、かえってわが国文学のすぐれた価値を傷つけるかもしれないと思うからである。ただ私は、わが国民性のあるいは無情冷淡と見え、あるいは笑いと落胆とのヒステリー性の混合と見られ、ときには正気が怪しまれることさえある、その心の奥底は、本当はどのような状態であるかを説明しようとしただけである。

　また、日本人が、苦痛に耐え、死を恐れないのは、日本人の神経がにぶいためではないか、という説がある。その限りにおいては、もっともらしく聞こえる。また「日本人の神経の緊張感は、なぜ外国人より低いのか」という疑問に対して

veils an effort to regain balance of temper when disturbed by any untoward circumstance. It is a counterpoise of sorrow or rage.

The suppression of feelings being thus steadily insisted upon, they find their safety-valve in poetical aphorisms. A poet of the tenth century writes "In Japan and China as well, humanity when moved by sorrow, tells its bitter grief in verse. A mother who tries to console her broken heart by fancying her departed child absent on his wonted chase after the dragon-fly hums,

> How far to-day in chase, I wonder,
> Has gone my hunter of the dragon-fly!"

I refrain from quoting other examples, for I know I could do only scant justice to the pearly gems of our literature, were I to render into a foreign tongue the thoughts which were wrung drop by drop from bleeding hearts and threaded into beads of rarest value. I hope I have in a measure shown that inner working of our minds which often presents an appearance of callousness or of an hysterical mixture of laughter and dejection, and whose sanity is sometimes called in question.

It has also been suggested that our endurance of pain and indifference to death are due to less sensitive nerves. This is plausible as far as it goes. The next question is,— Why are our nerves less tightly strung? It may be our cli-

は、わが国の気候風土が、たとえばアメリカのそれにくらべ
てさほど刺激的ではないためかもしれないし、またわが国の
君主政体が、共和政体のフランスにおけるように、国民を熱
狂興奮させることがないためかもしれない。また、わが国民
はイギリス国民ほど熱心にカーライルの『衣裳哲学』を読ま
なかったせいかもしれない。私個人の考えとしては、わが国
民は感情が敏感で、激情しやすいために、絶えず自分を押さ
える必要があり、これを励行してきたためだと思っている。
この点に関しては、いかなる説明も、日本民族が昔から受け
継いできた長年の克己の修練を考えに入れなくては、正確さ
を欠くであろう。

　克己の修養は、ややもすれば度が過ぎ、霊魂の溌剌とした
流れをさえぎることもあるし、また素直な天性をゆがめて、
偏狭な、奇形の人とすることもある。克己はまた、頑固な性
格を生み、偽善者をつくり、愛情をにぶらすこともある。い
かに高尚な徳であっても、その反面があり、にせものがある。
われわれは、それぞれの徳において、積極的にそれぞれの長
所を認識し、その理想を追求しなければならない。克己の理
想とするところは、わが国の表現で言えば心の平静を保つこ
とであり、ギリシャ語を借りて言えば、デモクリトスが至高善
と呼んだエウテミアの状態に到達することである。

　さて、克己の極致は、自殺の制度に、もっともよく表れて
いる。この自殺と敵討ちの制度について、次に述べることに
しよう。

mate is not so stimulating as the American. It may be our monarchical form of government does not excite us so much as the Republic does the Frenchman. It may be that we do not read *Sartor Resartus* so zealously as the Englishman. Personally, I believe it was our very excitability and sensitiveness which made it a necessity to recognise and enforce constant self-repression; but whatever may be the explanation, without taking into account long years of discipline in self-control, none can be correct.

Discipline in self-control can easily go too far. It can well repress the genial current of the soul. It can force pliant natures into distortions and monstrosities. It can beget bigotry, breed hypocrisy, or hebetate affections. Be a virtue never so noble, it has its counterpart and counterfeit. We must recognise in each virtue its own positive excellence and follow its positive ideal, and the ideal of self-restraint is to keep the mind level—as our expression is—or, to borrow a Greek term, attain the state of *euthymia*, which Democritus called the highest good.

The acme and pitch of self-control is reached and best illustrated in the first of the two institutions which we shall now bring to view, namely, the institutions of suicide and redress.

第12章

切腹および
敵討ち

　　の二つの制度（前者は腹切り、後者は敵討ちと言われ
　　　る）については、多くの外国人が、いくらか詳しく論
じている。

　まず自殺について述べようと思うが、ここでは俗にハラキ
リと呼ばれている、切腹もしくは割腹にあらかじめ限定して
考察することをまずお断りしておく。これは腹部を切って自
殺することであるが、はじめてこの言葉を聞く者は「腹を切
るとは、なんと不合理なことであるか！」と叫ぶであろう。
たしかに外国人の耳には、奇怪なものに聞こえるかもしれな
い。しかし、シェークスピアの『ジュリアス・シーザー』を読
んだ者は、そんなに奇異な感じを起こさないだろう。なぜな
らば彼はブルータスに言わせて「汝（カエサル）の霊魂があら
われ、わが剣を逆さまにして、わが腹を刺さしめる」と、言
っているではないか。また近代のイギリス詩人が、その著書

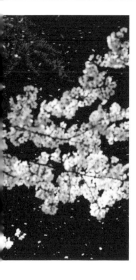

CHAPTER **XII**

THE INSTITUTIONS OF SUICIDE AND REDRESS

O F these two institutions (the former known as *hara-kiri* and the latter as *kataki-uchi*), many foreign writers have treated more or less fully.

To begin with suicide, let me state that I confine my observations only to *seppuku* or *kappuku*, popularly known as *hara-kiri*—which means self-immolation by disembowelment. "Ripping the abdomen? How absurd!"—so cry those to whom the name is new. Absurdly odd as it may sound at first to foreign ears, it cannot be so very foreign to students of Shakespeare, who puts these words in Brutus's mouth—"Thy [Cæsar's] spirit walks abroad and turns our swords into our proper entrails." Listen to a modern English poet who, in his *Light of Asia*, speaks of a sword piercing the bowels of a queen;—none blames him

『アジアの光』という作品の中で、女王の腹部に突き刺った剣のことをうたっているのを聞いても、誰も彼の英語が下品であり、慎みがないといって非難はしない。また他の例をあげるならば、ジェノヴァのパラッツォ・ロッサが収蔵している、グエルチーノがカトーの死を描いた絵画を見てみよう。アディソンがカトーに歌わせた臨終の歌を読む者は、彼の腹に深く刺さった剣をあざけったりはしないだろう。日本人の心には、切腹という死に方が最も高貴な行為で、最も感動的な哀感の実例を連想させ、なんらの嫌悪も感ずることもなく、まして嘲笑することなどはしないだろう。それが、徳性や、偉大さや、愛情に変化する力には、まことに驚くべきものがあって、最も醜い死の形式が、最も崇高なものとなり、新しい生命の象徴とさえなるのである。そうでなければ、コンスタンティヌス大帝が見た徴（十字架）が世界を征服することはなかったであろう！

　切腹が、われわれにはまったく不合理性を感じさせないのは、その連想によるだけではない。とくに身体のこの部分を選んで切るということは、そこが霊魂と愛情の宿るところだという古代の解剖学的信念に基づくものである。（旧約聖書の中で）モーゼは「ヨセフはその弟のために、はらわたがやけるがごとくいたむ」（創世紀43–30）と記し、また、ダビデは、「神がそのはらわたを忘れざらんこと」を祈り（詩篇26–6）、他にもイザヤ、エレミヤなど、旧約時代の霊感を受けた者たちが「はらわたが鳴る」とか「はらわたがいたむ」などと言った。これらのことは、腹に霊魂が宿っているものとした日本人の信仰を是認するものではなかろうか。セム族は、肝臓や腎臓やそのまわりの脂肪を、感情および生命の宿るところだとしていた。「腹」という語は、ギリシャ語のフレン（phren）もしくはツーモス（thumos）よりもその意味は広い

for bad English or breach of modesty. Or, to take still another example, look at Guercino's painting of Cato's death in the Palazzo Rossa, in Genoa. Whoever has read the swan-song which Addison makes Cato sing, will not jeer at the sword half-buried in his abdomen. In our minds this mode of death is associated with instances of noblest deeds and of most touching pathos, so that nothing repugnant, much less ludicrous, mars our conception of it. So wonderful is the transforming power of virtue, of greatness, of tenderness, that the vilest form of death assumes a sublimity and becomes a symbol of new life, or else—the sign which Constantine beheld would not conquer the world!

Not for extraneous associations only does *seppuku* lose in our mind any taint of absurdity; for the choice of this particular part of the body to operate upon, was based on an old anatomical belief as to the seat of the soul and of the affections. When Moses wrote of Joseph's "bowels yearning upon his brother," or David prayed the Lord not to forget his bowels, or when Isaiah, Jeremiah, and other inspired men of old spoke of the "sounding" or the "troubling" of bowels, they all and each endorsed the belief prevalent among the Japanese that in the abdomen was enshrined the soul. The Semites habitually spoke of the liver and kidneys and surrounding fat as the seat of emotion and of life. The term "*hara*" was more comprehensive than the Greek *phren* or *thumos*, and the Japanese

が、日本人もギリシャ人も同じように、人間の魂はこの部分のどこかに宿っていると考えていた。このような考えは決して古代とは限らない。フランス人の、最も優れた哲学者の一人であるデカルトが、霊魂は松果腺にあるという説を唱えたが、それでもなおお腹という意味のヴァントル（ventre）という言葉を「勇気」の意味にも使っており、この語は解剖学的にはあまりに漠然としているものの、生理学的には意味がある。同じくアントライユ（entrailles）（腹部）という言葉は、愛情あるいは憐憫（れんびん）の意味に用いられている。このような信仰はたんなる迷信などではなく、心臓をもって感情の中枢とする一般的な観念とくらべて、かえって科学的ではないか。日本人は、修道士に尋ねなくとも、「この臭骸のいずれの醜き部分に人の名が宿るのか」と言ったロメオよりも、そのことをよく知っていた。近世の神経学者は、腹部の脳とか骨盤の脳とか言って、その太陽神経叢（そう）の部分に自律神経の中枢があって、精神作用によってそれが多大な影響を受けると説いている。このような精神生理学説が容認されれば、切腹の論理は容易に構築することができる。「私はわが霊魂が座（ま）すところを開いて、あなたにその状態を見せよう。霊魂が汚れているか清浄か、その目で確かめてもらいたい」。

　私は宗教上からも道徳上からも、自殺の正当性を主張しているのではない。しかし、名誉を重んずる信念は、多くの武士に、自らその生命を絶つに充分な理由を与えたのである。（イギリスの詩人）ガースは、つぎのように歌っている。

　　　　名誉が失われたときは　死こそ救いなれ
　　　　死は恥辱よりの唯一の安らかなかくれ家

and Hellenese alike thought the spirit of man to dwell somewhere in that region. Such a notion is by no means confined to the peoples of antiquity. The French, in spite of the theory propounded by one of their most distinguished philosophers, Descartes, that the soul is located in the pineal gland, still insist in using the term *ventre* in a sense which, if anatomically too vague, is nevertheless physiologically significant. Similarly, *entrailles* stands in their language for affection and compassion. Nor is such a belief mere superstition, being more scientific than the general idea of making the heart the centre of the feelings. Without asking a friar, the Japanese knew better than Romeo "in what vile part of this anatomy one's name did lodge." Modern neurologists speak of the abdominal and pelvic brains, denoting thereby sympathetic nerve centres in those parts which are strongly affected by any psychical action. This view of mental physiology once admitted, the syllogism of *seppuku* is easy to construct. "I will open the seat of my soul and show you how it fares with it. See for yourself whether it is polluted or clean."

I do not wish to be understood as asserting religious or even moral justification of suicide, but the high estimate placed upon honour was ample excuse with many for taking one's own life. How many acquiesced in the sentiment expressed by Garth,

> "When honour's lost, 't is a relief to die;
> Death's but a sure retreat from infamy,"

　このような感情に同感して、いかに多くの者が自らの生命を絶ったか。武士道は、名誉にかかわる死をもって、多くの複雑な問題を解決する利剣としてきた。それ故に、功名心のある武士は、自然の死を、むしろ意気地のないものとして、男子の望む最期のものではないと考えてきた。あえて言えば、多くの良きキリスト者が、十分に正直でありさえすれば、カトーやブルータスやペトロニウスなど、多くの古代の偉人が、自己のこの地上における生命を自ら絶った崇高な態度に対して、積極的に賞賛することはなくとも、魅力を感じることを告白するだろう。哲学者の始祖ソクラテスの死も、半ば自殺であったといったら、言いすぎになろうか。彼は逃走の機会を拒否し、それが道徳上誤りであることを知っていながら、すすんで国家の命令に服従し、自ら毒杯を手に取り、その数滴をそそいで神に捧げまつったということを、彼の弟子たちが伝えた話から詳細に知ることができる。この話から、彼のとった全体の行動と態度に、自殺の行為が認められないだろうか？　たしかに通常の処刑のように、肉体的な強制はなかったが、裁判官の判決は強制的であって、「汝は死ぬべきである、それは汝自身の手によるべし」ということであった。自殺が自分の手によって死ぬことを意味するならば、ソクラテスの場合は明らかに自殺であった。しかし誰も彼にその罪を負わせないだろう。自殺を嫌悪したプラトンは、師ソクラテスを自殺者と呼ぼうとはしなかった。

　読者には、切腹がたんなる自殺の行為でないことがわかったであろうか。切腹は法律上ならびに礼法上の制度であった。切腹はわが国の中世にはじまって、武士がその罪をつぐない、過ちを謝し、恥をまぬがれ、友人につぐない、そして自分の

and have smilingly surrendered their souls to oblivion! Death involving a question of honour, was accepted in Bushido as a key to the solution of many complex problems, so that to an ambitious samurai a natural departure from life seemed a rather tame affair and a consummation not devoutly to be wished for. I dare say that many good Christians, if only they are honest enough, will confess the fascination of, if not positive admiration for, the sublime composure with which Cato, Brutus, Petronius, and a host of other ancient worthies terminated their own earthly existence. Is it too bold to hint that the death of the first of the philosophers was partly suicidal? When we are told so minutely by his pupils how their master willingly submitted to the mandate of the state—which he knew was morally mistaken—in spite of the possibilities of escape, and how he took the cup of hemlock in his own hand, even offering libation from its deadly contents, do we not discern, in his whole proceeding and demeanour, an act of self-immolation? No physical compulsion here, as in ordinary cases of execution. True, the verdict of the judges was compulsory: it said, "Thou shalt die,—and that by thine own hand." If suicide meant no more than dying by one's own hand, Socrates was a clear case of suicide. But nobody would charge him with the crime; Plato, who was averse to it, would not call his master a suicide.

Now my readers will understand that *seppuku* was not a mere suicidal process. It was an institution, legal and ceremonial. An invention of the middle ages, it was a process by which warriors could expiate their crimes,

誠実を証明する方法であった。それが法律上の刑罰として命じられたときには荘重な儀式をもって執り行われた。切腹は洗練された自殺であって、感情の冷静さと態度の沈着さとがなくては、誰もこれを実行することはできなかった。それ故に、切腹はとくに武士にとってふさわしい作法だったのである。

　好古的な好奇心からだけでも、すでに廃止されたこの儀式の描写をしようと思ったが、すでに、はるかにすぐれた作家によってその描写がなされているので、少し長いがそれを引用することにしよう。

　ミットフォードはその著書『旧日本の物語』の中で、日本の珍しい本から切腹に関する説を訳したあとで、彼自身が目撃した実例をくわしく描写している。

　　「われわれ（7人の外国代表者）は日本の検使役に案内されて、儀式が執行される寺院の本堂に入った。それはまことに荘厳なる光景であった。本堂は屋根が高く、黒い柱に支えられていた。天井からは仏教寺院に特有の燦然と輝く大きな金色の燈籠や装飾物がたれ下っていた。高い仏壇の前には、床から三、四インチの高さの座が設けられ、美しい白い畳が敷かれ、赤い毛氈が拡げられてあった。一定の間隔で並べられている高い燭台が、薄暗く神秘的な光を放って、ここで行われるすべての仕置きが、かろうじて見える程度の明るさだった。高座の左側に日本の検使役が、右側には外国人の検使役が着席した。他には誰もいなかった。

　　不安と緊張のうちに数分間待っていると、滝善三郎は麻

apologise for errors, escape from disgrace, redeem their friends, or prove their sincerity. When enforced as a legal punishment, it was practised with due ceremony. It was a refinement of self-destruction, and none could perform it without the utmost coolness of temper and composure of demeanour, and for these reasons it was particularly befitting the profession of bushi.

Antiquarian curiosity, if nothing else, would tempt me to give here a description of this obsolete ceremony; but seeing that such a description was made by a far abler writer whose book is not much read nowadays, I am tempted to make a somewhat lengthy quotation. Mitford, in his *Tales of Old Japan*, after giving a translation of a treatise on *seppuku* from a rare Japanese manuscript, goes on to describe an instance of such an execution of which he was an eye-witness:

"We (seven foreign representatives) were invited to follow the Japanese witnesses into the *hondo* or main hall of the temple, where the ceremony was to be performed. It was an imposing scene. A large hall with a high roof supported by dark pillars of wood. From the ceiling hung a profusion of those huge gilt lamps and ornaments peculiar to Buddhist temples. In front of the high altar, where the floor, covered with beautiful white mats, is raised some three or four inches from the ground, was laid a rug of scarlet felt. Tall candles placed at regular intervals gave out a dim mysterious light, just sufficient to let all the proceedings be seen. The seven Japanese took their places on the left of the raised floor, the seven foreigners on the right. No other person was present.

"After the interval of a few minutes of anxious sus-

裃の礼服を身に着け、しずしずと本堂に歩みでてきた。年齢は32歳、気品のある偉丈夫であった。一人の介錯人と、金糸の刺繍をほどこした陣羽織を着た三人の役人がこれに伴った。介錯という語は、英語の処刑人executionerと同じ意味ではないことを知っておく必要がある。この役目は立派な身分のある者の役であり、多くの場合、死刑を宣告された者の一族または友人によって行われ、この両者の関係は死刑囚と処刑人というよりはむしろ、主役と介添え役との関係である。この場合、介錯人は滝善三郎の門弟であって、剣道の達人であったがため、数ある友人の中から選ばれたのであった。

　滝善三郎は介錯人を左に従え、しずかに日本の検使役の方に進み出て、両人とも検使役に向かって挨拶をし、次に外国人の検使役の方に近づいて、なお一層の敬意をもって、同じように挨拶をした。どちらの検使役からも恭しい答礼がなされた。やがて善三郎は切腹の座に上り、静かに威儀を正し、本堂の仏壇の前に二度礼拝してから、仏壇を背にして毛氈の上に端坐[注1]し、介錯人は彼の左側にうずくまった。やがて三人の付き添い役の一人は、白紙に包んだ脇差を、神仏に供え物をするときに用いられる三宝の台の上に載せて、前に進み出た。脇差とは日本人の短刀もしくは匕首（あいくち）のことで、長さ9寸5分、その切っ先と刃は剃刀のように鋭利だった。付き添い人が一礼してこれを死刑囚に渡すと、彼は恭しくこれを受けとり、両手でもって頭の高さにまで捧げてから、自分の前に置いた。

　再び丁重な辞儀をした後、滝善二郎は、次のような口上を述べ、その声には痛ましい告白をする人が出すような、

[注1] 正坐——日本の行儀で、膝とつま先を床につけ、上体はかかとに掛かっている。これは一つの礼儀であり、彼は死に至るまでその姿勢を崩さなかった。

pense, Taki Zenzaburo, a stalwart man thirty-two years of age, with a noble air, walked into the hall attired in his dress of ceremony, with the peculiar hempen-cloth wings which are worn on great occasions. He was accompanied by a *kaishaku* and three officers, who wore the *jimbaori* or war surcoat with gold tissue facings. The word *kaishaku*, it should be observed, is one to which our word executioner is no equivalent term. The office is that of a gentleman; in many cases it is performed by a kinsman or friend of the condemned, and the relation between them is rather that of principal and second than that of victim and executioner. In this instance, the *kaishaku* was a pupil of Taki Zenzaburo, and was selected by friends of the latter from among their own number for his skill in swordsmanship.

"With the *kaishaku* on his left hand, Taki Zenzaburo advanced slowly toward the Japanese witnesses, and the two bowed before them, then drawing near to the foreigners they saluted us in the same way, perhaps even with more deference; in each case the salutation was ceremoniously returned. Slowly and with great dignity the condemned man mounted on to the raised floor, prostrated himself before the high altar twice, and seated[1] himself on the felt carpet with his back to the high altar, the *kaishaku* crouching on his left-hand side. One of the three attendant officers then came forward, bearing a stand of the kind used in the temple for offerings, on which, wrapped in paper, lay the *wakizashi*, the short sword or dirk of the Japanese, nine inches and a half in length, with a point and an edge as sharp as a razor's. This he handed, prostrating himself, to the condemned man, who received it reverently raising it to his head with both hands, and placed it in front of himself.

"After another profound obeisance, Taki Zenzaburo, in a voice which betrayed just so much emotion and

---

[1] Seated himself—that is, in the Japanese fashion, his knees and toes touching the ground and his body resting on his heels. In this position, which is one of respect, he remained until his death.

感情の高ぶりと躊躇する気持ちが現れてはいたが、顔色や態度には少しもそのような様子が見受けられなかった。

『私はただ一人、無分別にも誤ちをおかし、神戸において外国人に対して発砲の命令を下し、逃げようとするのを見て、再び撃ちかけました。今、その罪を負って切腹いたします。皆様には検使のお役目ご苦労に存じます』

そう言ってもう一度挨拶をすると、善三郎は上衣を帯のあたりまで脱ぎ下げ、上半身をあらわし、後方に仰向けに倒れないように、型に従って注意深く両袖を膝の下に敷き入れた。それは身分のある日本の武士は、前向けに伏して死ぬべきものとされていたからである。彼は短刀をおもむろに、しっかりととりあげ、それに思いをこめて、ほとんど愛情をこめてといってよいような眼差しで見つめた。そして一瞬の間、最後の時のために思いを集中させているようだったが、やがて左の腹の下を深く突き刺して、ゆっくりと右側に引きまわし、また元に返してやや上に切りあげた。このすさまじくも痛ましい動作の間、彼は顔の筋肉を一つも動かさなかった。彼は短刀を引き抜き、前にかがんで首を差しだした。苦痛の表情がはじめて彼の顔をよぎったが、まったく声は発しなかった。このとき、そばにじっとうずくまって彼の一挙一動を鋭く見つめていた介錯人は、やおら立ち上がって、一瞬のうちに大刀をふりあげた。刀が閃いたと思うと、重いどさっという倒れる音がし、一閃たちまち頭は体から切り離された。

この静寂のなかで、われわれの目の前にある、生命を失った肉塊からほとばしりでる血のすさまじい音がきこえるだけであった。その肉塊は、一瞬前までは勇敢で男らしい武士であった。それは見るも恐ろしい光景であった。

介錯人は平伏してから、用意の白紙を取り出して刀の血を拭い、切腹の座から下りた。血染めの短刀は、処刑の証拠として厳かに運び去られた。

その後、ミカドの二人の役人は席を離れて、外国人検使

hesitation as might be expected from a man who is making a painful confession, but with no sign of either in his face or manner, spoke as follows:—

"'I, and I alone, unwarrantably gave the order to fire on the foreigners at Kobe, and again as they tried to escape. For this crime I disembowel myself, and I beg you who are present to do me the honour of witnessing the act.'

"Bowing once more, the speaker allowed his upper garments to slip down to his girdle, and remained naked to the waist. Carefully, according to custom, he tucked his sleeves under his knees to prevent himself from falling backward; for a noble Japanese gentleman should die falling forwards. Deliberately, with a steady hand he took the dirk that lay before him; he looked at it wistfully, almost affectionately; for a moment he seemed to collect his thoughts for the last time, and then stabbing himself deeply below the waist in the left-hand side, he drew the dirk slowly across to his right side, and turning it in the wound, gave a slight cut upwards. During this sickeningly painful operation he never moved a muscle of his face. When he drew out the dirk, he leaned forward and stretched out his neck; an expression of pain for the first time crossed his face, but he uttered no sound. At that moment the *kaishaku*, who, still crouching by his side, had been keenly watching his every movement, sprang to his feet, poised his sword for a second in the air; there was a flash, a heavy, ugly thud, a crashing fall; with one blow the head had been severed from the body.

"A dead silence followed, broken only by the hideous noise of the blood throbbing out of the inert heap before us, which but a moment before had been a brave and chivalrous man. It was horrible.

"The *kaishaku* made a low bow, wiped his sword with a piece of paper which he had ready for the purpose, and retired from the raised floor; and the stained dirk was solemnly borne away, a bloody proof of the execution.

"The two representatives of the Mikado then left

役の前に来て、滝善三郎の処刑が滞りなく終わったので、
検使をしていただきたいと言った。儀式はこれで終わり、
われわれは寺院を去った」

　わが国の文学や、実見者の物語などによって、切腹の情景
を記したものが数多くあるが、もう一つその実例を挙げれば
十分であろう。
　左近と内記という兄弟がいた。兄は24歳、弟は18歳であっ
たが、父の敵を討とうとして、徳川家康をつけねらっていた
が、陣屋に忍び込もうとして捕えられてしまった。家康は自
分の命を狙った兄弟の勇気を賞めて「名誉の死を遂げさせよ」
と命じた。
　一族の男子は皆処刑されることになり、この兄弟の末弟の
八麿という8歳の少年も死ぬことに決まり、三人は刑場とな
った寺に引き立てられていった。そのときの情景が、その場
に居合せた一医師の日記に、次のように書かれている。

　「三人の兄弟が、最期の座に着いたとき、左近は末弟に向
い、『八麿よりまず腹を切れ、切り損じないように見届け
てくれようぞ』と言うと、幼いこの少年は、『私は今まで
切腹を見たことがないので、兄さんのする有様を見て、私
もその通りにいたしましょう』と答えた。兄二人は涙を浮
かべながら微笑して、『よくぞ申した、おまえは父の子に
恥じない健気な少年であるな』と言って、二人の間に八麿
を坐らせ、まず左近が、左側の腹に刀を突き立てながら言

their places, and crossing over to where the foreign witnesses sat, called to us to witness that the sentence of
death upon Taki Zenzaburo had been faithfully carried
out. The ceremony being at an end, we left the temple."

I might multiply any number of descriptions of *seppuku* from literature or from the relations of eye-wit-
nesses; but one more instance will suffice.

Two brothers, Sakon and Naiki, respectively twenty-
four and seventeen years of age, made an effort to kill
Iyéyasu in order to avenge their father's wrongs; but
before they could enter the camp they were made prison-
ers. The old general admired the pluck of the youths who
dared an attempt on his life and ordered that they should
be allowed to die an honourable death. Their little
brother Hachimaro, a mere infant of eight summers, was
condemned to a similar fate, as the sentence was pro-
nounced on all the male members of the family, and the
three were taken to a monastery where it was to be exe-
cuted. A physician who was present on the occasion has
left us a diary, from which the following scene is translated:

"When they were all seated in a row for final despatch,
Sakon turned to the youngest and said—'Go thou first,
for I wish to be sure that thou doest it aright.' Upon the
little one's replying that, as he had never seen *seppuku*
performed, he would like to see his brothers do it and
then he could follow them, the older brothers smiled
between their tears.—'Well said, little fellow! So canst
thou well boast of being our father's child.' When they
had placed him between them, Sakon thrust the dagger

った。『弟よ、よく見ておれ、あまり深く掻くと、仰向け
に倒れるぞ、うつ伏せして膝をくずすな』。内記も同じよ
うにして、腹を掻き切りながら言った。『いいか、かっと
目を開け、そうしなければ女の死に顔のようになってしま
うぞ。刀の切り先がぶって力が弱まっても、さらに勇気
を出して引きまわせよ』。八麿は、兄たちのする有様を見
て、二人が共に息絶えると、静かに衣服をぬいで、兄たち
に教えられたように、ものの見事に切腹して果てた」

　切腹をもって名誉としたことは、おのずからその乱用を生
んだ。まったく道理に合わない事柄のために、あるいはまっ
たく死に値しない理由で、気の早い若者は飛んで火に入る夏
の虫のように、死に急いだ。よく理解できないあいまいな動
機で死んでいった武士の数は、尼寺にかけ込んだ女の数より
も多かった。生命の価値は、世間の名誉の標準をもって計る
よりも、なお安かったのである。最も悲しむべきことは、名
誉には常にプレミアムがついたことである。それも正当の価
値に対してではなく、不当に水増しされた価値に対してであ
る。ダンテの『神曲』の「地獄篇」の中で、ダンテがすべて
の自殺者を入獄させた第7獄よりも、日本人ほどその数の多
さを誇るものはないであろう。

　しかし、真の武士にとっては、死に急ぎをしたり、死にお
もねたりすることは、卑怯なことだとされていた。ある一人
の典型的な武士は、幾度も戦いに敗れ、野から山へ、森から
洞穴へ追われ、そしてついに一人飢えに疲れて木の暗いうろ
に潜み、刀は欠け、弓は折れ、矢は尽き果てても——最も高
貴なローマ人（ブルータス）はフィリピで、これに似た状況で
ついに自刃したのではなかったか？——だがこの武士は、死

into the left side of his abdomen and said—'Look brother! Dost understand now? Only, don't push the dagger too far, lest thou fall back. Lean forward, rather, and keep thy knees well composed.' Naiki did likewise and said to the boy—'Keep thine eyes open or else thou mayst look like a dying woman. If thy dagger feels anything within and thy strength fails, take courage and double thy effort to cut across.' The child looked from one to the other, and, when both had expired, he calmly half denuded himself and followed the example set him on either hand."

The glorification of *seppuku* offered, naturally enough, no small temptation to its unwarranted committal. For causes entirely incompatible with reason, or for reasons entirely undeserving of death, hot-headed youths rushed into it as insects fly into fire; mixed and dubious motives drove more samurai to this deed than nuns into convent gates. Life was cheap—cheap as reckoned by the popular standard of honour. The saddest feature was that honour, which was always in the *agio*, so to speak, was not always solid gold, but alloyed with baser metals. No one circle in the Inferno will boast of greater density of Japanese population than the seventh, to which Dante consigns all victims of self-destruction!

And yet, for a true samurai to hasten death or to court it, was alike cowardice. A typical fighter, when he lost battle after battle and was pursued from plain to hill and from bush to cavern, found himself hungry and alone in the dark hollow of a tree, his sword blunt with use, his bow broken and arrows exhausted—did not the noblest of the Romans fall upon his own sword in Philippi under

ぬことを卑怯だと考え、キリスト教殉教者の精神に近い忍耐
の心をもって、

　　　憂きことのなおこの上に積れかし
　　　限りある身の力ためさん

と歌って、自分を励ました。

　武士道の教えるところは、実にこのことであった。つまり、
正しい信念と忍耐とをもって、あらゆる困難に立ち向かい、
耐えるということである。孟子[注2]も、次のように言っている
ではないか、「天がある人に大任をさずけようとするときは、
必ずその身も心も苦しめ、窮乏の境遇において、何を行って
も、すべてその人のしようとすることに逆らうような試練を
与えるものだ」と。真の名誉とは、天の命ずることを果すこ
とであって、このために死を招くことは、決して不名誉なこ
とではなかった。これに反して、天が与えようとするものを
避けるための死は、まったく卑怯なことなのである。
　（イギリスの医師で作家でもあった）サー・トマス・ブラウンの
奇書『医道宗教』の中に、わが武士道が教えていることと、
全く同じような一節がある。それを引用すると「死を軽んず
るのは勇気である。しかし、生が死よりも恐ろしい場合に、
あえて生きることこそ、真の勇気である」と。17世紀のある
名僧も、次のように言った。「平生はいくら口達者なことを
言っていても、死んだことがない武士は、まさかのときに逃
げかくれてしまうものだ。ひとたび心の中で死んだ者には、
真田の槍も、為朝の矢も通らないものである」と。

[注2] レッグ博士の逐語訳による。

like circumstances?—deemed it cowardly to die, but, with a fortitude approaching a Christian martyr's, cheered himself with an impromptu verse:

> "Come! evermore come,
>   Ye dread sorrows and pains!
> And heap on my burden'd back;
> That I not one test may lack
>   Of what strength in me remains!"

This, then, was the Bushido teaching—Bear and face all calamities and adversities with patience and a pure conscience; for, as Mencius[2] taught, "When Heaven is about to confer a great office on anyone, it first exercises his mind with suffering and his sinews and bones with toil; it exposes his body to hunger and subjects him to extreme poverty: and it confounds his undertakings. In all these ways it stimulates his mind, hardens his nature, and supplies his incompetencies." True honour lies in fulfilling Heaven's decree and no death incurred in so doing is ignominious, whereas, death to avoid what Heaven has in store is cowardly indeed! In that quaint book of Sir Thomas Browne's, *Religio Medici*, there is an exact English equivalent for what is repeatedly taught in our Precepts. Let me quote it: "It is a brave act of valour to condemn death, but where life is more terrible than death, it is then the truest valour to dare to live." A renowned priest of the seventeenth century satirically observed—"Talk as he may, a samurai who ne'er has died is apt in decisive

---

[2] I use Dr. Legge's translation verbatim.

　これらの言葉は、「わがためにおのれの生命を失う者は、これを見いだすであろう」と説いたキリストの教えに、なんと接近していることか。キリスト教徒と異教徒との差異をことさらに説く者があるが、右の例をみても、人類はすべて道徳的な一致点をもっているものなのである。

　切腹という武士道の制度は、一見するとその乱用に驚くことがあるかもしれないが、決して不合理で野蛮ではないことがわかったであろう。われわれはこれから、切腹の姉妹と言ってもいい敵討ちの制度の中にも、はたしてなんらかの美点があるかどうかを考えてみよう。私は、この問題は数語をもって片づけることができるように思う。このような制度もしくは風習は、すべての民族の間に行われていたもので、現代でもまったく廃れていないことは、決闘や私刑が今なお存続されていることでも証明されるであろう。最近でも、アメリカの軍人が、無実の罪に陥れられたドレフュスの敵を討とうとして、エステルハージに決闘を申し込んだ、ということがあったではないか。結婚制度がまだ行われていない未開民族の間では、姦通の罪はなくて、ただ愛人の嫉妬のみが女子を保護し危害から守ってきたように、刑事裁判の法廷がない時代には、殺人の罪はなく、ただ被害者の身寄りの者が行う敵討ちのみが、社会の秩序を維持してきたのである。（古代エジプトの神話の中で）オシリス[訳注10]が、わが子ホラスに「この地上にあって最も美しいものは何か」と問うと、「それは親の仇を討つことです」と答えているが、日本人はこれに「主君の仇」という言葉を付け加えるであろう。

moments to flee or hide." Again—"Him who once has died in the bottom of his breast, no spears of Sanada nor all the arrows of Tametomo can pierce." How near we come to the portals of the temple whose Builder taught "He that loseth his life for my sake shall find it"! These are but a few of the numerous examples that tend to confirm the moral identity of the human species, notwithstanding an attempt so assiduously made to render the distinction between Christian and Pagan as great as possible.

We have thus seen that the Bushido institution of suicide was neither so irrational nor barbarous as its abuse strikes us at first sight. We will now see whether its sister institution of Redress—or call it Revenge, if you will—has its mitigating features. I hope I can dispose of this question in a few words, since a similar institution, or call it custom, if that suits you better, prevailed among all peoples and has not yet become entirely obsolete, as attested by the continuance of duelling and lynching. Why, has not an American captain recently challenged Esterhazy, that the wrongs of Dreyfus be avenged? Among a savage tribe which has no marriage, adultery is not a sin, and only the jealousy of a lover protects a woman from abuse; so in a time which has no criminal court, murder is not a crime, and only the vigilant vengeance of the victim's people preserves social order. "What is the most beautiful thing on earth?" said Osiris to Horus. The reply was, "To avenge a parent's wrongs,"—to which a Japanese would have added "and a master's."

　敵討ちには、自分の正義感を満足させるというところがある。その復讐者の理屈は次のようである。「私の父は善人であって、非道に倒れる理由がなかった。父を殺したものは大悪事を行ったのである。父がもし生きていたならば、このような行為を決して許しはしないだろう。天もまた悪行を憎む。悪人にその行為を止めさせるのは、父の意志であり天の意志である。彼は私の手によって死ななければならない。なぜならば、彼は父の血を流したのだから、父の血肉を受け継いだ私は、父を殺した人間の血を流さなければならない。私は彼とともに天をいただくことはできないのである」。この理屈は簡単で幼稚である。（しかし、ハムレットもこれ以上の深い理由をもっていたわけではない。）それにもかかわらず、この理屈の中には、人間の生まれながらの正確な平衡感覚と平等な正義感があらわれている。それは「目には目を、歯には歯を」という復讐の感覚は数理のように正確であり、方程式の両項が満足させられない限り、何かをし忘れたような感覚をぬぐい去ることはできないのである。

　妬（ねた）みの神を信じるユダヤ教や、あるいは（復讐の女神）ネメシスをもっているギリシャ神話においては、敵討ちを、超人間的な力にゆだねることができたであろう。しかし武士道は、常識に基づいて敵討ちの制度を設け、普通法では裁判ができない事件を訴えることによって、道義的に裁くことができた。四十七士は主君を死罪にされたが、彼らは控訴できる裁判所をもっていなかったので、当時の唯一の最高裁判所であった敵討ちに訴えた。そうして彼らは普通法によって死罪となった。しかし民衆の本能はちがう裁定をくだし、だからこそ彼らの名は、泉岳寺の墓前の香華（こうげ）と共に、今に至るまで消えることがないのである。

　老子は「怨みに報いるに徳をもってせよ」と説き、孔子は

In revenge there is something which satisfies one's sense of justice. The avenger reasons:—"My good father did not deserve death. He who killed him did great evil. My father, if he were alive, would not tolerate a deed like this: Heaven itself hates wrong-doing. It is the will of my father; it is the will of Heaven that the evil-doer cease from his work. He must perish by my hand; because he shed my father's blood, I, who am his flesh and blood, must shed the murderer's. The same Heaven shall not shelter him and me." The ratiocination is simple and childish (though we know Hamlet did not reason much more deeply); nevertheless it shows an innate sense of exact balance and equal justice. "An eye for an eye, a tooth for a tooth." Our sense of revenge is as exact as our mathematical faculty, and until both terms of the equation are satisfied we cannot get over the sense of something left undone.

In Judaism, which believed in a jealous God, or in Greek mythology, which provided a Nemesis, vengeance may be left to super-human agencies; but common sense furnished Bushido with the institution of redress as a kind of ethical court of equity, where people could take cases not to be judged in accordance with ordinary law. The master of the forty-seven Ronins was condemned to death; he had no court of higher instance to appeal to; his faithful retainers addressed themselves to vengeance, the only Supreme Court existing; they in their turn were condemned by common law,—but the popular instinct passed a different judgment, and hence their memory is

さらに大きな声で「正義をもって怨みに報いる」ことを教えた。しかしながら、復讐は、目上の者か恩人の仇を報いるときにおいてのみ正しいとされ、自分自身や、または妻や子に加えられた危害に対しては、これを忍び、許すべきものであるとされた。

したがって武士は、祖国の仇を討とうとするハンニバルの誓いには全面的に共感することができるが、ジェイムズ・ハミルトンが妻の墓から取ってきた一握りの土を自分の帯につけ、摂政マレーに対する妻の仇を報いるための、たえざる刺激にしたことは軽蔑する。

切腹および敵討ちの二つの制度は、近代刑法が施行されると共に、その存在理由を失った。美しい乙女が、身をやつして父の敵を尋ねるロマンチックな冒険を耳にすることはもはやないし、家族の敵を討つ悲劇を見ることも、もはやない。宮本武蔵の武者修行は、今はただ昔話にすぎない。規律正しい警察が、被害者のために犯人を見つけだし、法律が正義を行う。国家および社会全体が不正を正すのである。社会の正義感が充たされれば、敵討ちの必要はなくなる。もし敵討ちが、ニューイングランドの神学者が言ったように、「犠牲者の生き血で満たしたいと、ひたすら望む心の飢え」を意味していたとすれば、刑法の数条によってこれほど完全になくなることはなかったであろう。

切腹もまた、法制上はすでにその存在を認められなくなっ

still kept as green and fragrant as are their graves at Sengakuji to this day. Though Lâo-tse taught to recompense injury with kindness, the voice of Confucius was very much louder, which taught that injury must be recompensed with justice;—and yet revenge was justified only when it was undertaken in behalf of our superiors and benefactors. One's own wrongs, including injuries done to wife and children, were to be borne and forgiven. A samurai could therefore fully sympathise with Hannibal's oath to avenge his country's wrongs, but he scorns James Hamilton for wearing in his girdle a handful of earth from his wife's grave, as an eternal incentive to avenge her wrongs on the Regent Murray.

Both of these institutions of suicide and redress lost their *raison d'être* at the promulgation of the Criminal Code. No more do we hear of romantic adventures of a fair maiden as she tracks in disguise the murderer of her parent. No more can we witness tragedies of family vendetta enacted. The knight errantry of Miyamoto Musashi is now a tale of the past. The well-ordered police spies out the criminal for the injured party and the law metes out justice. The whole state and society will see that wrong is righted. The sense of justice satisfied, there is no need of *kataki-uchi*. If this had meant that "hunger of the heart which feeds upon the hope of glutting that hunger with the life blood of the victim," as a New England divine has described it, a few paragraphs in the Criminal Code would not so entirely have made an end of it.

As to *seppuku*, though it too has no existence *de jure*,

たが、しばしば行われると聞いている。おそらく過去の記憶がつづいている限り、今後も耳にすることがあるだろう。自殺志願者の数が、非常な勢いで世界中に増加しているのをみれば、あまり苦痛のない、時間のかからない多くの自殺の方法が流行してゆくだろう。しかし、（『自殺論』の著者）モルセリ教授は多くの自殺方法の中で、その貴族的な地位を切腹に与えなければならないだろう。しかしモルセリ教授は、次のように主張している。「自殺が、最も苦痛な方法によって、あるいは長時間かかって行われる場合は、100件中99件が、狂信や、発狂や、または病的な興奮によって精神が錯乱したあげくの行為として認めることができる」[注3]と。しかしながら、尋常な切腹は、狂信も錯乱も、また興奮のかけらもなく、それを成功させるには、きわめて冷静な態度が必要だったのである。ストラハン博士[注4]は自殺を「合理的自殺または疑似的自殺」または「不合理的自殺もしくは真実の自殺」の二種類に分けているが、切腹は前者の型の最高の例である。

　以上述べたような、血なまぐさい制度より見ても、また武士道の一般的な傾向より見ても、刀が社会の規律および生活に重要な役割を占めていたことが、容易に推察できるであろう。「刀は武士の魂」というのは一つの格言とまでなったのである。

[注3] モルセリ著『自殺論』314ページ。
[注4] ストラハン著『自殺と狂気』。

we still hear of it from time to time, and shall continue to hear, I am afraid, as long as the past is remembered. Many painless and time-saving methods of self-immolation will come in vogue, as its votaries are increasing with fearful rapidity throughout the world; but Professor Morselli will have to concede to *seppuku* an aristocratic position among them. He maintains that "when suicide is accomplished by very painful means or at the cost of prolonged agony, in ninety-nine cases out of a hundred, it may be assigned as the act of a mind disordered by fanaticism, by madness, or by morbid excitement."[3] But a normal *seppuku* does not savour of fanaticism, or madness or excitement, utmost *sang froid* being necessary to its successful accomplishment. Of the two kinds into which Dr. Strahan[4] divides suicide, the Rational or Quasi, and the Irrational or True, *seppuku* is the best example of the former type.

From these bloody institutions, as well as from the general tenor of Bushido, it is easy to infer that the sword played an important part in social discipline and life. The saying passed as an axiom which called the sword the soul of the samurai.

---

[3] Morselli, *Suicide*, p. 314
[4] *Suicide and Insanity*.

第13章

刀・武士の魂

刀は、武士道における力と勇気の象徴であった。（イスラム教の始祖）マホメットは「剣は天国と地獄との鍵である」と宣言したが、この言葉は、まさに日本人の感情を反映している。武士は幼いときから剣を学び、5歳になると武士の礼装をさせられて、碁盤[注1]の上に立たせられ、それまでの玩具の小刀の代わりに真剣を腰にさして、はじめて武士の資格を認められた。こうして、武門に入る第一の儀式が終わった後は、彼の分身を示す刀をおびないで、家の門を出ることはなかった。もっとも日常生活においては、ふつう、銀塗りの木刀をもって代用とし、それから数年の後は、その子はたとえ鈍刀であっても、真剣を腰にさし、新しい力を得た喜びで、戸外に出てはその刀で木や石を切ったりなどして試みた。

[注1] 碁。日本のチェッカー（西洋飛び碁）と呼ばれることもあるが、より複雑。碁盤には361の目があり、その空間を取り合い、勝敗を競う。

CHAPTER XIII

THE SWORD, THE SOUL OF THE SAMURAI

BUSHIDO made the sword its emblem of power and prowess. When Mahomet proclaimed that "the sword is the key of Heaven and of Hell," he only echoed a Japanese sentiment. Very early the samurai boy learned to wield it. It was a momentous occasion for him when at the age of five he was apparelled in the paraphernalia of samurai costume, placed upon a *go*-board[1] and initiated into the rights of the military profession, by having thrust into his girdle a real sword instead of the toy dirk with which he had been playing. After this first ceremony of *adoptio per arma*, he was no more to be seen outside his father's gates without

---

[1] The game of *go* is sometimes called Japanese checkers, but is much more intricate than the English game. The *go*-board contains 361 squares and is supposed to represent a battle-field—the object of the game being to occupy as much space as possible.

　15歳で元服し成年に達し、独立した行動の自由を許される
と、彼はどのような時にも十分に役に立つ鋭い刀を持つこと
を誇りとすることができた。この危険な道具の所有こそが、
彼に自尊心や責任感をいだかせた。「刀は伊達にはささぬ」
もので、腰におびているものは、精神と心におびているもの、
つまりそれは忠義と名誉の象徴となった。

　大小二本の刀は、大刀と小刀または脇差と呼ばれ、いつも
身辺から離すことはなく、家にいるときは、書斎か客間のも
っとも目のつきやすい場所に置かれ、夜にはいつでも手の届
く枕辺におかれた。刀はこのように、日常の不断の伴侶（はんりょ）と
して愛され、愛称をつけられて、ほとんど崇拝と言えるほどに
尊ばれた。

　歴史の父（ヘロドトス）は、スキタイ人が鉄の新月刀に犠
牲をささげたことを、奇聞として記録している。わが国の神
社や名家においては、刀剣を礼拝の対象として秘蔵している
ところも少なくなかった。ごくありふれた短刀でさえも、ふさ
わしい尊敬を払わなければならなかった。刀をいやしめるの
は、その持主を侮ることと同じで、床の上に置かれた刀を不
注意にまたぐなどということは許されなかった。

　このように刀はまことに貴重なるものだったので、工芸家
の関心と技巧、あるいは所有者の虚栄心から長く逃れること

this badge of his status, even though it was usually substituted for everyday wear by a gilded wooden dirk. Not many years pass before he wears constantly the genuine steel, though blunt, and then the sham arms are thrown aside and with enjoyment keener than his newly acquired blades, he marches out to try their edge on wood and stone. When he reaches man's estate, at the age of fifteen, being given independence of action, he can now pride himself upon the possession of arms sharp enough for any work. The very possession of the dangerous instrument imparts to him a feeling and an air of self-respect and responsibility. "He beareth not the sword in vain." What he carries in his belt is a symbol of what he carries in his mind and heart,—loyalty and honour. The two swords, the longer and the shorter,—called respectively *daito* and *shoto* or *katana* and *wakizashi*,—never leave his side. When at home, they grace the most conspicuous place in the study or parlour; by night they guard his pillow within easy reach of his hand. Constant companions, they are beloved, and proper names of endearment given them. Being venerated, they are well-nigh worshipped. The Father of History has recorded as a curious piece of information that the Scythians sacrificed to an iron scimitar. Many a temple and many a family in Japan hoards a sword as an object of adoration. Even the commonest dirk has due respect paid to it. Any insult to it is tantamount to personal affront. Woe to him who carelessly steps over a weapon lying on the floor!

So precious an object cannot long escape the notice and the skill of artists nor the vanity of its owner, especially in

はできなかった。刀をおびることが、司教の笏杖や王の笏ほどの意味しかなくなった平和な時代になると、なおさらであった。柄には鮫の皮、絹の糸が巻かれ、鍔には金銀がちりばめられ、鞘にはさまざまな色合いの漆が塗られて、この恐ろしい凶器から恐ろしさが半分とりさられた。しかし、これらの飾りは刀身そのものと比べれば、たんなる遊びにすぎなかった。

　刀鍛冶もたんなる工人ではなく、霊感を受けた芸術家であって、彼の職場は神聖なところとされていた。彼は毎日神仏に祈り、斎戒沐浴をしてから仕事を始め、あるいはいわゆる「その心魂気迫を打って錬鉄鍛冶した」のである。槌をふるい、湯に入れ、砥石で研ぐなど、その一つ一つが厳粛な宗教的行事であった。日本刀が、鬼気を帯びているといわれるのは、そのような工人の精魂がのりうつったものか、あるいは神仏の霊気が宿ったものであろうか。それは美術品として完璧であり、トレドやダマスカスの名剣に劣らない日本刀には、すぐれた美術品以上のものがこめられていた。その氷のような刀身は、抜けばたちまち大気中の水蒸気をあつめ、その曇りない肌は青色に光り輝き、その比類のない刃には、歴史と未来への可能性が秘められ、その反りは、すぐれた美とすべての力を結合され、これらすべてから、われわれは畏敬と恐怖の入り交じった感情に襲われる。

　刀が、もし、美と喜びとの道具だけであったならば、それは無害なものであるだろう。が、それがいつも手に届くところにあったが故に、乱用されることも少なくなかった。ときには、新刀の切れ味を試そうと、無害な生き物の首を斬るようなことさえあったのである。

　しかし、最も気になる問題はそこにある。武士道は、みだり

times of peace, when it is worn with no more use than a crosier by a bishop or a sceptre by a King. Sharkskin and finest silk for hilt, silver and gold for guard, lacquer of varied hues for scabbard, robbed the deadliest weapon of half its terror; but these appurtenances are playthings compared with the blade itself.

The swordsmith was not a mere artisan but an inspired artist and his workshop a sanctuary. Daily he commenced his craft with prayer and purification, or, as the phrase was, "he committed his soul and spirit into the forging and tempering of the steel." Every swing of the sledge, every plunge into water, every friction on the grindstone, was a religious act of no slight import. Was it the spirit of the master or of his tutelary god that cast a formidable spell over our sword? Perfect as a work of art, setting at defiance its Toledo and Damascus rivals, there was more than art could impart. Its cold blade, collecting on its surface the moment it is drawn the vapour of the atmosphere; its immaculate texture, flashing light of bluish hue; its matchless edge, upon which histories and possibilities hang; the curve of its back, uniting exquisite grace with utmost strength;—all these thrill us with mixed feelings of power and beauty, of awe and terror. Harmless were its mission, if it only remained a thing of beauty and joy! But, ever within reach of the hand, it presented no small temptation for abuse. Too often did the blade flash forth from its peaceful sheath. The abuse sometimes went so far as to try the acquired steel on some harmless creature's neck.

The question that concerns us most is, however,—Did

に刀を用いることを認めたのか。いや断じてそうではない。武士道は刀の正当な使用を重んじたが、その乱用をいましめ、これを憎んだ。その時と場合を心得ずに、刀をふるう者は卑怯者あるいは傲慢な者であるとされた。冷静な武士は、刀を用いる正しい時をよく知っており、その時はきわめてまれであった。

　故・勝海舟伯は、わが国の歴史上、最も騒然とした時代の一つをくぐってきた人物であるが、当時は暗殺や自殺など、血なまぐさい事件が毎日のように行われていた。彼は一時期ほとんどひとりで政策を決定する権力を与えられていて、何度も暗殺の標的にされたが、一度も自分の刀に血を塗ることはしなかった。彼は、その特徴ある平民的な口調で、一友人に当時のことを次のように語っている。

　「私は人を殺すのが大嫌いで、一人でも殺したことはないよ。みんな逃がして、殺すべきものでも、マアマアと言って放っておいた。川上彦斎（佐久間象山を暗殺した）が私に『あなたは、そう人を殺しなさらぬが、それはいけません。南瓜でも茄子でも、あなたはとっておあがんなさるだろう。あいつらはそんなものです』と教えてくれたが、それはヒドイ奴だったよ。しかし川上は殺されたよ。私が殺されなかったのは、無実の者を殺さなかった故かもしれんよ。刀でも、ひどく丈夫に結わえて、決して抜けないようにしてあった。人に斬られても、こちらは斬らぬという覚悟だった。ナニ蚤や虱だと思えばいいのさ。肩につかまってチクリチクリ刺しても、ただ痒いだけだ。生命に関りはしないよ」（『海舟座談』）。

　これが艱難と勝利のはげしい時代の中で、武士道の訓練を受けた人の言葉である。ことわざにも「負けるが勝ち」という言葉がある。真の勝利は乱暴な敵に抵抗しないことにあり、やはりことわざで、「血を流さずに勝つのが最上の勝利であ

Bushido justify the promiscuous use of the weapon? The answer is unequivocally, no! As it laid great stress on its proper use, so did it denounce and abhor its misuse. A dastard or a braggart was he who brandished his weapon on undeserved occasions. A self-possessed man knows the right time to use it, and such times come but rarely. Let us listen to the late Count Katsu, who passed through one of the most turbulent times of our history, when assassinations, suicides, and other sanguinary practices were the order of the day. Endowed as he once was with almost dictatorial powers, chosen repeatedly as an object of assassination, he never tarnished his sword with blood. In relating some of his reminiscences to a friend he says, in a quaint, plebeian way peculiar to him: "I have a great dislike for killing people and so I haven't killed one single man. I have released those whose heads should have been chopped off. A friend said to me one day, 'You don't kill enough. Don't you eat pepper and egg-plants?' Well, some people are no better! But you see that fellow was slain himself. My escape may be due to my dislike of killing. I had the hilt of my sword so tightly fastened to the scabbard that it was hard to draw the blade. I made up my mind that though they cut me, I would not cut. Yes, yes! some people are truly like fleas and mosquitoes and they bite—but what does their biting amount to? It itches a little, that's all; it won't endanger life." These are the words of one whose Bushido training was tried in the fiery furnace of adversity and triumph. The popular apothegm—"To be beaten is to conquer," meaning true conquest consists in not opposing

る」と教えたのも、武士道の窮極の理想は、結局平和であっ
たことを示している。

　この高い理想が、もっぱら僧侶や道徳家の講釈にゆだねら
れて、武士は、武芸の訓練やその奨励を旨としたのは、大い
に惜しむべきことである。これによって、彼らは、婦人の理
想をも、アマゾン^{訳注1}的な、つまり男まさりの性格に色づけ
ようとしたのである。ここで、婦人の教育およびその地位に
ついて述べることにしよう。

a riotous foe; and "The best won victory is that obtained without shedding of blood," and others of similar import— will show that after all the ultimate ideal of knighthood was peace.

It was a great pity that this high ideal was left exclusively to priests and moralists to preach, while the samurai went on practising and extolling martial traits. In this they went so far as to tinge the ideals of womanhood with Amazonian character. Here we may profitably devote a few paragraphs to the subject of the training and position of woman.

第14章

婦人の教育と
地位

人類の半分を構成している女性は、しばしば矛盾の典型といわれている。女性の心理の直感的な働きは、男性のいわゆる数理的な理解力をもっては推し量ることができない場合があるからである。漢字で、不可思議とか、不可知とかを意味する「妙」という字は、「女」と、若いという意味の「少」によって構成されている。この言葉は、女性の容姿の美しさや繊細な思考は、男性の粗雑な心理では、うまく説明できないことを表わしている。

しかし、武士道の理想とする女性は、少しも不可思議なところはなく、その矛盾も外見的なものである。私はそれを男まさりであると言ったが、それだけでは真理の半分をとらえているにすぎない。妻を意味する漢字の「婦」は、箒を持っている女、という意味であるが、もっともその箒をふるって、夫に対して攻撃にでたり、あるいは防御したりするものではなく、また魔

CHAPTER XIV

THE TRAINING AND POSITION OF WOMAN

THE female half of our species has sometimes been called the paragon of paradoxes, because the intuitive working of its mind is beyond the comprehension of men's "arithemetical understanding." The Chinese ideogram denoting "the mysterious," "the unknowable," consists of two parts, one meaning "young" and the other "woman," because the physical charms and delicate thoughts of the fair sex are above the coarse mental calibre of our sex to explain.

In the Bushido ideal of woman, however, there is little mystery and only a seeming paradox. I have said that it was Amazonian, but that is only half the truth. Ideographically the Chinese represent wife by a woman holding a broom—certainly not to brandish it offensively or defensively against her conjugal ally, neither for witchcraft, but for the more

法をかけるためのものでもない。等の無害な本来の用途において
である。「婦」という言葉の観念は、英語の妻（wife）の語源
が、織る人（weaver）より出ており、娘（daughter）が牛乳し
ぼり（duhitar）より出ているのと同様に、家庭的である。ドイ
ツ皇帝は、婦人の活動の範囲は、台所（Küche）教会（Kirche）
ならびに子供（Kinder）にあると言ったそうだが、武士道の女
性の理想像は、その三つに限らず、とみに家庭的であった。男
まさりと家庭的とでは、一見矛盾するようであるが、武士道の
教訓からすれば、この二つは決して両立できないものではない。

　武士道はもともと男子のために設けられた教訓であったの
で、その婦人に求められた徳性も、いわゆる女性的なるもの
からかけ離れていた。（ドイツの美術史家）ウィンケルマンは、
「ギリシャ芸術の最高の美は、女性的であるよりもむしろ男
性的である」と言ったが、レッキーはそれにつけ加えて、こ
のことは、ギリシャ人の道徳観念からみても、芸術における
のと同じように真であると言った。武士道もまた同様に、
「女性の弱さより自分を解放して、最も強い最も勇敢な男性
に値するような、たくましさを発揮する婦人[注1]」を賞賛した。
それ故に、少女のころから自分の感情を押さえ、その神経を
強くすることを修練し、不慮の事態が起こったら、武器をも
って、ことに薙刀という長い柄の刀を用いて、自分の身を守
ることが訓練された。しかし女性の武芸は、戦場で用いるた
めではなく、むしろ一身のため家庭のためのものであった。
自分では主君を持たない女性は、自分で自分の身を守った。
女性は、夫が主君を守るのと同じ熱意で、自分の尊厳を自分
の武器で守った。女性の武芸が家庭で利用される機会は、息
子の教育であった。それについては後述する。

レッキー著『ヨーロッパ道徳史』第2巻383ページ。

harmless uses for which the besom was first invented—the idea involved being thus not less homely than the etymological derivation of the English wife (weaver) and daughter (*duhitar*, milkmaid). Without confining the sphere of woman's activity to *Küche, Kirche, Kinder*, as the present German Kaiser is said to do, the Bushido ideal of womanhood was pre-eminently domestic. These seeming contradictions—domesticity and Amazonian traits—are not inconsistent with the Precepts of Knighthood, as we shall see.

Bushido being a teaching primarily intended for the masculine sex, the virtues it prized in woman were naturally far from being distinctly feminine. Winckelmann remarks that "the supreme beauty of Greek art is rather male than female," and Lecky adds that it was true in the moral conception of the Greeks as in their art. Bushido similarly praised those women most "who emancipated themselves from the frailty of their sex and displayed an heroic fortitude worthy of the strongest and the bravest of men."[1] Young girls, therefore, were trained to repress their feelings, to indurate their nerves, to manipulate weapons—especially the long-handled sword called *nagi-nata*, so as to be able to hold their own against unexpected odds. Yet the primary motive for exercise of this martial character was not for use in the field; it was twofold—personal and domestic. Woman owning no suzerain of her own, formed her own body-guard. With her weapon she guarded her personal sanctity with as much zeal as her husband did his master's. The domestic utility of her warlike training

---

[1] Lecky, *History of European Morals*, ii, p. 383.

　婦人は剣術などの武芸を実際に用いることはほとんどなかったが、彼女らの家庭における非活動的な習慣を補う、健康上の効用があった。しかしこれらの武芸は健康上の目的からのみ習練されたのではなく、有事の場合には実際に用いることができた。少女は成年に達すれば短刀を与えられ、それによって自分を襲う者の胸を刺し、場合によっては自分の胸を刺すこともあった。後者の場合は実際にしばしば起こったが、そのことで彼女たちを厳格に裁こうとは思わない。キリスト教の良心は自殺を嫌悪するとはいえ、彼女たちに厳しい非難はしないだろう。自殺したペラギアとドミニナの二人を、その純潔と敬虔のゆえに聖者に加えられたのだから。（古代ローマにおいて、独裁者の無法な要求を拒否した美少女ヴァージニア[訳注12]の父は、独裁者の暴虐を怒り、公衆の面前で娘を刺した。）日本のヴァージニアは自分の貞操に危険がせまったようなときは、父親の剣を待つまでもなかった。自分の武器は常に懐中にあったのだ。自害の作法を知らなければ、それは彼女の恥とされた。彼女らは、解剖学は学ばなかったが、喉のどこの部分を刺せばよいかを正確に知っておかねばならなかった。死の苦痛がいかに激しくても、死体が発見されたときに、最大の慎みを示して、脚が乱れず正しい姿勢を保っているように、帯紐で自分の膝を固く縛ることも知らねばならなかった。このような身だしなみは、キリスト者ペルペチュアや貞女コルネリアに比すべきではないだろうか。私がこのようなことを唐突に言い出すのは、日本の入浴の習慣などの些細なことを見て、わが国には貞操観念がないという誤解があるからである[注2]。それどころか、貞操は武士の婦人の主要

[注2] 裸体および入浴について、フィンク著『日本の蓮の花時(はすのはなどき)』286–297ページが十分に理解して説明をしている。

was in the education of her sons, as we shall see later.

Fencing and similar exercises, if rarely of practical use, were a wholesome counterbalance to the otherwise sedentary habits of women. But these exercises were not followed only for hygienic purposes. They could be turned into use in times of need. Girls, when they reached womanhood, were presented with dirks (*kai-ken*, pocket poniards), which might be directed to the bosom of their assailants, or, if advisable, to their own. The latter was very often the case; and yet I will not judge them severely. Even the Christian conscience with its horror of self-immolation, will not be harsh with them, seeing Pelagia and Dominina, two suicides, were canonised for their purity and piety. When a Japanese Virginia saw her chastity menaced, she did not wait for her father's dagger. Her own weapon lay always in her bosom. It was a disgrace to her not to know the proper way in which she had to perpetrate self-destruction. For example, little as she was taught in anatomy, she must know the exact spot to cut in her throat; she must know how to tie her lower limbs together with a belt so that, whatever the agonies of death might be, her corpse be found in utmost modesty with the limbs properly composed. Is not a caution like this worthy of the Christian Perpetua or the Vestal Cornelia? I would not put such an abrupt interrogation were it not for a misconception, based on our bathing customs and other trifles, that chastity is unknown among us.[2] On

---

[2] For a very sensible explanation of nudity and bathing see Finck's *Lotos Time in Japan*, pp. 286–297.

な徳であって、生命以上に重んじられた。ある若い女性が、
敵に捕えられて荒々しい武士たちに暴行を加えられようとし
たとき、彼女は「このたびの戦いに、散り散りになった母や
姉に一筆の便りを書くことが許されるならば、あなた方の意
に従いましょう」と申し出て、手紙を書き終ると、すぐ近く
の井戸に走り、身を投じて彼女の貞操を守った。遺された手
紙のはしには、次のような一首が書かれていた。

　　世にへなばよしなき雲もおおひなん
　　いざ入りてまし山の端の月

　男性的であることのみが、わが国の女性の最高の理想であ
ったと読者に思わせるのは公平ではない。いやむしろ、芸能
などの優雅な習慣は、彼女らに最も必要とされ、音楽、舞踊、
文学などもおろそかにされなかった。実際わが国の文学史上、
最もすぐれた和歌や俳句などにも、彼女らの感情を表現して
いるものが数多くあり、重要な役割を果している。舞踊
（芸者の踊りではなく武士の娘の踊り）は、主としてその立
居振舞いを優雅にするためであり、音楽は、父や夫の気持ち
を慰めるためのものであって、芸術そのもののためではなか
った。

　要するに、それらの究極の目的は心を清めることであり、
心が平らかでなければ、音もおのずから整わないといわれた。
私は前に、青年武士の教育においては、芸道は、常に道徳的

the contrary, chastity was a pre-eminent virtue of the samurai woman, held above life itself. A young woman, taken prisoner, seeing herself in danger of violence at the hands of the rough soldiery, says she will obey their pleasure, provided she be first allowed to write a line to her sisters, whom war has dispersed in every direction. When the epistle is finished, off she runs to the nearest well and saves her honour by drowning. The letter she leaves behind ends with these verses:

"For fear lest clouds may dim her light,
    Should she but graze this nether sphere,
    The young moon poised above the height
    Doth hastily betake to flight."

It would be unfair to give my readers an idea that masculinity alone was our highest ideal for woman. Far from it! Accomplishments and the gentler graces of life were required of them. Music, dancing, and literature were not neglected. Some of the finest verses in our literature were expressions of feminine sentiments; in fact, woman played an important role in the history of Japanese *belles-lettres*. Dancing was taught (I am speaking of samurai girls and not of *geisha*) only to smooth the angularity of their movements. Music was to regale the weary hours of their fathers and husbands; hence it was not for the technique, the art as such, that music was learned; for the ultimate object was purification of heart, since it was said that no harmony of sound is attainable without the player's heart

価値に対し、それに付属する地位にある、と言ったが、女性の場合にも同様であった。舞踊や音楽は、生活に優雅さと明るさを付け加えればそれで充分であって、決して虚栄心や、ぜいたく心を養うためではなかった。ペルシャ王がロンドンの舞踏会に招かれ、舞踏に加わるようにすすめられたとき、「わが国では、このような技能の仕事をする特別な女子をやとっている」と憮然として言ったというが、私はこの王に同情する。

　武家の女性の芸事は、見せるためのものでもなく、出世のために学んだものでもなかった。それは、家庭における娯楽であって、社交の席でその技を示すことはあっても、それは主婦の務めとして、家の客を歓待する一つの方法にすぎなかった。彼女らの教育で最も重要なことは家を治めることにあって、旧日本の婦人の芸事は、文武を問わず、主として家庭のためであった。彼女らはいかに遠く離れていても、決して炉辺を忘れることなく、家の名誉と体面を保持してゆくために、苦労して働き、それに一生を捧げた。彼女らは、強くやさしく、そして勇ましく、ときには哀しい調べをもって、日夜彼女らの小さな巣のために歌いつづけた。娘としては父のために、妻としては夫のために、母としては子供のために、彼女らはおのれを犠牲にした。こうして女性は幼少のころより、おのれを空しくすることを教えられた。彼女らの一生は独立の生涯ではなく、従属的な奉仕の生涯であって、男子の内助者として彼女の存在が役に立てば、夫と共に晴れの舞台に立ち、もし役に立たなければ彼女は幕のかげに退くのである。一人の青年が一人の娘を愛し、その娘もその青年に同じ熱愛で応えた。しかし、その青年が自分への愛に気をとられ

being in harmony with itself. Here again we see the same idea prevailing which we notice in the training of youths—that accomplishments were ever kept subservient to moral worth. Just enough of music and dancing to add grace and brightness to life, but never to foster vanity and extravagance. I sympathise with the Persian Prince, who, when taken into a ball room in London and asked to take part in the merriment, bluntly remarked that in his country they provided a particular set of girls to do that kind of business for them.

The accomplishments of our women were not acquired for show or social ascendancy. They were a home diversion; and if they shone in social parties, it was as the attributes of a hostess,—in other words, as a part of the household contrivance for hospitality. Domesticity guided their education. It may be said that the accomplishments of the women of Old Japan, be they martial or pacific in character, were mainly intended for the home; and, however far they might roam, they never lost sight of the hearth as the centre. It was to maintain its honour and integrity that they slaved, drudged, and gave up their lives. Night and day, in tones at once firm and tender, brave and plaintive, they sang to their little nests. As daughter, woman sacrificed herself for her father, as wife for her husband, and as mother for her son. Thus from earliest youth she was taught to deny herself. Her life was not one of independence, but of dependent service. Man's helpmeet, if her presence is helpful she stays on the stage with him: if it hinders his work, she retires behind the curtain. Not

て義務を怠っているのに気づき、自分の魅力を失わせるため、その美貌を傷つけるといったようなことは、めずらしくなかった。武士の娘たちの鑑とされた吾妻（14歳で源渡に嫁した袈裟御前）は、自分が夫の失脚をたくらむ男に愛されていることに気づく。彼女はその悪事に加担するふりをして、闇にまぎれて夫の身代わりにたち、自分を恋する刺客の刃にその貞潔な首を刺し貫かせたのである。一人の若い大名（木村重成）の妻が自刃する前に夫に遺した次の手紙にはなんの説明も必要ないだろう。

「一樹の陰、一河の流れ、これをも他生の縁ということですが、一昨年より私は貴方と夫婦の契りを結びました。私は今までただ貴方の影にそうようにして生きてまいりました。聞くところによりますと、此度の合戦は、この世限りのことでございます由。中国の項王とか申す人は、世にも勇猛な武士でしたが、虞美人のために名残を惜しみ、木曽義仲は松殿の局との別れを惜しんだといいます。この世にもう何の望みもない私は、せめて貴方が生きておられる間に最後の覚悟をいたし、貴方を死出の道とかいうところでお待ち申しあげております。必ず必ず、秀頼公の多年にわたる海山の御恩を、何とぞお忘れなきようにお願い申しあげます」

infrequently does it happen that a youth becomes enamoured of a maiden who returns his love with equal ardour, but, when she realises his interest in her makes him forgetful of his duties, disfigures her person that her attractions may cease. Adzuma, the ideal wife in the minds of samurai girls, finds herself loved by a man who is conspiring against her husband. Upon pretence of joining in the guilty plot, she manages in the dark to take her husband's place, and the sword of the lover-assassin descends upon her own devoted head. The following epistle written by the wife of a young *daimio*, before taking her own life, needs no comment:

"I have heard that no accident or chance ever mars the march of events here below, and that all is in accordance with a plan. To take shelter under a common bough or a drink of the same river, is alike ordained from ages prior to our birth. Since we were joined in ties of eternal wedlock, now two short years ago, my heart hath followed thee, even as its shadow followeth an object, inseparably bound heart to heart, loving and being loved. Learning but recently, however, that the coming battle is to be the last of thy labour and life, take the farewell greeting of thy loving partner. I have heard that Kowu, the mighty warrior of ancient China, lost a battle, loth to part with his favorite Gu. Yoshinaka, too, brave as he was, brought disaster to his cause, too weak to bid prompt farewell to his wife. Why should I, to whom earth no longer offers hope or joy—Why should I detain thee or thy thoughts by living? Why should I not, rather, await thee on the road which all mortal kind must sometime tread? Never, prithee, never, forget the many benefits which our good master Hidéyori hath heaped upon thee. The gratitude we owe him is as deep as the sea and as high as the hills."

　女性がその夫や家庭や、その家族のために身を捨てるのは、男子がその主君のために身を捨てるのと同様に、喜んで立派になされた。おのれを空しくすること、それなくしては、人生の不可解な点は一つも解決できず、すなわち女性にとっては家のためであり、男子にとっては主君のため、これが基調であった。妻が夫に尽すのは、夫が主君に尽すのと同様で、女性は男性の奴隷ではなかった。女性の果す役割は、「内助」すなわち「内側からの助け」であった。妻はおのれを空しくして夫に仕え、夫はおのれを空しくして主君に仕え、主君はさらにこれをもって天の意に服従したのである。私はこれらの教訓の欠陥を知っている。キリスト教のすぐれている点が最も明白に現われているのは、すべての人間ひとりひとりが、創造主に対する直接の責任がある、と教えていることである。この奉仕の教義に関するかぎり、つまり自分の個性を犠牲にして、自己よりも高い目的に仕えるということは、キリストの教えの中でも最大の教えである。それにもかかわらず使命の神聖な基調をなしている、奉仕の教義は、これに関するかぎり武士道も永遠の真理に基づいていると言ってもよいではなかろうか。

　読者は、私に対して不当な偏見をもち、意志の奴隷的な屈従を是認しているなどと、非難していただきたくない。私は学識思想ともに高い（哲学者）ヘーゲルが主張し、弁護した「歴史とは自由の発展であり、その実現である」という説におおむね賛成である。私の明らかにしようとする点は、武士道の教訓はすべて自己犠牲の精神によって充たされており、それは女子についてのみでなく男子についても要求された、ということである。したがって、武士道の感化が、まったく消滅する日が来ない限り、あるアメリカ人の女権拡張論者が

Woman's surrender of herself to the good of her husband, home, and family, was as willing and honourable as the man's self-surrender to the good of his lord and country. Self-renunciation, without which no life-enigma can be solved, was the key-note of the loyalty of man as well as of the domesticity of woman. She was no more the slave of man than was her husband of his liege-lord, and the part she played was recognised as *naijo*, "the inner help." In the ascending scale of service stood woman, who annihilated herself for man, that he might annihilate himself for the master, that he in turn might obey Heaven. I know the weakness of this teaching and that the superiority of Christianity is nowhere more manifested than here, in that it requires of each and every living soul direct responsibility to its Creator. Nevertheless, as far as the doctrine of service—the serving of a cause higher than one's own self, even at the sacrifice of one's individuality; I say the doctrine of service, which is the greatest that Christ preached and was the sacred key-note of His mission—so far as that is concerned, Bushido was based on eternal truth.

My readers will not accuse me of undue prejudice in favour of slavish surrender of volition. I accept in a large measure the view advanced and defended with breadth of learning and profundity of thought by Hegel, that history is the unfolding and realisation of freedom. The point I wish to make is that the whole teaching of Bushido was so thoroughly imbued with the spirit of self-sacrifice, that it was required not only of woman but of man. Hence, until the influence of its precepts is entirely done away with,

「すべての日本婦人は、旧来の習慣に反逆して起（た）ち上がれ」
と軽率に主張した見解に、わが国の社会は賛同はしないだろ
う。このような反逆は成功しうるだろうか。それで、女性の
地位が向上するだろうか。そのような手軽に獲得した権利は、
女性が今日まで受け継いできた柔和な性質、やさしい動作の
喪失に見合うものなのだろうか。ローマの主婦が家庭への愛
着を失ったあとに、道徳の腐敗は言語に絶するほどひどくな
らなかったのか。アメリカの改革論者は、わが国の娘たちの
反逆が真に歴史的発展のとるべき経路であると、われわれを
納得させられるのか。これは重大な問題である。変化は、そ
のような反抗によらなくても起るべきであり、起るものであ
る。それでは、武士道の制度下での女性の地位は、はたして
反逆を正当化するほど悪いものであったろうか。

　われわれは、ヨーロッパの騎士が「神とレディ」に捧げた
外見的な尊敬についてしばしば耳にしている。この二つの言
葉の釣り合わないことは、ギボンを赤面させたほどである。
また、ハラムによれば、騎士道の道徳は粗野であり、婦人に
対する慇懃（いんぎん）には不義の愛が含まれていたという。騎士道の女
性に及ぼした影響は、哲学者に思索の糧（かて）を与えた。（フランス
の歴史家）ギゾー氏は、封建制度と騎士道は、後世に健全な
る影響を与えたと論じたのに対して、スペンサー氏は、封建
制下の軍事社会（そして封建社会は、軍事的でなくて何であ
ろう）においては、婦人の地位は必然的に低く、社会の産業
の発達に伴ってのみ改良されると言った。
　さて、日本については、ギゾー氏の説とスペンサー氏の説
とのいずれを正しいとするだろうか。私はその二つとも正し
いと思う。日本における封建制下の軍事階級は、およそ200

our society will not realise the view rashly expressed by an American exponent of woman's rights, who exclaimed, "May all the daughters of Japan rise in revolt against ancient customs!" Can such a revolt succeed? Will it improve the female status? Will the rights they gain by such a summary process repay the loss of that sweetness of disposition, that gentleness of manner, which are their present heritage? Was not the loss of domesticity on the part of Roman matrons followed by moral corruption too gross to mention? Can the American reformer assure us that a revolt of our daughters is the true course for their historical development to take? These are grave questions. Changes must and will come without revolts! In the meantime let us see whether the status of the fair sex under the Bushido regimen was really so bad as to justify a revolt.

We hear much of the outward respect European knights paid to "God and the ladies,"—the incongruity of the two terms making Gibbon blush; we are also told by Hallam that the morality of chivalry was coarse, that gallantry implied illicit love. The effect of chivalry on the weaker vessel was food for reflection on the part of philosophers, M. Guizot contending that feudalism and chivalry wrought wholesome influences, while Mr. Spencer tells us that in a militant society (and what is feudal society if not militant?) the position of woman is necessarily low, improving only as society becomes more industrial. Now is M. Guizot's theory true of Japan, or is Mr. Spencer's? In reply I might aver that both are right. The military class in Japan was restricted to the samurai, comprising nearly

万の武士に限られていた。その上に軍事貴族の大名と宮廷貴族の公卿がいた。これらの身分の高いぜいたくな貴族たちは、ただ名前だけの武士に過ぎなかった。武士の下には平民階級である、農、工、商があって、これらの者たちは、もっぱら平和的な仕事に従事していた。したがって、ハーバート・スペンサーが軍事的社会の形態の特色としてあげた点は、もっぱら武士階級に限られたことであった。これに対し、産業的社会形態の特色は、その上層と下層の階級においてのみ、見られたといってよい。

このことは婦人の地位を見ればよくわかる。すなわち、婦人の自由が最も拘束されたのは武士階級においてであった。奇態なことに社会階級が下になればなるほど、例えば職人の間においては、夫婦の地位は平等であった。身分の高い貴族の間においてもまた両性間の差はそれほど著しくはなかった。これは、有閑貴族の生活が女性化したことにその主な原因があって、そのため性の差異を明らかにする機会が少かった故である。すなわちスペンサーの説は、旧日本において例証されたといってよいだろう。ギゾーの説は、彼がとくに身分の高い貴族を考察の対象としているがために、わが国では大名や公卿のみに適用されるであろう。

もし私の説明が、武士道の下における婦人の地位が、はなはだ低いものに思わせたとするならば、私は歴史的な真理に対して、大きな不正を犯したことになる。私は女子が男子と対等の待遇をされなかったと述べることにためらいはない。しかし、差異と不平等の相違点をよく理解しない限り、この問題についての誤解はまぬかれないであろう。

two million souls. Above them were the military nobles, the *daimio*, and the court nobles, the *kugé*—these higher, sybaritical nobles being fighters only in name. Below them were masses of the common people—mechanics, tradesmen, and peasants—whose life was devoted to arts of peace. Thus what Herbert Spencer gives as the characteristics of a militant type of society may be said to have been exclusively confined to the samurai class, while those of the industrial type were applicable to the classes above and below it. This is well illustrated by the position of woman; for in no class did she experience less freedom than among the samurai. Strange to say, the lower the social class—as, for instance, among small artisans—the more equal was the position of husband and wife. Among the higher nobility, too, the difference in the relations of the sexes was less marked, chiefly because there were few occasions to bring the differences of sex into prominence, the leisurely nobleman having become literally effeminate. Thus Spencer's dictum was fully exemplified in Old Japan. As to Guizot's, those who read his presentation of a feudal community will remember that he had the higher nobility especially under consideration, so that his generalisation applies to the *daimio* and the *kugé*.

I shall be guilty of gross injustice to historical truth if my words give one a very low opinion of the status of woman under Bushido. I do not hesitate to state that she was not treated as man's equal; but, until we learn to discriminate between differences and inequalities, there will always be misunderstandings upon this subject.

　男性でさえ、お互いに平等であることは、法廷や選挙などきわめて少数の場合に限られることを思えば、両性の平等に関する議論に身を労するのは無駄に思えてくる。アメリカの独立宣言において、すべての人は平等に創造せられたと言っているのは、人間の精神的あるいは肉体的能力を指しているものではない。それは昔（ローマの法律家）アルピアンが「法の前には万人は平等である」と言ったことを、繰り返し述べたにすぎない。この場合においては、法律的な権利が平等の尺度であるとされた。もし法律が、社会における婦人の地位を計るただ一つのはかりであるとすれば、彼女らの地位の高低を知るのは、彼女らの体重を計るのと同様に容易なことである。しかし問題はこの点である。

　男女の相対的な社会的地位を比較しようとするとき、正確な尺度はあるのであろうか。金や銀の価値を比較するように、男女の地位を比較して、その比率を数字にあらわせば、それで正しく、また十分なのであろうか。そのような計算方法は、人間の持つ最も重要な価値、すなわち本質的価値を考えに入れないことになってしまう。男女それぞれが、この世にうけている使命を果すためのさまざまな要件がきわめて多いことを考えれば、両性の総体的地位を計る尺度は、複合的な性質のものでなければならない。あるいは、経済学の用語を借りていえば、多元的本位でなければならない。武士道は独自の基準を持っており、それは二項方程式の基準であった。女子の価値を、戦場とそして家庭との二つにおいて計れば、前者においては女子の価値ははなはだ軽いが、後者においては完全であった。女性に与えられる待遇はこの二重の評価に対応していた。すなわち、社会的あるいは政治的な単位としては高くなかったけれども、妻あるいは母としては最も高い尊敬と最も深い愛情を払われた。古代ローマ人のような軍事的国

When we think in how few respects men are equal among themselves, *e.g.*, before law courts or voting polls, it seems idle to trouble ourselves with a discussion on the equality of sexes. When the American Declaration of Independence said that all men were created equal, it had no reference to their mental or physical gifts; it simply repeated what Ulpian long ago announced, that before the law all men are equal. Legal rights were in this case the measure of their equality. Were the law the only scale by which to measure the position of woman in a community, it would be as easy to tell where she stands as to give her avoirdupois in pounds and ounces. But the question is: Is there a correct standard in comparing the relative social position of the sexes? Is it right, is it enough, to compare woman's status to man's, as the value of silver is compared with that of gold, and give the ratio numerically? Such a method of calculation excludes from consideration the most important kind of value which a human being possesses, namely, the intrinsic. In view of the manifold variety of requisites for making each sex fulfil its earthly mission, the standard to be adopted in measuring its relative position must be of a composite character; or to borrow from economic language, it must be a multiple standard. Bushido had a standard of its own and it was binomial. It tried to gauge the value of woman on the battle-field and by the hearth. There she counted for very little; here for all. The treatment accorded her corresponded to this double measurement:—as a social-political unit not much, while as wife and mother she received highest respect and deepest

民の間でも、婦人が高い尊敬を払われたのは、彼女らが、マトロネー（matronae）すなわち、母だったからではなかったか。戦士あるいは政治家としてではなく、母であるが故に、ローマ人は婦人の前に身をかがめた。わが国民においても同様である。父や夫が戦場に出れば、家庭を治めるのは母や妻であって、子供の教育はもとより、その子供を守る責任も彼女らにまかせられていた。私が前に述べた婦人の武芸も、要するに、その将来に悔いのないように、子供らを教育するためであった。

　日本人について生半可（なまはんか）な知識しかない外国人の中には、日本人が俗に自分の妻を「愚妻」などと呼ぶのを見て、妻を軽蔑して少しも尊敬していない証拠だなどと、表面的な見方をしている者がいる。しかし「愚夫」「豚児（とんじ）」「拙者」などの言葉も日常使われていることを知ってもらいたいものである。

　私は、わが国民の結婚観が、ある点においてはキリスト教徒よりも進んでいると考えている。聖書では、「男と女は合して一体となるべし」と言っているが、アングロ・サクソンの個人主義は、夫と妻とは二人の人格であるという観念から抜け出すことはできない。したがって、彼らが相争うときは、別々の権利を認め、相和するときは、ばかばかしいほどの相愛の言葉や無意味なへつらいの言葉を尽くす。それでも足りず、夫もしくは妻が第二者に対し、その半身を——それが善き半身であるか悪き半身であるかは別として、その半身に対して、愛らしいとか、聡明だとか、親切だとか言うのを、日本人が聞いたならば、きわめて不合理に思うであろう。自分

affection. Why, among so military a nation as the Romans, were their matrons so highly venerated? Was it not because they were *matronae,* mothers? Not as fighters or lawgivers, but as their mothers did men bow before them. So with us. While fathers and husbands were absent in field or camp, the government of the household was left entirely in the hands of mothers and wives. The education of the young, even their defence, was entrusted to them. The warlike exercises of women, of which I have spoken, were primarily to enable them intelligently to direct and follow the education of their children.

I have noticed a rather superficial notion prevailing among half-informed foreigners, that because the common Japanese expression for one's wife is "my rustic wife" and the like, she is despised and held in little esteem. When it is told that such phrases as "my foolish father," "my swinish son," "my awkward self," etc., are in current use, is not the answer clear enough?

To me it seems that our idea of marital union goes in some ways farther than the so-called Christian. "Man and woman shall be one flesh." The individualism of the Anglo-Saxon cannot let go of the idea that husband and wife are two persons;—hence when they disagree, their separate *rights* are recognised, and when they agree, they exhaust their vocabulary in all sorts of silly pet-names and nonsensical blandishments. It sounds highly irrational to our ears, when a husband or wife speaks to a third party of his or her other half—better or worse—as being lovely, bright, kind, and what not. Is it good taste to speak of

自身のことを「聡明なる私」とか「愛すべき私の性質」などと
言うのは良い趣味だといえるだろうか。われわれは、自分の妻
を賞めるのは、自分自身の一部分を賞めることだと考えてい
る。そして、わが国民は、自分のことを賞讃することは、少
くとも悪趣味だと見なしている。私はキリスト教徒の国民の
間にも、そうあってほしいと希望したい。礼儀正しく自分の
妻をけなして呼ぶことは、武士の間には通常行われていた習
慣であったから、私はあえて横道に入って論じた次第である。
　チュートン人種は、女性をきわめて畏敬する迷信をもって、
その種族的な生活を始めた。（現在のドイツにおいては消滅
しつつある）またアメリカ人は、女子の人口不足を痛感しな
がら、その社会的生活を始めた[注3]。（今はアメリカでは、女子
人口が増加し、植民地時代の母性の特権は、急速に失われつ
つあるのではなかろうか）したがって、西洋文明においては、
男子が女子に対して払う尊敬が、道徳の主要な標準となった
のである。しかし武士道の道徳においては、善悪を分ける分
水嶺を他に求めた。それは、人間が自分の内なる神聖な霊魂
と結びつき、そののちに本書で前述した五倫の道にしたがっ
て、他者の霊魂と結びつくという、義務とよく似た位置に存
在した。私はこの五倫の道の中で忠義、すなわち臣下と主君
の関係について本書で述べたが、その他の点については、武
士道の特質ではないため付言したにすぎない。それは自然的
な愛情に基づいているもので、当然全人類の人間関係に共通
するものであった。ただし、武士道の教訓から導き出された
状況によって、それらが特に強調された部分がいくつかあっ
た。これらのことに関連して、私は男同士の友情について固
有の力と美があることが思いおこされる。このような友情が

[注3] イギリスから娘たちが船で運ばれ、煙草などと交換に結婚が行われた時
代のこと。

one's self as "my bright self," "my lovely disposition," and so forth? We think praising one's own wife is praising a part of one's own self, and self-praise is regarded, to say the least, as bad taste among us,—and I hope, among Christian nations, too! I have diverged at some length because the polite debasement of one's consort was a usage most in vogue among the samurai.

The Teutonic races beginning their tribal life with a superstitious awe of the fair sex (though this is really wearing off in Germany!), and the Americans beginning their social life under the painful consciousness of the numerical insufficiency of women[3] (who, now increasing, are, I am afraid, fast losing the prestige their colonial mothers enjoyed), the respect man pays to woman has in Western civilisation become the chief standard of morality. But in the martial ethics of Bushido, the main watershed dividing the good and the bad was sought elsewhere. It was located along the line of duty which bound man to his own divine soul and then to other souls in the five relations I have mentioned in the early part of this paper. Of these, we have brought to our reader's notice loyalty, the relation between one man as vassal and another as lord. Upon the rest, I have only dwelt incidentally as occasion presented itself; because they were not peculiar to Bushido. Being founded on natural affections, they could but be common to all mankind, though in some particulars

---

[3] I refer to those days when girls were imported from England and given in marriage for so many pounds of tobacco, etc.

義兄弟の盟約となり、さらにロマンチックな愛慕を伴う情と
なることもしばしばあった。これは、青年時代の男女別居の
習慣によって強められたことは疑いない。つまり、男女の別
居が、ヨーロッパの騎士道あるいはアングロ・サクソン諸国
の男女の自由交際におけるような、愛情の自然的な流露の道
をふさいできたためである。われわれは、（古代ギリシャに
おける）ダモン[訳注13]とピシアスあるいはアキレウスとパトロ
クロスの物語の日本版で多くの紙数を費やすこともきれ
ば、あるいは（『旧訳聖書』の中の羊飼いの）ダビデ[訳注14]と、
（王子）ヨナタンとの友情におとらぬ深い友情を、武士道の
物語として語ることもできる。

さて、武士道特有の道徳と教訓は、武士階級のみに行われ
たのではない。私はこのことを、つまり武士道の国民全般に
及ぼした感化について、次に述べようと思う。

they may have been accentuated by conditions which its teachings induced. In this connection there comes before me the peculiar strength and tenderness of friendship between man and man, which often added to the bond of brotherhood a romantic attachment doubtless intensified by the separation of the sexes in youth,—a separation which denied to affection the natural channel open to it in Western chivalry or in the free intercourse of Anglo-Saxon lands. I might fill pages with Japanese versions of the Story of Damon and Pythias or Achilles and Patroclos, or tell in Bushido parlance of ties as sympathetic as those which bound David and Jonathan.

It is not surprising, however, that the virtues and teachings unique in the Precepts of Knighthood did not remain circumscribed to the military class. This makes us hasten to the consideration of the influence of Bushido on the nation at large.

第15章

武士道の感化

武士道の道徳は、わが国民生活の一般的な水準よりも、はるかに高い山脈を形成しているが、私はこれまで、その中のさらに高いいくつかの峯を考察したにすぎない。太陽が昇るときは、まず最も高い峯の頂上を紅に染めて、それから次第にその光を谷間に投げかけてくるように、まず武士階級を照らした道徳の体系は、時間がたつにしたがって、一般民衆の間からも、それに追従する者が出てきた。民主主義は天成の指導者としての王者を育て、貴族主義は王者の精神を民衆の間にゆきわたらせる。道徳は罪悪に劣らず伝染しやすい。（アメリカの思想家）エマーソンは、「仲間の中には、ただ一人の賢者がおればよい。そうなれば仲間みんなが賢くなる。伝染の力はそれほど速いものである」と言ったが、いかなる社会階級でも、道徳的感化の伝播を阻止することはできない。

THE INFLUENCE OF BUSHIDO

THUS far we have brought into view only a few of the more prominent peaks which rise above the range of knightly virtues, in themselves so much more elevated than the general level of our national life. As the sun in its rising first tips the highest peaks with russet hue, and then gradually casts its rays on the valley below, so the ethical system which first enlightened the military order drew in course of time followers from amongst the masses. Democracy raises up a natural prince for its leader, and aristocracy infuses a princely spirit among the people. Virtues are no less contagious than vices. "There needs but one wise man in a company, and all are wise, so rapid is the contagion," says Emerson. No social class or caste can resist the diffusive power of moral influence.

　われわれはアングロ・サクソン民族の、自由の勝利とその進歩については、いくらでも言うことができるが、そこに、一般民衆の動かす力が働いたことは、きわめて少なかった。それはむしろ、郷士でありジェントルメンの功績ではなかったろうか。（フランスの思想家）テーヌ氏が、「海峡の彼方（イギリス）で用いられている三音節の言葉（gentlemen）は、イギリス社会の歴史を要約するものである」と言っているのは、まさに然りである。民主主義はそのような発言に対して、自信に満ちた反駁をして、こう問い返すだろう。「アダムが耕してイヴが紡いでいた時、一体ジェントルマンはどこにいたのか？」と。悲しいかな、ジェントルマンはエデンの園にはいなかった。人類の始祖は彼の不在により、ひどく苦しみ、高い代償を払った。もし、ジェントルマンがいたなら、楽園はもっと豊かなうるおいに充ちたものになっていたであろうし、この人類の始祖は苦痛を体験することなく、エホバに対して不従順でないこと、不忠であって不名誉、また裏切りであって反逆であることを学んでいただろう。

　過去の日本は、武士の賜によってつくられてきた。武士はわが国の花であったばかりでなく、その根源でもあった。天のあらゆる恵み、深い賜は、武士を通してもたらされていった。武士は民衆と社会的な階級によって離れていたけれども、民衆の間に道徳の標準をもたらし、自らが模範となってこれを導いていった。武士道には対外的教訓と対内的教訓の二つを認めることができるが、前者は社会の安寧と幸福を願う善なる意志であり、後者は徳のためにそれを強く実践しようとする規律であった。

　ヨーロッパにおいては、騎士道の最盛期においても、騎士の数は人口の小部分を占めるにすぎなかった。しかし、エマーソンが言ったように、「イギリス文学におけるサー・フィリッ

Prate as we may of the triumphant march of Anglo-Saxon liberty, rarely has it received impetus from the masses. Was it not rather the work of the squires and *gentlemen*? Very truly does M. Taine say, "These three syllables, as used across the channel, summarise the history of English society." Democracy may make self-confident retorts to such a statement and fling back the question—"When Adam delved and Eve span, where then was the gentleman?" All the more pity that a gentleman was not present in Eden! The first parents missed him sorely and paid a high price for his absence. Had he been there, not only would the garden have been more tastefully dressed, but they would have learned without painful experience that disobedience to Jehovah was disloyalty and dishonour, treason and rebellion.

What Japan was she owed to the samurai. They were not only the flower of the nation, but its root as well. All the gracious gifts of Heaven flowed through them. Though they kept themselves socially aloof from the populace, they set a moral standard for them and guided them by their example. I admit Bushido had its esoteric and exoteric teachings; these were eudemonic, looking after the welfare and happiness of the commonalty; those were aretaic, emphasising the practice of virtues for their own sake.

In the most chivalrous days of Europe, knights formed numerically but a small fraction of the population, but, as Emerson says,—"In English literature half the drama and

プ・シドニー（16世紀の詩人）より、サー・ウォルター・スコット（18世紀の小説家）にいたるまで作られた戯曲の半分と、小説の全部は、この人物、つまりジェントルマンを描写した」のである。もし、シドニーおよびスコットの代わりに、近松門左衛門および滝沢馬琴の名をあげれば、日本文学史の主なる特色は一目瞭然であろう。

　民衆は娯楽によっていろんな教訓を与えられ、そして学んだが、それらの方法、たとえば芝居、寄席、講談、浄瑠璃、小説などは、その主題の多くは武士の物語から採用された。農民は囲炉裏の火をかこんで、義経と忠臣弁慶の物語、あるいは勇ましい曽我兄弟の物語などを繰り返し語り、あきることがなかった。そのかたわらで、腕白小僧どもは、口を開いて耳をそばたて、炉の薪が燃え尽きても、その物語に心はまだ燃えつづけた。商家の番頭や小僧たちは、一日の仕事を終えて店の雨戸[注1]を閉じると、膝をよせ合って、信長や秀吉の物語に夜をふかし、疲れきって眠ると、夢の中では、昼間の仕事の辛さから解き放たれ、戦場をかけまわるのであった。また、よちよち歩きの幼児さえも、桃太郎の鬼ケ島征伐の昔話を、まわらぬ舌で語ることを覚え、女の子供でさえ、武士の武勇とその美徳を慕い、武士の物語を熱心に聞きたがるその有様は、あたかもデズデモナのようであった。

　武士は、国民全体の美しい理想であって、「花は桜木、人は武士」と民衆の間に広くうたわれるほどであった。武士階

注1 家の外側の扉。

all the novels, from Sir Philip Sidney to Sir Walter Scott, paint this figure (gentleman)." Write in place of Sidney and Scott, Chikamatsu and Bakin, and you have in a nut-shell the main features of the literary history of Japan.

The innumerable avenues of popular amusement and instruction—the theatres, the story-tellers' booths, the preacher's dais, the musical recitations, the novels,—have taken for their chief theme the stories of the samurai. The peasants around the open fire in their huts never tire of repeating the achievements of Yoshitsuné and his faithful retainer Benkéi, or of the two brave Soga brothers; the dusky urchins listen with gaping mouths until the last stick burns out and the fire dies in its embers, still leaving their hearts aglow with tale that is told. The clerks and the shop boys, after their day's work is over and the *amado*[1] of the store are closed, gather together to relate the story of Nobunaga and Hidéyoshi far into the night, until slumber overtakes their weary eyes and transports them from the drudgery of the counter to the exploits of the field. The very babe just beginning to toddle is taught to lisp the adventures of Momotaro, the daring conqueror of ogreland. Even girls are so imbued with the love of knightly deeds and virtues that, like Desdemona, they would seriously incline to devour with greedy ear the romance of the samurai.

The samurai grew to be the *beau ideal* of the whole race. "As among flowers the cherry is queen, so among

---

[1] Outside shutters.

級は、商業に従事することを禁じられていたので、直接には
商業の進歩の助けにはならなかった。しかし、いかなる人間
の活動の在り方も、思考の方法も、いくらかでも武士道の影
響を受けないものはなかった。知的な、あるいは道徳的な日
本は、直接にも間接にも、武士道がつくりあげてきたもので
あった。

　マロック氏は、そのすぐれて示唆に富んだ著書『貴族主義
と進化』の中で、「社会進化は、生物進化と異なっている限
りにおいて、傑出した人物の意志より生まれた、無意識的結
果であると定義できる」と雄弁に語り、さらに歴史上の進歩
は「社会一般の生存競争によるものではなくて、むしろ社会
の少数者の間で、大衆を最良の方法で指導し、支配し、使役
しようとする競争によって生まれてきたものである」と言っ
ている。この説の適切さに対して批判の余地がないわけでは
ない。だがわが帝国の社会進歩には、武士の果した役割のい
かに大きかったことを例証するものである。

　武士道の精神が、いかにすべての社会階級に浸透していっ
たかは、男達とよばれている、ある特定階級の人物、すなわ
ち民主主義のこれら天性の指導者の発達からもよくうかがう
ことができる。彼らは義俠心にあふれた男子であって、その
頭から爪先まで豪快な活力にみちており、平民の権利の保護
者であり代弁者でもあった。彼らはそれぞれ数百数千の子分
をかかえていたが、これらの子分たちは、武士が大名に仕え
るように「身体と生命と、財産および現世の名誉」の一切を
親分にささげ、喜んで親分に仕えた。ともすれば短気で過激
な市井の労働者である大衆の絶大な支持を得て、これらの天
成の親分たちは、二本差階級（武士階級）のわがままなふる

men the samurai is lord," so sang the populace. Debarred from commercial pursuits, the military class itself did not aid commerce; but there was no channel of human activity, no avenue of thought, which did not receive in some measure an impetus from Bushido. Intellectual and moral Japan was directly or indirectly the work of Knighthood.

Mr. Mallock, in his exceedingly suggestive book, *Aristocracy and Evolution*, has eloquently told us that "social evolution, in so far as it is other than biological, may be defined as the unintended result of the intentions of great men"; further, that historical progress is produced by a struggle "not among the community generally, to live, but a struggle amongst a small section of the community to lead, to direct, to employ, the majority in the best way." Whatever may be said about the soundness of his argument, these statements are amply verified in the part played by bushi in the social progress, so far as it went, of our Empire.

How the spirit of Bushido permeated all social classes is also shown in the development of a certain order of men, known as *otoko-daté*, the natural leaders of democracy. Staunch fellows were they, every inch of them strong with the strength of massive manhood. At once the spokesmen and the guardians of popular rights, they had each a following of hundreds and thousands of souls who proffered, in the same fashion that samurai did to *daimio*, the willing service of "limb and life, of body, chattels, and earthly honour." Backed by a vast multitude of rash and impetuous working men, these born "bosses" formed a

まいに対し、それを阻止する恐るべき大きな力を構成していた。

　武士道は、その最初に発生した社会階級より、いろんな道に分かれて流れ下り、大衆の間に酵母として作用し、すべての人民に道徳の標準を供給した。武士道は、その初めはエリートの栄光であったが、時が経つにしたがい国民全般が熱望するインスピレーションとなった。大衆は、武士の道徳的な高さまでは達することができなかったけれども、「大和魂」という言葉は、ついにはこの島国の帝国の民族精神を象徴するものとなったのである。宗教というものが、もし（イギリスの詩人）マシュー・アーノルドが定義したように「情緒によって感動された道徳」にすぎないものであるとすれば、武士道以上に、宗教の資格をもっている道徳体系は、ほかにあるだろうか。本居宣長は、わが国民の無言の言葉を表現して、つぎのように歌った。

　　　敷島の大和心を人間はば
　　　朝日に匂ふ山桜花

　然り、桜[注2]は古来わが国民の愛した花であって、わが国民性の象徴であった。とくにこの歌人が言っている「朝日に匂ふ山桜花」という言葉に注意せよ。

　大和魂は、柔弱な花ではなくて、自然という意味で野性のものであり、わが国土に特有のものである。その付随的な性

注2 サクラの学名は、リンドレイによるとCerasus pseudo-cerasus。

formidable check to the rampancy of the two-sworded order.

In manifold ways has Bushido filtered down from the social class where it originated, and acted as leaven among the masses, furnishing a moral standard for the whole people. The Precepts of Knighthood, begun at first as the glory of the *élite*, became in time an aspiration and inspiration to the nation at large; and though the populace could not attain the moral height of those loftier souls, yet *Yamato Damashii*, the Soul of Japan, ultimately came to express the *Volksgeist* of the Island Realm. If religion is no more than "Morality touched by emotion," as Matthew Arnold defines it, few ethical systems are better entitled to the rank of religion than Bushido. Motoöri has put the mute utterance of the nation into words when he sings:

"Isles of blest Japan!
    Should your Yamato spirit
  Strangers seek to scan,
      Say—scenting morn's sunlit air,
      Blows the cherry wild and fair!"

Yes, the *sakura** has for ages been the favourite of our people and the emblem of our character. Mark particularly the terms of definition which the poet uses, the words the *wild cherry flower scenting the morning sun.*

The Yamato spirit is not a tame, tender plant, but a wild—in the sense of natural—growth; it is indigenous to

---

² *Cerasus pseudo-cerasus*, Lindley.

質には他国の花と同じものがあるかもしれないが、本質においてはあくまでもわが国だけに自生するものである。しかし、わが国の原産だからという理由だけでわれわれは桜を愛好するものではない。その優雅な姿がわが国民の美的な感覚に訴えることは、他のいかなる花も及ばない。

　ヨーロッパ人は薔薇の花を愛好するが、われわれは違う。薔薇は桜の単純さをもっていない。さらに薔薇は甘美な花の下に棘をかくしていて、あたかも、その生命に強い執着をもち、死を嫌い恐れて、咲いたまま落ちるよりも、枝についたまま朽ちることを選ぶかのようである。その華美な色と濃厚な香りは、わが国の花と著しく異なる特徴である。わが国の桜はその美の下に短剣も毒も潜ませてはおらず、自然のままに散り、その色彩は少しも華麗ではなく、その香りは淡くて、人を飽きさせない。

　形態や色彩の美は外観的なもので、その花固有の性質をもっているが、その香りは生命の息吹のように浮動して、神聖な清らかさを持っている。それ故に多くの宗教上の儀式には、乳香と没薬は重要な役割を果たしているのである。香気には霊的なものがある。太陽が東から昇って、この極東の島国を照らし、桜の花の香りが大気を匂わすとき、その美しい日の香気を胸一杯に吸うことほど、われわれの気分を清澄爽快にするものはないだろう。

（『旧訳聖書』の創世記にも見られるように）創造主すらも、（ノア訳注15の捧げた）かぐわしい香りをかいで、（この地上を呪うことはすまいと）新しい決意をなされたというではないか（創世紀8-32）。そうであるならば、桜の花の匂う季節に

the soil; its accidental qualities it may share with the flowers of other lands, but in its essence it remains the original, spontaneous outgrowth of our clime. But its nativity is not its sole claim to our affection. The refinement and grace of its beauty appeal to *our* æsthetic sense as no other flower can. We cannot share the admiration of the Europeans for their roses, which lack the simplicity of our flower. Then, too, the thorns that are hidden beneath the sweetness of the rose, the tenacity with which she clings to life, as though loth or afraid to die rather than drop untimely, preferring to rot on her stem; her showy colours and heavy odours—all these are traits so unlike our flower, which carries no dagger or poison under its beauty, which is ever ready to depart life at the call of nature, whose colours are never gorgeous, and whose light fragrance never palls. Beauty of colour and of form is limited in its showing; it is a fixed quality of existence, whereas fragrance is volatile, ethereal as the breathing of life. So in all religious ceremonies frankincense and myrrh play a prominent part. There is something spirituelle in redolence. When the delicious perfume of the sakura quickens the morning air, as the sun in its course rises to illumine first the isles of the Far East, few sensations are more serenely exhilarating than to inhale, as it were, the very breath of beauteous day.

When the Creator Himself is pictured as making new resolutions in His heart upon smelling a sweet savour (Gen. viii. 21), is it any wonder that the sweet-smelling season of the cherry blossom should call forth the whole

は、わが国土のすべての人民を、その小さな住処から外へ誘い出されるのも、何も不思議なことではない。こうして彼らはしばしの間、日頃の苦労や悲哀を忘れ果てても、何もとがめることはないであろう。この短い快楽が終ると、彼らは新しい力と新しい決意をもって、日常の仕事に戻るのである。これらのことによっても、桜の花は実にわが国民の花といってもよいだろう。

しかし、このように美しく、かつ、はかなく散りやすく、風のままに舞いながら、ひとすじの香気を放ちながら永久に消えてゆくこの花は、はたして大和魂の象徴なのか、日本の魂はこのようにもろく、そして消えやすいものであるのだろうか。

nation from their little habitations? Blame them not, if for a time their limbs forget their toil and moil and their hearts their pangs and sorrows. Their brief pleasure ended, they return to their daily task with new strength and new resolutions. Thus in ways more than one is the sakura the flower of the nation.

Is, then, this flower, so sweet and evanescent, blown whithersoever the wind listeth, and, shedding a puff of perfume, ready to vanish forever, is this flower the type of the Yamato spirit? Is the soul of Japan so frailly mortal?

第16章

武士道はなお
生きられるか

わが国における驚くべき西洋文明の進入は、わが古来の教訓のあらゆる痕跡を、すでに拭い去ってしまったであろうか。一国民の魂が、もしそのように早く死滅するものならば、はなはだ悲しいことである。そのように外来の感化によって屈服するようでは、それは貧弱な魂にほからならない。

国民性を構成する心理的な要素の集合体がその国民性と切り離せないのは、「魚のひれや鳥のくちばし、肉食動物の歯といったその種属に欠かせない要素」と同じである。ル・ボン氏は皮相な見解の独言と、すばらしい概括とに満ちている近著[注1]で、「知性がもたらした発見は、人類共有の遺産であるが、性格の長所短所はそれぞれ国民が継承してきた専有の遺産である。それは堅い岩のように、何世紀にもわたって日夜、

[注1] ル・ボン著『民族心理学』33ページ。

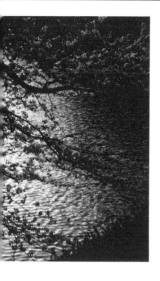

CHAPTER **XVI**

IS BUSHIDO
STILL ALIVE?

H AS Western civilisation, in its march through our
land, already wiped out every trace of its ancient
discipline?

It were a sad thing if a nation's soul could die so fast.
That were a poor soul that could succumb so easily to
extraneous influences.

The aggregate of psychological elements which constitute a national character is as tenacious as the "irreducible
elements of species, of the fins of the fish, of the beak of
the bird, of the tooth of the carnivorous animal." In his
recent book, full of shallow asseverations and brilliant
generalisations, M. LeBon[1] says: "The discoveries due to
the intelligence are the common patrimony of humanity;

---

[1] *The Psychology of Peoples*, p. 33.

水で洗われなければ、外面の荒さを削りとることはできない」
と言っている。これは強固な言い方である。しかし、それぞれ
れの国民が「専有する遺産を構成する」性格の短所長所とい
うものがあるとするならば、一考に値するだろう。この種の
図式化された学説は、ル・ボンがその著書を書き始めるはる
か以前から提出されており、しかもだいぶ前にテオドール・
ワイツやヒュー・マレーなどによって論破されている。武士
道が徐々に教えてきたさまざまな徳目を研究するにあたっ
て、われわれはヨーロッパの事例から比較の対象とその例証
を探したが、その性格のどの一つの性質をとってみても、そ
れが武士道のみの「専有」遺産でないことを見てきた。道徳
性が集合すると、まったく独自の様相を呈することはたしか
である。エマーソンが「あらゆるすぐれた力が分子となって
集合した、複合的結果である」と名づけたのは、この集合で
ある。しかし、コンコルドの哲学者（エマーソン）は、ル・ボ
ンのように、これを一民族あるいは一国民の専有遺産とはせ
ず、「それぞれの国の最も有力な人物を結びつけ、お互いに
理解し合い、同感せしめ、それはフリーメイソンのような秘
密結社の符号を用いなくとも、即座に感得できるほど明確な
要素である」としている。

　武士道が、わが国民、とくに武士に刻みつけた性格は「そ
の種族にとって欠かせない要素」を形成しているとは言えな
いが、その活力をもっていることは疑いない。仮に武士道が、
たんなる物理的な力に過ぎなかったとしても、過去700年の
間に蓄積されたエネルギーは、急に停止させようと思っても
できるものではない。また、武士道がたんに遺伝のみによっ

qualities or defects of character constitute the exclusive patrimony of each people: they are the firm rock which the waters must wash day by day for centuries, before they can wear away even its external asperities." These are strong words and would be highly worth pondering over, provided there were qualities and defects of character which *constitute the exclusive patrimony* of each people. Schematising theories of this sort had been advanced long before Le Bon began to write his book, and they were exploded long ago by Theodor Waitz and Hugh Murray. In studying the various virtues instilled by Bushido, we have drawn upon European sources for comparison and illustrations, and we have seen that no one quality of character was its *exclusive* patrimony. It is true the aggregate of moral qualities presents a quite unique aspect. It is this aggregate which Emerson names a "compound result into which every great force enters as an ingredient." But, instead of making it, as LeBon does, an exclusive patrimony of a race or people, the Concord philosopher calls it "an element which unites the most forcible persons of every country; makes them intelligible and agreeable to each other; and is somewhat so precise that it is at once felt if an individual lack the Masonic sign."

The character which Bushido stamped on our nation and on the samurai in particular, cannot be said to form "an irreducible element of species," but nevertheless as to the vitality which it retains there is no doubt. Were Bushido a mere physical force, the momentum it has gained in the last seven hundred years could not stop so

て継承されてきたとしても、その影響は広大な範囲に及んでいるに違いない。フランスの経済学者シェイソン氏の計算したところによると、1世紀に3世代の交替があると仮定すれば、「それぞれの人間の血管の中には、少なくとも西暦1千年の間に生存した2千万人の血液が流れている」という。「世紀の重荷に腰をかがめて」土を耕している貧しい農民も、その血管の中には、幾時代もの血液が流れており、彼らは「牛」と兄弟であるだけでなく、われわれとも兄弟なのである。

武士道は、無意識的な、かつ抵抗しがたい力として、われわれ国民やそれぞれの個人を動かしてきた。新生日本の最も輝かしい先駆者の一人である吉田松陰が、刑に処せられる前夜に詠んだ歌は、日本民族の偽らざる告白であった。

かくすればかくなるものと知りながら
やむにやまれぬ大和魂

武士道は、形式こそ備えてはいなかったが、わが国の活動精神であったし、また推進力でもあった。そして現在でもそうである。

（アメリカの詩人）ランサム氏は、「今、三つの別々の日本が、相並んで存在している。旧日本はいまだ全く死滅せず、新日本は、その精神においてようやく誕生したにすぎず、過渡的日本は、現在最も危機的な試練を経験している」と言ったが、この説は多くの点、とくにわが国の具体的な諸制度に関して言えば、たしかに適切だと言える。が、これを根本的な道徳観念に応用するときは、多少の修正を加えなければならない。

abruptly. Were it transmitted only by heredity, its influence must be immensely widespread. Just think, as M. Cheysson, a French economist, has calculated, that, supposing there be three generations in a century, "each of us would have in his veins the blood of at least twenty millions of the people living in the year 1000 A.D." The merest peasant that grubs the soil, "bowed by the weight of centuries," has in his veins the blood of ages, and is thus brother to us as much as "to the ox."

An unconscious and irresistible power, Bushido has been moving the nation and individuals. It was an honest confession of the race when Yoshida Shôin, one of the most brilliant pioneers of Modern Japan, wrote on the eve of his execution the following stanza:

"Full well I knew this course must end in death;
It was Yamato spirit urged me on
To dare whate'er betide."

Unformulated, Bushido was and still is the animating spirit, the motor force of our country.

Mr. Ransome says that "there are three distinct Japans in existence side by side today,—the old, which has not wholly died out; the new, hardly yet born except in spirit; and the transition, passing now through its most critical throes." While this is very true in most respects, and particularly as regards tangible and concrete institutions, the statement, as applied to fundamental ethical notions,

なぜならば、旧日本の建設者であり、また、そこから生み出された武士道は、今でもなお過渡期的日本を指導する原理であり、さらに新時代の日本を形成してゆく力があるからである。

王政復古の暴風雨の真只中（まっただなか）を、わが国の舵取り（かじ）をしてきた偉大な指導者たちは、武士道以外に道徳的な教訓を知らない人たちであった。

最近二、三の外国人著者[注2]が、新生日本の建設にあたって、キリスト教の宣教師がいかに、多大な貢献をしてきたか、ということを証明しようと試みた。私はもとより、名誉あるところには喜んで名誉を与えようと思う。しかし、このような名誉は、これら善良なる宣教師たちにはまだまだ与えがたい。彼らがなんら裏打ちされた証拠もない要求をもち出すよりも、「お互いに、名誉は他に帰すべきである」という聖書の教訓を守ることこそ、彼ら宣教師たちの職務に似つかわしい。私個人としては、キリスト教の宣教師が、わが国の教育、とくに道徳教育においては、大いに力を尽くしていると信じている。しかし聖霊の活動は確実ではあるが、いまだ神秘的であって、神聖な秘密の中に隠されている。それ故に宣教師の働きはいまだ間接的な影響でしかありえない。つまり、今日までのところ、キリスト教の伝道が新日本の性格を形成する上で貢献した点は、ほとんど見られないといってよい。いや、善かれ悪しかれ、われわれを刺激し動かしてきたものは、純粋で単純な武士道そのものであった。新日本の建設者であった、佐久間象山、西郷隆盛、大久保利通、木戸孝允らの伝記をひもといてみよう。さらに、伊藤博文、大隈重信、板垣退助など現存の人物の回顧談は言うまでもない。彼らの思想お

[注2] スピーア著『アジアにおける伝道と政治』第4講189–192ページ。デンニス著『キリスト教伝道と社会進化』第1巻32ページ、第2巻70ページほか。

requires some modification; for Bushido, the maker and product of Old Japan, is still the guiding principle of the transition and will prove the formative force of the new era.

The great statesmen who steered the ship of our state through the hurricane of the Restoration and the whirlpool of national rejuvenation, were men who knew no other moral teaching than the Precepts of Knighthood. Some writers[2] have lately tried to prove that the Christian missionaries contributed an appreciable quota to the making of New Japan. I would fain render honour to whom honour is due; but this honour can as yet hardly be accorded to the good missionaries. More fitting it will be to their profession to stick to the scriptural injunction of preferring one another in honour, than to advance a claim in which they have no proofs to back them. For myself, I believe that Christian missionaries are doing great things for Japan—in the domain of education, and especially of moral education:—only, the mysterious though not the less certain working of the Spirit is still hidden in divine secrecy. Whatever they do is still of indirect effect. No, as yet Christian missions have effected but little visible in moulding the character of New Japan. No, it was Bushido, pure and simple, that urged us on for weal or woe. Open the biographies of the makers of Modern Japan—of Sakuma, of Saigo, of Okubo, of Kido not to mention the reminiscences of living men such as Ito,

---

[2] Speer: *Missions and Politics in Asia*, Lecture IV, pp. 189–192; Dennis: *Christian Missions and Social Progress*, vol. I, p. 32, vol. II, 70, etc.

よび行動は、武士道の刺激の下に養われたことを知るであろう。

　極東の研究家である、ヘンリー・ノーマン氏は、日本が他の東洋専制国と異なる唯一の点は「人類がこれまで案出した名誉の掟の中で、最も厳格で、最も高く、最も正確なるものが、国民の間に支配的な勢力をもっていたこと」であると言明したが、これは、今日の日本を建設し、将来の日本の運命を達成する原動力に触れた言葉である[注3]。

　日本の変貌は、今や全世界にあまねく知られている事実である。このような大事業を成すに当たっては、おのずからさまざまな動力が入りこんだが、もしその主なる力を挙げよと言われたら、誰も武士道を挙げることにためらいはしないだろう。わが国が海外諸国との通商を開き、生活の各方面を刷新し、西洋の政治や科学を学びはじめたとき、われわれの指導的な原動力となったものは、物質的な資源の開発や、富の増加などではなく、まして西洋の習俗やその模倣でもなかった。

　東洋の制度やその民族をくわしく観察したタウンゼンド氏は、

　　「われわれはいつも、ヨーロッパがいかに日本に影響を及ぼしたかということを聞かされて、この島国の変化は、まったく自発的であったことを忘れている。ヨーロッパが日本に教えたのではなくて、日本は自分からヨーロッパの文武の制度を学び、大きな成功をおさめてきたのである。数年前、トルコがヨーロッパから大砲を輸入したように、日本は

[注3] ヘンリー・ノーマン著『極東』375ページ。

Okuma, Itagaki, etc.,—and you will find that it was under the impetus of samuraihood that they thought and wrought. When Mr. Henry Norman declared, after his study and observation of the Far East, that the only respect in which Japan differed from other oriental despotisms lay in "the ruling influence among her people of the strictest, loftiest, and the most punctilious codes of honour that man has ever devised," he touched the main-spring which has made New Japan what she is, and which will make her what she is destined to be.[3]

The transformation of Japan is a fact patent to the whole world. Into a work of such magnitude various motives naturally entered; but if one were to name the principal, one would not hesitate to name Bushido. When we opened the whole country to foreign trade, when we introduced the latest improvements in every department of life, when we began to study Western politics and sciences, our guiding motive was not the development of our physical resources and the increase of wealth; much less was it a blind imitation of Western customs.

A close observer of oriental institutions and peoples has written:

> "We are told every day how Europe has influenced Japan, and forget that the change in those islands was entirely self-generated, that Europeans did not teach Japan, but that Japan of herself chose to learn from Europe methods of organisation, civil and military, which have so far proved successful. She imported European mechanical science, as the Turks years before

---

[3] *The Far East*, p. 375.

ヨーロッパの機械科学を輸入した。しかし、それは正確に言えば影響ではない。イギリスが中国からお茶を輸入することによって中国の影響を受けたとは言えないからである」と言っており、さらにまた次のように述べている。
　「日本を改造したヨーロッパの使徒や、哲学者や、政治家や、もしくは扇動者が、どこにいったのか」と[注4]。

　タウンゼンド氏が、日本に変化をもたらした原動力は、すべてわれわれ日本人自身の中にあったことを認識したのは、たしかに卓見である。そしてもし、彼がさらに詳しく日本人の心理を観察したならば、氏の鋭い観察力は、その原動力が武士道にほかならなかったことを容易に確認することができたであろう。要するにわれわれ日本人が、外国から劣等民族であると見下されることに耐えることができない名誉心──これが最大の動機だったのである。わが国の産業を振興しようとする考えは、国家変革の過程において、次第に自覚されてきた問題だったのである。
　武士道の影響が、今日でもなお明らかに残っていることは、すぐにもわかる。日本人の生活の一端を見ただけでも明白であろう。さらに、日本人の心を最も雄弁にかつ忠実に代弁した、ラフカディオ・ハーン（小泉八雲）の著書を読めば、彼の描く日本人の心の働きが、武士道の働きの一例であることがよくわかるだろう。国民が一般的に礼儀正しいのも、武士道の遺産であるが、これは改めて取りあげるまでもなく、周知の事実であろう。「小さな日本人」が持っている、肉体的な耐久力、我慢強さ、勇気は、日清戦争において十分に証明された[注5]。「日本人以上に忠君愛国の国民がほかにいるだろう

<hr>

[注4] メレディス・タウンゼンド著『アジアとヨーロッパ』28ページ。
[注5] この問題に関してはイーストレイク・山田共著『英雄的日本』、およびダイオシー著『新極東』を勧める。

imported European artillery. That is not exactly influence," continues Mr. Townsend, "unless, indeed, England is influenced by purchasing tea in China. Where is the European apostle," asks our author, "or philosopher or states man or agitator, who has re-made Japan?"[4]

Mr. Townsend has well perceived that the spring of action which brought about the changes in Japan lay entirely within our own selves; and if he had only probed into our psychology, his keen powers of observation would easily have convinced him that this spring was no other than Bushido. The sense of honour which cannot bear being looked down upon as an inferior power,—that was the strongest of motives. Pecuniary or industrial considerations were awakened later in the process of transformation.

The influence of Bushido is still so palpable that he who runs may read. A glimpse into Japanese life will make it manifest. Read Hearn, the most eloquent and truthful interpreter of the Japanese mind, and you see the working of that mind to be an example of the working of Bushido. The universal politeness of the people, which is the legacy of knightly ways, is too well known to be repeated anew. The physical endurance, fortitude, and bravery that "the little Jap" possesses, were sufficiently proved in the Chino-Japanese war.[5] "Is there any nation more loyal and

---

[4] Meredith Townsend, *Asia and Europe*, p. 28.

[5] Among other works on the subject, read Eastlake and Yamada on *Heroic Japan*, and Diosy on *The New Far East*.

か？」と多くの人が問い、その誇り高い答として、「否」と言うことができるわれわれは、武士道に感謝しなくてはならないだろう。

しかし公平を期するために、日本人の性格の欠点や短所もまた、武士道が大いに責任があるということも、認めなければならない。わが国民が、深遠な哲学に欠ける原因は――つまりわが国の青年が、科学の研究においてはすでに世界的な名声を博しているにもかかわらず、哲学の領域においてはなんらの貢献をもしていない原因は――それは武士道の教育制度において、形而上の学問の訓練をおろそかにしてきた故である。わが国民が、感情に激しやすい性格をもっているのは、われわれの名誉心に責任がある。外国人がしばしばわれわれを非難するように「自負尊大」が、もしわが国民の性格であるとすれば、それは名誉心の病的な行きすぎにほかならない。

海外から日本を訪れた人は、乱れた髪で、まことに粗末な衣服を着て、手に大きな杖か本を持ち、世俗のことにはまったく無関心な様子で、大道を闊歩する若者を何人も見かけたことがあるだろう。これは「書生」（学生）であり、彼にとっては地球はあまりにも小さく、天もまた十分に高くはない。彼には独自の宇宙論と人生論がある。そして、空中を漂う楼閣に住み、天上の知恵の言葉を常食として生きており、目は野心の光に輝き、精神は知識に飢えている。赤貧は彼を前進させる刺激にすぎず、世俗的な財産は彼の目には品性を束縛するものだと映る。彼は忠君愛国の権化であり、国家の名誉の番人を自認する。このような彼らの長所と短所のすべてもまた、武士道の最後の断片であろう。

patriotic?" is a question asked by many; and for the proud answer, "There is not," we must thank the Precepts of Knighthood.

On the other hand, it is fair to recognise that for the very faults and defects of our character, Bushido is largely responsible. Our lack of abstruse philosophy—while some of our young men have already gained international reputation in scientific researches, not one has achieved anything in philosophical lines—is traceable to the neglect of metaphysical training under Bushido's regimen of education. Our sense of honour is responsible for our exaggerated sensitiveness and touchiness; and if there is the conceit in us with which some foreigners charge us, that, too, is a pathological outcome of honour.

Have you seen in your tour of Japan many a young man with unkempt hair, dressed in shabbiest garb, carrying in his hand a large cane or a book, stalking about the streets with an air of utter indifference to mundane things? He is the *shoséi* (student), to whom the earth is too small and the heavens are not high enough. He has his own theories of the universe and of life. He dwells in castles of air and feeds on ethereal words of wisdom. In his eyes beams the fire of ambition; his mind is athirst for knowledge. Penury is only a stimulus to drive him onward; worldly goods are in his sight shackles to his character. He is the repository of loyalty and patriotism. He is the self-imposed guardian of national honour. With all his virtues and his faults, he is the last fragment of Bushido.

　武士道の影響が、今日でもなお深く強く根ざしているのは、すでに私が述べたように、無意識的かつ暗黙の影響である。わが国民の心情は、継承してきた観念に訴えられると、その理由の何であるかにかかわらず、ただちに反応するであろう。それ故に、外国と日本と、たとえ同一の道徳観念があったとしても、新しい訳語によって表現された場合と、旧い武士道の用語によって表現された場合には、その効力には大きな差異があるのである。信仰の道から遠ざかったキリスト者がいて、牧師のどんな忠告でも彼を堕落へ向かうことから救うことができなかった。しかし彼がかつて主君に誓った誠実、すなわち忠義に訴えられると、彼は信仰に復帰せざるを得なかった。「忠義」の一語が、なまぬるく、あいまいな状態にさせられていた彼の高貴な感情を復活させたのである。あるカレッジでは、ある教授に対する不満を理由に、乱暴な青年の一団が長くストライキを行っていたが、校長が出した二つの簡単な質問によって解散した。それは、「諸君の批判する教授は、価値ある人物であるか。もしそうならば、諸君は彼を尊敬して学校に留まらせるべきである。彼は弱い人物であるか。もしそうであるならば、倒れた人間を押し倒すのは男らしくないのではないか」と問うたのであった。その教授の学力不足が、騒動の始まりであったのだが、それは校長が示した道徳的な問題に比べれば、重要な問題ではなくなってしまったのである。このように、武士道によって培われた感情を刺激することによって、偉大な道徳的革新を成就することができたのである。

　わが国におけるキリスト教の伝道事業の失敗の一原因は、宣教師の大半が、わが国の歴史についてまったく無知なことである。ある者は言う、「異教徒の歴史的記録など、なんの役に立つのか」と。その結果、彼らの宗教を、われわれとわ

Deep-rooted and powerful as is still the effect of Bushido, I have said that it is an unconscious and mute influence. The heart of the people responds, without knowing a reason why, to any appeal made to what it has inherited, and hence the same moral idea expressed in a newly translated term and in an old Bushido term, has a vastly different degree of efficacy. A backsliding Christian, whom no pastoral persuasion could help from downward tendency, was reverted from his course by an appeal made to his loyalty, the fidelity he once swore to his Master. The word "Loyalty" revived all the noble sentiments that were permitted to grow lukewarm. A party of unruly youths engaged in a long continued "students' strike" in a college, on account of their dissatisfaction with a certain teacher, disbanded at two simple questions put by the Director,—"Is your professor a worthy character? If so, you ought to respect him and keep him in the school. Is he weak? If so, it is not manly to push a falling man." The scientific incapacity of the professor, which was the beginning of the trouble, dwindled into insignificance in comparison with the moral issues hinted at. By arousing the sentiments nurtured by Bushido, moral renovation of great magnitude can be accomplished.

One cause of the failure of mission work is that most of the missionaries are entirely ignorant of our history—"What do we care for heathen records?" some say—and consequently estrange their religion from the habits of

れわれの祖先が、数百年の長い間継承してきた思索の習慣から切り離してしまうのである。なんと、一国民の歴史を嘲笑するとは！——いかなる民族の経歴でも、なんら記録したものをもっていないアフリカの先住民の経歴でさえも、神自らの手によって記述された人類の歴史の一ページをなしているのではなかったのか。この世から滅亡した種族でさえも、具眼の士によって解読されるべき古文書である。敬虔な哲学的な心には、人種自体が、神の書きたまいし記号であって、その皮膚の色を、あるいは白くあるいは黒く、それぞれに明記されたものであるという。——この比喩にしたがって言えば、黄色人種は金色の象形文字をもって記された貴重な一ページではないのか。彼ら宣教師たちは、一国民の過去の歴史を無視して、キリスト教は新宗教であると宣言する。しかし私の考えでは、それは「むかしむかしの物語」であって、もしキリスト教を伝道しようとするならば、理解しやすい言葉、つまりそれぞれの国の人々の道徳的発達にふさわしい言葉で表現したならば、人類や民族の如何にかかわらず、それらの人びとの心の中に深く宿ることができるであろう。アメリカ的あるいはイギリス的形式をもっているキリスト教——すなわちキリストの恩寵と純粋とは裏腹に、アングロ・サクソン的性癖と妄想を含んでいるキリスト教——は、武士道の幹に接木をするには、きわめて貧弱な芽にすぎない。彼ら新宗教の教師たちは、幹、根、枝などを根こそぎにして、福音の種子を荒れ果てた土地に播くようなことをするべきであろうか。そのような英雄的な方法は、ハワイでは可能かもしれない。そこでは戦闘的教会が、富の搾取と先住民の種族の絶滅とに、完全な成功をおさめたといわれている。しかし、このような方法は、日本においては断じて不可能である。いや、それはキリスト自身が、この地上に彼の王国を建設しようとするとき

thought we and our forefathers have been accustomed to for centuries past. Mocking a nation's history?—as though the career of any people—even of the lowest African savages possessing no record—were not a page in the general history of mankind, written by the hand of God Himself. The very lost races are a palimpsest to be deciphered by a seeing eye. To a philosophic and pious mind the races themselves are marks of Divine chirography clearly traced in black and white as on their skin; and if this simile holds good, the yellow race forms a precious page inscribed in hieroglyphics of gold! Ignoring the past career of a people, missionaries claim that Christianity is a new religion, whereas, to my mind, it is an "old, old story," which, if presented in intelligible words,—that is to say, if expressed in the vocabulary familiar in the moral development of a people,—will find easy lodgment in their hearts, irrespective of race or nationality. Christianity in its American or English form—with more of Anglo-Saxon freaks and fancies than grace and purity of its Founder—is a poor scion to graft on Bushido stock. Should the propagator of the new faith uproot the entire stock, root, and branches, and plant the seeds of the Gospel on the ravaged soil? Such a heroic process may be possible—in Hawaii, where, it is alleged, the Church militant had complete success in amassing spoils of wealth itself, and in annihilating the aboriginal race; such a process is most decidedly impossible in Japan—nay, it is a process which Jesus Himself would never have adopted in founding His kingdom on earth.

に、決して採用しなかったであろう方法である。

　私はここで、聖徒であり、敬虔なるキリスト教徒で、かつ
深遠な学者（であるジョエット）の述べた、次のような言葉
をあげておこう。

　　　「人はこの世界を、異教徒とキリスト教徒に分けた。そし
　　　て前者にどれほどの善が隠され、後者にどれほど悪が混じ
　　　っているかを、十分に考えもしなかった。彼らは自分の最
　　　善なるものをあげて、隣人の最悪なるものと較べて、キリ
　　　スト教の理想を、ギリシャもしくは東洋の堕落と比較する。
　　　彼らは公平であろうとはしなかった。かえって自己の宗教
　　　の美点といわれているもののみをとり集めて、他の宗教の
　　　形式を大いにけなすために用い、それでもって満足してい
　　　る」と[注6]。

　しかしながら、個人的にはいろんな誤りを犯したにせよ、
彼ら宣教師たちの信ずる宗教の根本的な原理は、われわれが
武士道の将来を考える上に、必ず研究しなければならない一
大勢力であることには疑いない。武士道の時代はすでに残り
少ない。その将来を示す不吉な徴候も見られる。いや、徴候
ばかりでなく、多くの強大な勢力が働いて、これをおびやか
しつつあるのである。

[注6] ジョエット著『信仰と教義についての説教集』第2章。

It behooves us to take more to heart the following words of a saintly man, devout Christian, and profound scholar:

> "Men have divided the world into heathen and Christian, without considering how much good may have been hidden in the one or how much evil may have been mingled with the other. They have compared the best part of themselves with the worst of their neighbours, the ideal of Christianity with the corruption of Greece or of the East. They have not aimed at impartiality, but have been contented to accumulate all that could be said in praise of their own, and in disprais of other forms of religion."[6]

But, whatever may be the error committed by individuals, there is little doubt that the fundamental principle of the religion they profess is a power which we must take into account in reckoning the future of Bushido, whose days seem to be already numbered. Ominous signs are in the air that betoken its future. Not only signs, but redoubtable forces are at work to threaten it.

---

[6] Jowett, *Sermons on Faith and Doctrine*, II.

武士道の将来

ヨーロッパの騎士道と、日本の武士道の歴史を比較してみたとき、これほどよく似ているものはまれである。もし歴史が繰り返すものだとすれば、武士道の運命は、必ず騎士道がたどってきた運命を繰り返すであろう。サン・パレーの挙げる、騎士道が衰退した特殊な、かつ地方的原因は、もちろん日本の状態には当てはまらない。しかし、中世紀以後における騎士および騎士道を覆すことになった主なる原因も、また一般的なさまざまな原因も、今や武士道の衰退の原因として、たしかに働きつつある。

ヨーロッパと日本との、歴史的な経験において、最も顕著な差異と見られるのは、ヨーロッパにおいては、騎士道は封建制度のふところから離れ、キリスト教によって養い育てられ、新しい生命を得たことである。これに反して、日本の武

CHAPTER **XVII**

THE FUTURE OF BUSHIDO

FEW historical comparisons can be more judiciously made than between the Chivalry of Europe and the Bushido of Japan, and, if history repeats itself, it certainly will do with the fate of the latter what it did with that of the former. The particular and local causes for the decay of chivalry which St. Palaye gives, have, of course, little application to Japanese conditions; but the larger and more general causes that helped to undermine knighthood and chivalry in and after the Middle Ages are as surely working for the decline of Bushido.

One remarkable difference between the experience of Europe and of Japan is, that whereas in Europe, when chivalry was weaned from feudalism and was adopted by the Church, it obtained a fresh lease of life, in Japan no

士道には、これを養育するほどの大宗教がなかったことであった。したがって、その生みの親である封建制度が崩れ去ると、武士道は孤児として取り残され、やむを得ず自立して生きてゆかねばならなかったのである。現在のよく整備された軍事組織は、武士道をその保護下に置くかもしれないが、現代の戦争は武士道が成長しつづけていく余地をほとんど与えないことは、よく知られている。武士道を、その幼児のころから養育してきた神道は、それ自体すでに老い、中国古代の聖賢の教えはしりぞけられて、ベンサムやミルのタイプの知的成り上り者にとって代わられた。時代の好戦的、排他傾向に迎合し、それゆえに、今日の要求によく適合すると考えられた快楽主義的な傾向の道徳論が発明され、提供された。しかし今日なお、それらの騒々しい声は通俗的なジャーナリズムのコラムによって聞かされているにすぎない。

　さまざまな勢力や権力が、一緒になって武士道に対抗している。ヴェブレンが言うように、すでに「本来の労働者階級の間における儀礼的規律の衰退、言い換えれば生活の通俗化は、鋭敏な感受性をもつすべての人々の目からみれば、当世の文明の重大な誤りの一つとして映った」。目ざましく抵抗しがたい民主主義の潮流は、いかなる形式あるいは形態の、独立した結合の精神をも許さなかった。武士道が本来もっているものは、知性と文化を充分にたくわえた権力を独占する人々によって組織された、道徳的な性質の等級とその価値を定める、独立した結合の精神であった。それゆえに、民主主義の潮流によってだけでも、生き残った武士道を呑み込むのに十分な力があった。現代の社会勢力は、狭量な階級精神を容認しない。しかし、騎士道は、フリーマンが鋭く批評するように、明らかに一つの階級精神であった。現代社会は、その統一を計るなんらかの旗じるしを掲げている限り、「特権

religion was large enough to nourish it; hence, when the mother institution, feudalism, was gone, Bushido, left an orphan, had to shift for itself. The present elaborate military organisation might take it under its patronage, but we know that modern warfare can afford little room for its continuous growth. Shintoism, which fostered it in its infancy, is itself superannuated. The hoary sages of ancient China are being supplanted by the intellectual parvenu of the type of Bentham and Mill. Moral theories of a comfortable kind, flattering to the Chauvinistic tendencies of the time, and therefore thought well adapted to the need of this day, have been invented and propounded; but as yet we hear only their shrill voices echoing through the columns of yellow journalism.

Principalities and powers are arrayed against the Precepts of Knighthood. Already, as Veblen says, "the decay of the ceremonial code—or, as it is otherwise called, the vulgarisation of life—among the industrial classes proper, has become one of the chief enormities of latter-day civilisation in the eyes of all persons of delicate sensibilities." The irresistible tide of triumphant democracy, which can tolerate no form or shape of trust,—and Bushido was a trust organised by those who monopolised reserve capital of intellect and culture, fixing the grades and value of moral qualities,—is alone powerful enough to engulf the remnant of Bushido. The present societary forces are antagonistic to petty class spirit, and chivalry is, as Freeman severely criticises, a class spirit. Modern society, if it pretends to any unity, cannot admit "purely personal

階級の利益のために工夫された純粋な個人的な義務注1」を容認することはできない。それに加えて普通教育の普及や、産業技術の発達、それによってもたらされる富や都市生活の発達などが、それらの特権階級を衰微させていった。今や、武士の鋭い刀の切れ味も、最強の弓から放たれた鋭い矢も、なんの役にも立たないことは火を見るよりも明らかである。名誉の巌の上に建てられ、名誉によって守られてきた国家は、──これを名誉国家、あるいはカーライル流に英雄国家と呼ぶべきか──今は屁理屈の武器でもって武装した三百代言の法律家や、饒舌の政治家の手に落ちようとしている。一人の大思想家（古代ギリシャの悲劇詩人ソフォクレス）は、テレーサとアンチゴーネ訳注16について「彼女の熱烈な行為を生み出した環境は、もはや永久に去ってしまった」と述べているが、その言葉は、まさにわが国の武士についてもいえるであろう。

　悲しいかな、武士の道徳！　悲しいかな武士の誇り！　かつては、鉦や太鼓の響きと共に大声をもってこの世に迎え入れられた道徳は、（ソフォクレスが）「将軍も去り、王者も去りぬ」（と歌った）ように、今や消え去らんとする運命にある。

　歴史が、もしわれわれに何ものかを教えることができるとすれば、武徳の上に建設された国家は、たとえスパルタのような都市国家であれ、ローマのような大帝国であれ、この地上に「永遠の都」を保持することはできないということである。人間の中にある闘争本能は、自然であってかつ普遍性をもっており、それが高尚な感性や男らしい徳性を生むものであるとしても、それだけでは完全なる人格を形成することはできない。闘争の本能のかげには、より神聖な本能がひそんでいる。それは愛である。神道や、孟子、および王陽明は、明らかにそのことを教えてきたことは、前に述べた通りであ

注1 フリーマン著『ノーマン征服』第5巻482ページ。

obligations devised in the interests of an exclusive class."[1]
Add to this the progress of popular instruction, of industrial arts and habits, of wealth and city life,—then we can
easily see that neither the keenest cuts of samurai sword
nor the sharpest shafts shot from Bushido's boldest bows
can aught avail. The state built upon the rock of Honour
and fortified by the same—shall we call it the *Ehrenstaat*,
or, after the manner of Carlyle, the Heroarchy?—is fast
failing into the hands of quibbling lawyers and gibbering
politicians armed with logic-chopping engines of war.
The words which a great thinker used in speaking of
Theresa and Antigone may aptly be repeated of the samurai, that "the medium in which their ardent deeds took
shape is forever gone."

Alas for knightly virtues! alas for samurai pride!
Morality ushered into the world with the sound of bugles
and drums, is destined to fade away as "the captains and
the kings depart."

If history can teach us anything, the state built on
martial virtues—be it a city like Sparta or an Empire like
Rome—can never make on earth a "continuing city." Universal and natural as is the fighting instinct in man, fruit-
ful as it has proved to be of noble sentiments and manly
virtues, it does not comprehend the whole man. Beneath
the instinct to fight there lurks a diviner instinct—to love.
We have seen that Shintoism, Mencius, and Wan Yang
Ming, have all clearly taught it; but Bushido and all other
militant types of ethics, engrossed doubtless, with questions

---

[1] *Norman Conquest*, vol. V, p. 482.

る。だが、武士道やその他のすべての武士的な道徳は、目の前の実際的な問題にのみ取り組まざるを得なかった。そのため、しばしばこの愛するという本能を正当に強調することを忘れてきたのである。近年は人間の生活の幅が大きく拡がってきた。今日、われわれが必要とするものは、武士の使命よりもさらに高く、さらに広い使命である。広い意識をもつ人生観、民主主義の成長、他の国民や他の国家に対する知識の増大と共に、孔子の仁の思想や仏教の慈悲の思想は、キリスト教のいう愛の観念へと拡がってゆくであろう。すなわち、人は臣民以上のものとなり市民の地位にまで達し、いやそれだけに止まらず、つまりは人間そのものになるのである。たとえわが地平線上に、戦雲が暗く覆うようなことがあっても、私は平和の天使の翼が、これを払い去るであろうことを信じている。世界の歴史は、「柔和なる者はこの地を嗣ぐであろう」という予言を確信する。生まれたときからもっている平和の権利を売り渡して、産業主義の前線から後退し、侵略主義の戦線へと移行してゆく国民は、まったく仕様がない取引をするものではないか！

　社会の状況が大きく変化して、武士道に反対するだけでなく、それに敵対するようにさえなった今日、その名誉ある葬送の準備をしなければならない時である。武士道が死滅した時を知ることは、その生まれた時を明らかにするのと同じように難しい。ミラー博士は、次のように言っている。「騎士道は、1559年に、フランスのアンリ2世が、武芸試合で殺された時をもって、公に廃止された」と。わが国においては、1870年（明治3年）廃藩置県が公布されたことは、まさに武士道の弔いの鐘を知らせる信号であった。それから5年後の廃刀令の公布は「なんの代償もなくて手に入れた人生の恩典、男子らしい情操と英雄的な行動の保護者」であった旧時代を

of immediate practical need, too often forgot duly to emphasise this fact. Life has grown larger in these latter times. Callings nobler and broader than a warrior's claim our attention to-day. With an enlarged view of life, with the growth of democracy, with better knowledge of other peoples and nations, the Confucian idea of benevolence—dare I also add the Buddhist idea of pity?—will expand into the Christian conception of love. Men have become more than subjects, having grown to the estate of citizens; nay, they are more than citizens—being men. Though war clouds hang heavy upon our horizon, we will believe that the wings of the angel of peace can disperse them. The history of the world confirms the prophecy that "the meek shall inherit the earth." A nation that sells its birthright of peace, and backslides from the front rank of industrialism into the file of fillibusterism, makes a poor bargain indeed!

When the conditions of society are so changed that they have become not only adverse but hostile to Bushido, it is time for it to prepare for an honourable burial. It is just as difficult to point out when chivalry dies, as to determine the exact time of its inception. Dr. Miller says that chivalry was formally abolished in the year 1559, when Henry II. of France was slain in a tournament. With us, the edict formally abolishing feudalism in 1870 was the signal to toll the knell of Bushido. The edict, issued five years later, prohibiting the wearing of swords, rang out the old, "the unbought grace of life, the cheap defence

高らかに送って、「詭弁家、経済家、勘定屋」の新時代を鳴りもの入りで迎えた。

　日本が先の中国との戦争（日清戦争）に勝ったのは、村田銃とクルップ砲によってであると言われている。また、この勝利は近代的な学校制度の教育による成果であるとも言われている。しかし、これらは真実の半分をも満たしていない。たとえば、エールバーやスタインウエイの最高の職人の技術で作られたピアノでも、名演奏家の手がなくては、リストのラプソディやベートーヴェンのソナタが、見事に鳴り響くものだろうか。あるいは、もし銃が戦争の勝利をもたらすなら、なゼルイ・ナポレオンはミトライユーズ式機関銃でプロシア軍を撃破しなかったのか。また、スペイン人はモーゼル銃でもって、旧式のレミントン銃で武装したにすぎないフィリピン人を破れなかったのか。言い古された言葉を繰り返すまでもないが、活力を与えるのは精神であり、それなしでは最高の道具もなんら利点とはならないのである。最新の銃でも、使い手がいなければ発射できず、最も近代的な教育制度も臆病者を英雄にすることはできない。いや、鴨緑江において、また朝鮮および満州において戦争に勝ったのは、われわれを導き、われわれの心に生きている父祖の威霊であった。これらの、武勇に富んだ私たちの先祖の霊魂は、死に絶えてはいない。見る目がある人たちには、彼らがはっきりと見える。最も進んだ思想を持つ日本人であっても、一皮むけばそこにサムライが現れる。名誉と勇気、そしてすべての武徳の偉大な遺産は、クラム教授がまさに適切に表現したように、それは「われわれが預かっている遺産にすぎず、今は亡き先祖とわれわれの子孫のもので、誰にも奪うことはできない永遠の遺産」である。したがって、現在われわれに課せられた使命は、こ

of nations, the nurse of manly sentiment and heroic enterprise," it rang in the new age of "sophisters, economists, and calculators."

It has been said that Japan won her late war with China by means of Murata guns and Krupp cannon; it has been said the victory was the work of a modern school-system; but these are less than half-truths. Does ever a piano, be it of the choicest workmanship of Ehrbar or Steinway burst forth into the Rhapsodies of Liszt or the Sonatas of Beethoven, without a master's hand? Or, if guns win battles, why did not Louis Napoleon beat the Prussians with his *Mitrailleuse,* or the Spaniards with their Mausers the Filipinos, whose arms were no better than the old-fashioned Remingtons? Needless to repeat what has grown a trite saying,—that it is the spirit that quickeneth, without which the best of implements profiteth but little. The most improved guns and cannon do not shoot of their own accord; the most modern educational system does not make a coward a hero. No! What won the battles on the Yalu, in Corea and Manchuria, were the ghosts of our fathers, guiding our hands and beating in our hearts. They are not dead, those ghosts, the spirits of our warlike ancestors. To those who have eyes to see, they are clearly visible. Scratch a Japanese of the most advanced ideas, and he will show a samurai. The great inheritance of honour, of valour, and of all martial virtues is, as Professor Cramb very fitly expresses it, "but ours on trust, the fief inalienable of the dead and of the generations to come," and the summons of the present is to

の遺産を守り、古来の精神を少しもそこなわないことであり、そして未来に課せられた使命は、古来の精神の範囲を大きく拡げてゆき、人生のすべての行動とそれらとのいろんな関係に応用してゆくことである。

　封建日本の道徳体系は、その城壁や武器と同じように崩れ去り、灰となってしまった。しかし、新しい日本の進路を照らす新しい道徳は、その灰の中から不死鳥のように生まれ出るであろうと予言され、この予言は過去半世紀におきた出来事によって確認された。このような予言の成就は望ましく、また可能であろうと信じている。しかし、不死鳥は自分で灰の中から生まれ飛び立つのであって、それは渡り鳥でもなければ、他の鳥の翼を借りて飛ぶのでもない、ということを忘れてはならない。「神の国は汝らの中にあり」という。神の国は、その山がいくら高くても、ひとりでにそこから降りてくるものでもなく、その海がいくら広くても、ひとりでにそれを渡ってくるものでもない。（イスラム教の聖典）『コーラン』では「神はそれぞれの国民に、その国の言葉をもって語る予言者をさずけている」と、言っている。日本人の心にそのあかしをたて、理解されてきた神の国の種子は、武士道の中にその花を咲かせた。しかし、悲しいことに、その実が充分に成熟する日を待たないで、今や武士道の時代は終わろうとしている。われわれは今、あらゆる方向に目を向けて、美と光明、力と慰めの源泉を探し求めている。しかし、いまだ武士道に代わるものを見つけることができないでいる。功利主義者や唯物主義者の損得哲学は、魂を半分失ったような屁理屈屋の好むところとなった。これに対抗できうるだけの強力な道徳体系は、ただキリスト教があるのみであり、これに比べれば武士道は、「わずかに燃え残った灯心」のようである、と告白せざるをえない。その灯心を、救い主はこれを消

guard this heritage, nor to bate one jot of the ancient spirit; the summons of the future will be so to widen its scope as to apply it in all walks and relations of life.

It has been predicted—and predictions have been corroborated by the events of the last half-century—that the moral system of Feudal Japan, like its castles and its armouries, will crumble into dust, and new ethics rise phœnix-like to lead New Japan in her path of progress. Desirable and probable as the fulfilment of such a prophecy is, we must not forget that a phœnix rises only from its own ashes, and that it is not a bird of passage, neither does it fly on pinions borrowed from other birds. "The Kingdom of God is within you." It does not come rolling down the mountains, however lofty; it does not come sailing across the seas, however broad. "God has granted," says the Koran, "to every people a prophet in its own tongue." The seeds of the Kingdom, as vouched for and apprehended by the Japanese mind, blossomed in Bushido. Now its days are closing—sad to say, before its full fruition —and we turn in every direction for other sources of sweetness and light, of strength and comfort, but among them there is as yet nothing found to take its place. The profit-and-loss philosophy of utilitarians and materialists finds favour among logic-choppers with half a soul. The only other ethical system which is powerful enough to cope with utilitarianism and materialism is Christianity, in comparison with which Bushido, it must be confessed, is like "a dimly burning wick" which the Messiah was pro-

さずに、あおいで炎とするように宣言された。キリストの先駆者であるヘブライの予言者たち、とりわけイザヤ、エレミヤ、アモス、ハバラクと同じように、武士道は、支配するものや、公の立場にいる者、ならびに国民の道徳的な行為に重点をおいた。これに反し、キリストの道徳は、ほとんどまったく個人ならびに、信じる者に関するものである。したがって個人主義が道徳の要素として勢力を増していけば、キリスト教の道徳の実際的なその効力も、ますます拡がってゆくであろう。自我中心思想、すなわちニーチェの言う個人道徳は、いくつかの点においては武士道に似ているが、もし私がはなはだしく誤解していないならば、これはニーチェが病的な歪曲によって、ナザレ人の謙虚で自己否定的な奴隷道徳と呼んだものに対する、過渡的な現象あるいは一時的な反動の結果である。

　キリスト教と唯物主義（功利主義を含む）——あるいは将来、ヘブライズムとヘレニズムというさらに古い形式に還元されることになるのだろうか——は、将来世界を二分することであろう。小さな道徳体系は、このいずれかの側に組して、その存続を計るであろう。武士道はいずれの側に組するであろうか。武士道には、必ずそれを守るべきとする教義も形式もないために、その実体はいつかは消え去ってしまうかもしれない。桜の花が、朝風に吹かれて散ってしまうように。しかし、完全な絶滅がその運命であることは決してあり得ない。ストイック主義が滅んでしまったと、誰が言い得ようか。体系としてはたしかに滅んだ。しかし道徳としてはなお生きている。その精力と活力とは、今日でもなお人生のあらゆる方向において——西洋諸国の哲学において、文明世界の法律において——それを知り感ずることができる。それのみならず、人が自らを高めようと奮闘するとき、自分の努力によって霊魂が肉体に勝つとき、（古代ギリシャの哲人）ゼノンの不滅

claimed not to quench, but to fan into a flame. Like His Hebrew precursors, the prophets—notably Isaiah, Jeremiah, Amos, and Habakkuk —Bushido laid particular stress on the moral conduct of rulers and public men and of nations, whereas the ethics of Christ, which deal almost solely with individuals and His personal followers, will find more and more practical application as individualism, in its capacity of a moral factor, grows in potency. The domineering, self-assertive, so-called master-morality of Nietsche, itself akin in some respects to Bushido is, if I am not greatly mistaken, a passing phase or temporary reaction against what he terms, by morbid distortion, the humble, self-denying slave-morality of the Nazarene.

Christianity and materialism (including utilitarianism)—or will the future reduce them to still more archaic forms of Hebraism and Hellenism?—will divide the world between them. Lesser systems of morals will ally themselves to either side for their preservation. On which side will Bushido enlist? Having no set dogma or formula to defend, it can afford to disappear as an entity; like the cherry blossom, it is willing to die at the first gust of the morning breeze. But a total extinction will never be its lot. Who can say that stoicism is dead? It is dead as a system; but it is alive as a virtue: its energy and vitality are still felt through many channels of life—in the philosophy of Western nations, in the jurisprudence of all the civilised world. Nay, wherever man struggles to raise himself above himself, wherever his spirit masters his flesh by his own exertions, there we see the immortal discipline of Zeno at work.

の教訓がそこに働いているのを見ることができるのである。

　武士道は、一個の独立した道徳の掟としては、消え去ってしまうかもしれない。しかしその力は、この地上より滅びはしないであろう。その武勇と文徳の教訓は、体系としては崩れ去るかもしれない。しかしその光明と栄光は、その廃虚を乗り越えて永遠に生きてゆくであろう。その象徴である桜の花のように、四方の風に吹かれて散り果てても、その香気は、人生を豊かにして、人類を祝福するであろう。100年の後、武士道の習慣が葬り去られ、その名さえ忘れられてしまう日がきても、その香気は、「路辺に立ちて眺めやれば」目に見えない遠い彼方の丘から、風と共に漂ってくるであろう。それはまさに、あるクエーカーの詩人が歌った、美しい言葉のように。

　　　　いずこよりかは知らねど　近き香りに
　　　　旅人はしばしやすらい　歩をとめて
　　　　ゆたかなる　その香りをなつかしみ
　　　　高き御空の　いのりをぞ聞く

Bushido as an independent code of ethics may vanish, but its power will not perish from the earth; its schools of martial prowess or civic honour may be demolished, but its light and its glory will long survive their ruins. Like its symbolic flower, after it is blown to the four winds, it will still bless mankind with the perfume with which it will enrich life. Ages after, when its customaries will have been buried and its very name forgotten, its odours will come floating in the air as from a far-off, unseen hill, "the wayside gaze beyond";—then in the language of the Quaker poet,

> "The traveller owns the grateful sense
>   Of sweetness near, he knows not whence,
>   And, pausing, takes with forehead bare
>   The benediction of the air."

訳注

訳注1　11世紀後半、北フランスのノルマンディー公ウィリアムが、イングランドを征服して、ノルマン王朝を開き、封建制度を確立した。

訳注2　ギリシャ哲学の一派にストア学派というのがあって、道徳的には厳格な義務の遵守を説いた。克己的、禁欲的な処世の態度をいう。

訳注3　『旧約聖書』の創世紀にある。人類の祖アダムが神の命に背いて犯した罪。人間は皆アダムの子孫として、生まれながらに原罪を負っているという教え。

訳注4　ギリシャの古代都市デルフィの神殿は、地球の中心として考えられていて、神託をうかがう者は質問を書いて神官に渡すと、巫女がその神託を語ったという。

訳注5　コリント王、シジフォスは、ゼウスの神に憎まれて、死後、険しい山からころげ落ちる大石を、頂上にもち上げる苦役を命じられた。限りなく続く苦役のたとえ。

訳注6　古代ギリシャの都市国家スパルタの国民は、幼少の頃より厳しい訓練と厳格な教育を施された。そのような教育方法をいう。

訳注7　ギリシャの王ディオニュソスの家臣ダモクレスは、あるとき王によって、頭上に細い糸で剣をつるされた。これは王の境遇がいかなるものかを知らせるための暗示である。つまり、いつも精神を緊張させて、おそれつつしむことのたとえである。

訳注8　1894年、ユダヤ系フランス人の砲兵大尉アルフレッド・ドレフュスは、陸軍の機密書類をドイツに売ったという嫌疑で逮捕され、ギニアの悪魔島に終身禁錮の刑に処せられた。その後、真犯人は参謀本部のエステルハージ少佐だということがわかったが、陸軍当局は当時のユダヤ人排斥の思想に迎合し、ドレフュスの無実を認めなかった。作家エミール・ゾラなど知識人がこれを弾劾し、世界的な政治問題となり、ついに再審となって、1906年、ドレフュスはやっと釈放された。

訳注9　アブラハムが神の命令に従い、ひとり息子イサクを犠牲にして献げるため、モリアの山に登りイサクをしばって祭壇の上にのせて殺そうとしたとき、神はアブラハムの信仰をみてこれを止め、代りに牡羊を犠牲として与えたといわれる。

訳注10　天の神と地の神の子であるオシリスは、弟セトのために殺されたが、妻ホシスとその子ホルスが、オシリスの敵を討った。

訳注11　ギリシャ神話に出てくる、女だけの武者からなる部族、ペニテシレイアという女王に統率されて勇猛をふるい戦った。女丈夫、女傑、勇婦などの意味に用いる。

訳注12　ローマの独裁者クラウディアスは、美少女ヴァージニアを見て、奴隷として自分に侍らせようとした。彼女の父ヴァージニアスは、クラウディアスの暴虐を怒り、公衆の面前で「わが娘よ、こうしてお前を救おう」と叫んで、娘ヴァージニアの胸を刺した。これが動機となってクラウディアスの独裁制は転覆したという。

訳注13　ダモンの親友ピシアスは、罪によって暴君ディオニシオスから死刑の宣告を受けたが、その前に一度故郷に帰り父母に会いたいと願い、ダモンはその身代りとなり捕えられた。ピシアスは故郷への往復にさまざまな難に会い、身代りのダモンが死刑になる直前にようやく到着し、死刑を願った。ディオニシオスは、この二人の友情と信義とに感じて、その罪を許したと伝えられている。

訳注14　羊飼いのダビデは、巨人ゴライアスと戦ってこれを倒し、サウル王にそのことを語ったとき、王子ヨナタンはダビデと心を結び、自分の生命のようにダビデを愛したという。

訳注15　『旧約聖書』の創世記に出てくる洪水伝説の中の主人公。神が人類の堕落を怒り、洪水を起こそうとしたとき、信仰の篤いノアに命じて箱舟を造らせた。ノアは妻子と一つがいずつのこの世のあらゆる動物をこの箱舟に乗せて難をのがれた。そのため人類は滅亡しなかったといわれる。

訳注16　ギリシャ神話の中にある。テーベ王オイディプスは、盲目となり叔父に追放された。娘のアンチゴーネは父に従って放浪し、父の死後、テーベ王の叔父の命令に背き、戦死した兄の死体を葬ったため、彼女は生き埋めの刑にされた。ソフォクレスはこれを題材として悲劇を作った。

武士道
BUSHIDO

1998 年 6 月 10 日　第 1 刷発行
2022 年 5 月 10 日　第 30 刷発行

著　者	新渡戸稲造
訳　者	須知徳平
はしがき	波多野敬雄
写　真	一村哲也
発行者	鈴木章一
発行所	株式会社講談社

〒112-8001　東京都文京区音羽2-12-21
販売　　東京03-5395-3606
業務　　東京03-5395-3615

編　集　株式会社講談社エディトリアル
代表　堺　公江
〒112-0013　東京都文京区音羽1-17-18　護国寺SIAビル
編集部　東京03-5319-2171

印刷・製本所　大日本印刷株式会社

KODANSHA